This book is dedicated to the memory of the following old boys from the 'Last Intake' who are no longer with us; Michael Browne, Shaun Daly, Andrew Dixon, Miles Hartland, David Rigby, Anthony Royle, Ronan Sargeant and Michael Watterson.

CONTENTS

Appendices

'Term's Jottings' – Preston Catholic College magazine, January 1978

5 September 1977 – 'All too soon, the return to College life and the entry of the last first form.'

Headmaster's Report – Preston Catholic College Magazine, June 1978

'Finally, we must try not to see this year as the end of an age of cherished traditions but rather the eventual flowering of 110 years of experienced dedication and devotion to the educational needs of the Catholics of Preston and the large districts surrounding it. The good seed has been sown, the ground well prepared and nourished, the harvest is ready for the gathering. We must look ahead to this final achievement that could be the crown of all that has gone before.' – *Fr Wren*

The Metalwork Department – Preston Catholic College Magazine, June 1978

'One cannot but regard the future with mixed feelings. The days of the present workshop are numbered (only four more groups to O level) and then a quarter of a century's production must cease. Still, there is a fair amount to be done before the fire cools for the last time and the final handful of Swarfega is dispensed.' – *Mr Talbot*

PREFACE

In October 2016, a group of 47 former Preston Catholic College students attended a school reunion, to mark our 50th birthdays and our unique position within the history of the school. It was a great evening, filled with lots of laughter and many a story shared, not only of our time at the Cath Coll but of what we have all gone on to do since. It got me thinking about how we could record all these memories and stories before they were lost forever. I mulled it over for some time. Would anyone be able to remember that far back? And more importantly, would I be run out of town for even suggesting such a crazy idea?

In late summer 2018 I decided to 'bite the bullet' and asked for some feedback about the idea from the old boys who constituted this 'Final Intake,' to find out if they'd be interested in contributing to a book on the final years of Preston Catholic College. The brief was simple: 'Can you write down your memories and experiences of what it was like to be part of the final year at the Cath Coll and what you have gone on to do since then? Me and Jonesy (Adrian Jones) will edit it.' (While we're at it, I'd like to take this opportunity to thank Jonesy for his help, assistance and patient counsel throughout this venture!)

Getting the old boys' accounts together has been a real labour of love; some might say it's been like herding cats! Life has continued apace while we have been busy recording our memories and experiences. A further number of teachers and one old boy have sadly passed away. At the time of writing, the world is still going through a pandemic, with schools closed to many and home schooling the norm for most. I wonder what our teachers and parents would have said about that?!

What I'm most proud of in the pages that follow is the candour of my peer's recollections and thoughts, both positive and negative, about their time at the school. If they hadn't been so honest this would not have been a genuine account of a unique time. And what a myriad of stories, experiences and lives we have all gone on to lead since we left the school. Maybe our Catholic education has had more of a lasting impact than we could have ever imagined!

Here it is, in all its glory – I hope you enjoy it.

Jim Clune

August 2020

FOREWORD

This book consists of the memories and reminiscences of some of the boys who were part of the very last intake into Preston Catholic College (PCC) in 1977. The school was a typical RC Grammar School of the Victorian era, one of many such institutions up and down the country. The College was opened and run by the Society of Jesus in the mid-1860s; its purpose was to educate boys of good ability so as to give them access to the professions where, as well-educated Catholic boys, they would influence society for the good. The syllabus deemed to be most likely to achieve these aims was based on English, Maths and the Classics (Latin and Greek), and the study of the Catholic faith. In the early years of the school, the Sciences did not count for much. Staff consisted mainly of Jesuit priests and brothers (14 at one time), and a few laymen, though it was thought fitting that the first year (aged 11) should be taught by women.

The boys who have written these reminiscences were the last to complete this five-year course of studies, so they will have their place in the history of Catholic education. Their reunion in October 2016 took place quite near to the Catholic College site, and, since I also 'went through the mill' and completed the course, and finally taught in the school, I was invited to attend. I met and spoke to quite a number of them, and was very pleased to see how well they had turned out. Most seemed to be in useful and influential employment, and many were in the professions, including one genuine Professor! I'm sure that the Jesuits who set it all up would have been very satisfied with the final results of all their efforts.

Joe Bamber (Scholar 1944-1951; Teacher 1962-1997)

A BRIEF HISTORY OF PRESTON CATHOLIC COLLEGE GRAMMAR SCHOOL, 1865 – 1978

Compiled by Ralph Cooper, Old Boy 1958-1963

On 1 September 1865, Fr William Cobb, Rector of St. Wilfrid's, a former Provincial of the Jesuit Society, opened a Catholic Grammar School at the corner of Garden Street, No. 25 Winckley Square, for which he paid an exorbitant rent of £50 a year. The College opened with only 11 pupils – a number which never rose above 30 in its first five years. The fee for boys under ten years old was six guineas a year, those aged 10-14 years, eight guineas, and those over 14 years, ten guineas, with a reduction for brothers.

The number of pupils whose parents could afford to pay for their sons to have this education in the 1860s was greatly limited, as during this period over 22,000 people – more than 25 per cent of the town's population – were on Poor Relief. This was largely a result of the 'Cotton Famine', directly attributable to the American Civil War, which paralysed the cotton trade in which a large number of Prestonians worked.

Fr William Syrett of St Wilfrid's Church (which is still positioned in Chapel Street, and borders on to Winckley Square) kept a meticulous, copperplate St Wilfrid's Logbook, in which he outlined the reasons why the Jesuit Fathers of St Wilfrid's had long felt the need for Preston to have a Catholic Grammar School. It was necessary, in the first place, 'to counteract the evil effects of a well-founded and richly-endowed Protestant Grammar School', to which any freeman of the borough could send his son to obtain a good classical education at 'trifling cost'. Some Catholic tradesmen and others were apparently sending their boys to this school to receive 'a classical education', but were having 'the poison of heresy in their minds, and were obliged to listen to calumny and ridicule that was cast upon their Faith and practice of the Holy Catholic Church'. A Catholic Grammar School was needed, he wrote, so that the Catholic boys of Preston could obtain an education equal to that available to the Protestant boys, without putting their spiritual welfare in jeopardy.

St Wilfrid's clergy hoped that the primary benefit in having a Catholic Grammar School would be that a greater number of local boys would be called to the priesthood, and that the school in Preston would provide them with the opportunity to pursue their preliminary studies, and test their vocations, without the need to leave home. It was also hoped that the school would not only benefit the Catholic citizens of Preston, but also those of other nearby Lancashire towns including Blackburn and Chorley.

Winckley Square, full of elegant Georgian mansions, was the most fashionable part of the town at this time. On the site of the main entrance to the College, between Nos. 34 and 35, there was a narrow passage which gave access to a short row of South-facing humble cottages, called Mount Pleasant. In August 1866 Fr Cobb purchased the middle cottage, No. 2 Mount Pleasant, together with a small cottage in Mount Street, with £500 of St Wilfrid's Parish money, and transferred the tiny school there in the following month. In November 1866, Elizabeth and Helen (Ellen) Roper gave £500 to set-up foundations to educate two boys at the new grammar school, requesting that a Mass be said annually for them, and that the boys should be induced to 'say the beads' daily for their benefactresses. The first boys awarded the Roper foundations were George Postlewhite and Sylvin Gillet. Gillet was later ordained a priest – probably the first College Old Boy to become a Jesuit – and joined his three elder brothers, all Jesuits, in the mission fields, dying in British Guinea in 1910.

Fr Cobb used the Ropers' money to purchase No. 3 Mount Pleasant for £300. In August 1867 he purchased No. 1 Mount Pleasant for £335. Six years later, he purchased the ground rents of the three cottages from Lady Shelley, the heiress to the Winckley estates. He had thereby purchased the entire property block, which provided the site, 30 years later, for the Upper School building. Once Fr Cobb had completed his purchases, the College Grammar School was based at Nos. 2 and 3 Mount Pleasant from 1866-1875, with No. 1 initially being occupied by a music teacher.

Fr Henry Martin, who replaced Fr Cobb, appointed Thomas Mackenzie, who resided with his family at No. 2 Mount Pleasant, and opened the new school year in July 1870, with 20 scholars, which, largely through his efforts, quickly grew to 40 and then 82 pupils by the time of his departure, to become a Rector of a newly opened Jesuit College in Malta on 24 October 1878. A photograph taken circa 1875 shows a total of 61 boys in attendance, with an assistant Master, Mr Swainson. also present. The original schoolroom was a back room on the first floor of Nos. 2 and 3 Mount Pleasant cottages; as pupil numbers increased, an additional room downstairs was used, until the cottages were no longer big enough.

No. 29 Winckley Square was purchased for £1,450 in December 1874; the school transferred here on 6 July 1875, following its refitting, and remained at the address until 1897. A further two south-facing small cottages were later purchased, in a small cul-de-sac off Mount Street, called Lythgoe Place. Then in November 1878, another cottage in Mount Street, adjacent to Mount Pleasant and Lythgoe Place, was purchased for £276 by the Province for the grammar school's benefit. The number of pupils attending in 1878 was between 70 and 80.

Fr Charles De Lapasture joined the School in 1878, replacing Fr Martin; there were 82 pupils in attendance when he took over, but by September 1884, this number had fallen to only 24. Fr De Lapasture's tenure was almost fatal to the School. He inherited unsatisfactory financial arrangements from his predecessor, faced intense rivalry from the very successful Xaverian Brothers' School in St Ignatius' Parish, and oversaw the eventual dismissal, owing to ill health, of Mr Mackenzie, who had done so much to build up the School. Mr Mackenzie was replaced in 1882 by Fred Dewhurst, a former member of the Preston North End 'Invincibles' football team, and an international player of some reputation. When Preston North End won the FA Cup in 1888 without conceding a goal, Mr Dewhurst brought it to the School, allowing the boys to drink from it. He left the School in 1893 and died, aged 35, in April 1895.

In August 1882 the School opened for the new school year, with only 37 pupils. There seems to be little doubt that the main obstacle to its progress at this time was the existence of the Middle or Select School, run by the Xaverian Brothers at St Ignatius' Parish, which offered a *commercial* education at a much lower cost of only £1.13s.0d a year, versus the *classical* education provided by the Grammar School at six guineas a year. This sometimes bitter rivalry didn't end until 1898, when the Brothers' School was absorbed by the Grammar School into the new Catholic College.

Fr De Lapasture was replaced in 1884 by Fr Francis Payne. The new headmaster skilfully steered the school away from the rocks towards which it was so clearly headed, leaving 14 years later, by which time it had emerged as a full Catholic College. Fr Payne's humorous, frank and hearty manner revealed the true man, and the sincere friend of all, irrespective of their religious persuasion.

One of Fr Payne's first great achievements came in 1886, when he leased the playing field at Riverside from the Railway Company, building a small pavilion on the site. Sports games were soon in full swing on Wednesdays and Saturdays, and shortly afterwards the Annual Athletic Sports competition began, attended by the elites of Preston.

There is a letter, written by Fr Payne, which contains a brief Statement of the School Accounts in August 1887. It shows Total Receipts of £348.15s.6d, and Total Expenditure of £358.4s.3d, which included debts of £52. He accounts for the deficit of nearly £10 as being due to repairs needed for school top rooms, the cellar, and the playground, where the rockery had collapsed, and to the drainage of the Riverside field, which was unfit for use until it was drained but would only cost £8 a year thereafter. The Pavilion cost £30 but would, he hoped, be paid for by subscriptions.

Fr Payne will also be remembered for forming the Catholic Grammar School Association in 1894 for past school pupils, which became the Catholic College Association in 1909. The Association leased a Club room in Chapel Street for regular meetings, where talks and debates took place on the great questions of the day. There was also a Dramatic section, and Vincent Park was asked by Fr Payne to reform an Old Boys' Football Club in 1911. Later, Smoking Concerts, dances at the Geisha Ballroom (on the top floor of the Miller Arcade) and country excursions by 'waggonette' were also organised. The Association's second secretary was Oswald Goodier, the Chapel Street solicitor, who kept a fascinating scrapbook of newspaper cuttings, tickets and programmes of the Association's early activities, which still survives.

It was during the Rectorship of Fr Frederick O'Hare from 1894-1901, that the biggest change in the Grammar School's development came about, with the construction of the new Catholic College building. Along with the sale of No. 29 Winckley Square (for £1000), this project meant that the school needed to move to temporary accommodation in the Shepherd Library at the corner of Cross Street. The work, for which he had negotiated a loan of £4,000 in July 1897, necessitated the demolition of 11 houses and cottages in December 1897 and January 1898, which were either owned by the school or St Wilfrid's.

In September 1898 Fr Payne transferred to Glasgow. A new headmaster, Fr Patrick Flynn, was appointed. He stayed for one year and his only notable action was the appointment of a new teacher, Herbert Bolton ('Big Ben'), who came straight from College and served until 1947.

The new Catholic College building was opened with great solemnity in May 1899 by the Bishop of Liverpool, and constructed where the Mount Pleasant Cottages were originally located. To facilitate a frontage to Winckley Square, number 34 was purchased for £1, 000, (the amount received for number 29 Winckley Square which was sold at the same time). The frontage was constructed of Longridge brown stone in a Dutch style, quite unlike most of the other buildings in the Square, replacing the demolished No. 34 but preserving the familiar narrow frontage to Winckley Square. The gable is crowned by the Jesuit symbol and the letters *I.H.S.*, the Paschal Lamb, and the *P.P.* of Preston, and the date 1898. The College entrance also retained the passage between Nos. 34 and 35, which previously led to Mount Pleasant, but now continued in a straight line to Mount Street, and was most frequently used by the St Wilfrid's Fathers, who acted as Chaplains to St Joseph's Hospital.

The 1898 building consisted of the Upper School Block on the North side of the playground, with four classrooms on the ground floor, and one classroom and the Hall above, which connected by a broad corridor to the Entrance Hall, over which were the Headmaster's Room and the Governors' Room. In total there were nine classrooms, a Science Lecture Room, and a Practical Laboratory, as well as the Hall, which could be converted into three classrooms with the aid of moveable partitions if necessary. The building had electric lighting and was 'heated by hot water'.

On 1 October 1899 the Brothers' School in St Ignatius' Parish was closed, and on the same day a *Commercial Course* was opened at the Catholic College, where the original 70-80 Catholic Grammar School boys were now known as the '*Classical Course*'. The amalgamation terms stipulated that the 109 boys of the St Ignatius' School should join the Commercial Course in a body, accompanied by their school masters, and that all their furniture and apparatus should be temporarily transferred to the College. The existing Brothers' School fees of 26 shillings a year were to be retained for the transferred pupils, and the school was to continue in the new premises exactly as it had before for one year. After Christmas 1899 responsibility for the cohort was taken over by the new Catholic College Headmaster, Fr John Wright, who had just arrived to replace Fr Flynn. Fr Wright had been educated at St Francis Xavier's, in Liverpool, and was a most prolific writer of letters and memoranda, mostly in his neat longhand. He was also Rector of St Wilfrid's and chaired the College Board of Governors, formed in 1903. He was ostensibly the *proprietor* of the College. He later became the English Jesuit Provincial, serving during the years of the Great War, and died in 1926.

Fr Wright's time as Headmaster was fraught with many difficulties, particularly financial issues. First, he had to integrate the boys from the Commercial Course, paying 26 shillings per year (later two guineas) with those on the Classical Course, who were paying six guineas, along with their respective teachers (and their inadequate salaries). At the same time, he had to contend with changes to the education system, with the implementation of the Education Act of 1902. The College received a Full Inspection, on 28 and 29 April 1904, by the Board of Education, who recommended that all boys should pay six guineas a year, and that further building works were required. A large new extension was constructed on the Mount Street side of the playground in 1905-6. The top floor contained a large carpentry workshop, an art room, and a classroom, while below this was a dining room and a covered playground, which cost £1,300. Early in 1907 a large wooden workshop was also erected in the lower playground, at right-angles to the new building, approximately on the site of the later gymnasium, which was subsequently converted into an Art Studio. This enabled the carpentry workshop, with the construction of sliding-screens, to be converted into three classrooms.

Fr Henry Meyer, an assistant Jesuit master, then became the acting Headmaster for the Spring and Summer terms under Fr Wright's supervision, until the arrival of Fr Joseph Welsby, a Preston man, in September 1907. This was also the year that the large playground was drained and paved. The number of Jesuit staff, which included Fr Aloysius Gillow, an Old Boy, and Fr Francis Grafton, also steadily increased.

The ten years before the outbreak of the Great War in 1914, saw little increase in pupil numbers, which fluctuated around the 130 mark, still well below the full capacity of the existing buildings. The College's financial position gradually improved following new grants from the

Education Board, and Local Authority payments on behalf of their pupils. However, there was still a yearly deficit in the School's running costs. In 1909 the School Inspectors suggested an increased fee was justifiable, but the Governors decided to leave things at the level they were, six guineas for the Upper School, and £4.10s.0b for the Lower School.

In 1910 Fr Welsby introduced a distinctive cap-badge in metal gilt, representing the Imperial Eagle, with the Gonzaga motto *'Fides', (meaning Faith).* The College Arms were those of St. Aloysius Gonzaga, its Patron. The main part consists of four eagles divided by a red cross; these are the arms borne by the family in virtue of their title of Princes of the Holy Roman Empire. Two years later, in December 1912, the first College magazine appeared, taking inspiration from the motto in its title, *'Sons of the Eagle'.* The first ten publications of the magazine, covering the period from 1912-1916, were entirely cyclostyled, with a blocked cover showing boys at work and play. Its contents included long accounts of football matches, not least one in the first edition of a fixture against local rivals, Stonyhurst College on 15 December 1912, entitled *The Duel of the Eagles.*

The outbreak of the Great War in August 1914 greatly increased the magazine's readership, as the large number of College Old Boys serving all over the world in the Armed Forces subscribed to receive it, hungry for any news of home, and familiar places and people. The War became the publication's main content, with long and interesting Old Boys letters appearing in its pages, giving details of their authors' exploits from various battlefronts, enquiring about each other's fortunes, and saying how much the College Magazine was appreciated. Sadly, with each issue came another five or six names to be added to the Roll of Honour, of Old Boys who had died for their country. By the end of the War, the list had grown to 54 names. By the end of the Second World War this figure had risen to about 108 (exact figures cannot be confirmed).

From July 1916 the College Magazine was professionally printed by Mather Bros, who produced it until its cessation, when the Preston Catholic College became Newman College in September 1978. Denis

Mather was an Old Boy, who played for Preston North End at centre-forward, and later for Preston Catholic College Old Boys, latterly as a goalkeeper.

Fr Welsby was replaced as Headmaster in 1915 by Fr James Bridge, a Wigan man. The Golden Jubilee of the School received no special celebration, occurring as it did in the middle of the War and with a new Headmaster recently installed, though it did not go unnoticed. The Prize Distribution that year was presented by the Archbishop of Liverpool, who continued to perform the role until 1924 when the Lancaster Diocese was formed, and among the guests who attended were Fr Wright, Fr O'Hare, and Fr Welsby, all of whom had much input in the planning and early development of the College.

A most useful publication, the College Calendar, made its first appearance in 1915, containing class-lists of all the boys, and all the year's football fixtures. One of the most eagerly anticipated of these games was the annual Stonyhurst match, which entailed a two and a half hour drive each way by 'brake or baguette' (or Charabanc), which was traditionally broken by the players refreshing themselves with cups of hot Oxo at the Corporation Arms, Longridge. The fixture appeared until Stonyhurst abandoned *Soccer* in favour of *Rugger* in 1920. The St Francis Xavier match then took its place as the 'best day out.'

The end of the Great War in November 1918 saw the College unfurl its flag and celebrate with one and a half days' holiday. A Requiem Mass was celebrated for the Old Boys who had lost their lives in the War (a tradition that went on to be proudly maintained at the College annually), and a special commemorative edition of the College Magazine, containing photographs and details of the College War Dead, was produced.

A new Headmaster, Fr Henry Irwin, was appointed, following Fr Bridge's return to Liverpool. He was considered one of the Society's most brilliant scholars, but was unable to deal with the intricacies of timetables and the school organisation, and was very absent-minded. After three years he left to become Professor of Classics at St Mary's Hall, Stonyhurst, where he lived until 1957.

The College Magazine became thin and infrequent during this

period, with one interval between issues extending to 18 months. This was largely due to the greatly increased printing costs in the immediate post-war years. The College had to pay 40 per cent of the production cost of each issue as well, while the interest of Old Boys in contributing or subscribing to the Magazine had also declined considerably.

The numbers of boys attending the College was increasing rapidly compared with the Edwardian period, with the 150-mark being passed in September 1913, and the 200-mark celebrated with a holiday in June 1918. By September 1918, 210 boys were registered at the College, and to make an extra classroom, the platform that had served as a stage at the end of the Hall was removed. The College had grown to 250 boys by September 1920, but only about a dozen entered the sixth form.

These rapidly rising numbers saw the College become seriously overcrowded. There was an urgent need for extra accommodation, and although Fr Irwin addressed the Provincial authorities in 1922, presenting strong arguments for the purchase of the offices of Garlick and Sykes at 33 Winckley Square, it wasn't until nearly 40 years later, in 1962, that these premises were purchased by Fr Carty.

The Preston Guild Merchant, celebrated in September 1922, saw more than 200 College boys taking part in recreations of town life as it had been five hundred years previously. The Guild was established in 1179, after King Henry II awarded Preston its first royal charter, along with the right to have a Guild Merchant – an event which takes place once every 20 years to this day. The Guild was an organisation of traders, craftsmen and merchants, all with a monopoly trade in the town. Only members of the Guild could carry out a craft or business and newcomers could only trade with permission from the Guild.

The students wore outfits representing the Mayor and members of the Preston Corporation in 1450, together with those of 18 Trade Guilds, each with its own banner, and all were attired in contemporary costume and were suitably bearded. The players also co-operated with the Winckley Square Convent Girls in one scene in which a medieval Mystery Play was presented. The whole production was overseen by a new Headmaster, Fr Francis Grafton.

Fr Grafton initially joined the College as an Assistant Master in

1912, until he enlisted as a Military Chaplain in November 1915. He returned to the College as Headmaster in 1922, inheriting a school of some 280 boys. He anticipated this would increase to 350 boys, with a maximum annual intake of 70 pupils; most boys would remain until they were at least 16, with a good number staying on to the sixth form. The magic number of 300 boys, meriting a half-holiday, eluded them for a few years, and was only attained in September 1926, largely due to the growing size of the yearly intake being cancelled out by large numbers of early leavers.

Fr Grafton repeatedly said that he regarded the College as a Preston school, existing primarily to serve the Catholics of Preston, and he gave every encouragement to the establishment of Catholic Secondary Schools in Blackburn (St Mary's College), Blackpool (St Joseph's College), and Bolton (Thornleigh College), to better serve the boys from those areas who currently had to travel to the College by train on a daily basis. Due to the depression and the establishment of these new Catholic Colleges, numbers dropped in 1927 and 1928, and only passed 300 again in 1929, when my father Ralph Cooper, along with Louis Caton, (who later taught Technical Drawing, Metalwork, Mathematics, and Mechanics at the school), and James Harrison, were the three pupils who arrived from St Augustine's primary school. The 350 pupil target was only reached in September 1931, with numbers fluctuating around that level for the remainder of Fr Grafton's time at the College.

In 1926 the construction of the stage was completed in the Hall, where it was regarded by Fr Grafton as a great help to education. It was one of the finest and best-equipped stages for amateur performers in northern England, occasioning a great number of complimentary remarks from the professional artistes and companies who made use of it over the years. The stage was, however, primarily designed for the boys' use, and was in constant demand for all types of entertainment, dramatic and musical, presented by pupils and various Old Boys organisations. The first staging of a school concert took place in December 1926, and after that the school presented an annual Cabaret Concert to the public, the proceeds of which went to the Building

Fund.

The first of what was to become an annual Shakespeare Play performance, *Julius Caesar*, took place on 28 February 1927, and from then the original cycle of seven plays continued: *Merchant of Venice, 1928, Midsummer Night's Dream, 1929, Macbeth, 1930, Henry IV, 1931, The Tempest, 1932*, and *Richard II, 1933*, in a pattern which was repeated until war intervened in 1939.

The physical side of education was not neglected by Fr Grafton. One of his first actions on becoming Headmaster was to construct a new Pavilion at Riverside in 1923, and to lease several extra football pitches on the Bull field (located between the Riverside pitch and the Tram Road, by the River Ribble), from Preston Borough Council (BC) for games on Wednesday and Saturday afternoons. Cricket was in the doldrums until 1924, when it was steadily revived by Mr Lee and Mr Dowling, and the College was able to field two teams for the first time. A match between the Staff and the First XI was recorded as having taken place in 1937.

The construction of the gymnasium was one of the first of Fr Grafton's various projects, and the swimming bath was among his last, reflecting his well-known views about '*mens sana in corpore sano*' – '*A sound mind in a sound body.*' In 1936, the Lower School, apart from their field games, were having no less than five periods of PT weekly, including swimming and, incredibly, tap-dancing! In the summer of 1937, the first Annual Swimming Gala took place in the College baths.

Adjoining the Riverside Pavilion, at the top of the playing fields, three grass tennis courts were laid out, with a grass cricket net alongside them, primarily for use of the Catholic College Association (CCA) members or, later, for the College boys' use.

One of Fr Grafton's most famous institutions was the Annual Lent Steeplechase, which was first run on the Monday of Holy Week 1928. The original course was one and a half miles long, and included a water jump, several fences and ditches. There were two races, one for the Upper, and one for the Lower School. In 1940 the water jump was excluded, much to the dismay of spectators, particularly when watching the 'undignified wallowings' of the Upper School Seniors.

The Lent Steeplechase continued each year until 1956, while the annual School Sports Day continued to be held in June, frequently – judging by Magazine accounts – in the most atrocious weather.

Scouting, which started at the College in 1915 when the Scouting Movement was only seven years old, was initiated by Fr Grafton, then an assistant master, and Mr Wilfrid Park, a young master on his first appointment. Both left the College in Autumn 1915, though Mr Park continued to run the 16th Preston Scout Troop from elsewhere. In order to maintain numbers, it had to be opened to outsiders as well as College Boys, and was renamed the 16th Preston Loyola Troop (named after Saint Ignatius of Loyola, founder of the Jesuits). In January 1931, Wilfrid Park returned to the College Staff. The following month three troops of College Scouts were formed; the Loyolas, his own troop, the Xavier troop under Mr Charles Kinleside, and the Gonzolas under Mr Frank Stone, which broke-up soon after he was called up to the Forces in 1940.

Shortly after forming these new troops, Mr Park withdrew the non-College scouts to form their own troop based elsewhere. He later started the '*Foreign Legion*' for those boys who wished to be scouts but lived too far away to attend meetings regularly. He acted as their Scoutmaster until Mr Stainthorp took them over shortly after joining the staff in 1936, but when he joined the Forces, the *Foreign Legion* became a casualty of the war.

Annual summer camps had been established by Fr Grafton long before scouting returned to the College. There were usually two: No. 1 Camp for Senior boys being held abroad, almost always in France or Belgium and usually led by the Headmaster at a cost of five guineas, and No. 2 Camp, for younger boys, at a cost of 30/-, which was held more locally. Dunsop Bridge, Hornby, St. Bueno's, and Lee House were some of the earliest camping sites. They appear to have been very popular, being attended by large numbers of boys.

The General Strike of May 1926 threatened to prevent the hundred or so College boys who travelled daily by train, from attending school. Concerned their studies might suffer a serious set-back, Fr Grafton made arrangements to accommodate them in the house he had recently purchased, No. 27 Winckley Square. Thus, for a week or so the Catholic College became a boarding-school for the 'train-boys'.

Fr Grafton's College capital debt for his extensive building operations had increased to a figure of about £23,000, on which the interest payable was in excess of £700 per annum. His Annual Report frequently showed the steadily increasing deficit on the current account, with annual receipts never matching expenditure, and the deficit increase on the Maintenance Account steadily rose to £5,833. The annual cost of a College Boy's education during this period was between £20-£24, whereas costs in similar types of schools elsewhere were normally more than £30. The difference came about because the College Jesuit masters were still taking no salary, while the lay masters were receiving less than they would elsewhere.

College finances were derived from three main sources: *the fee*, which was nine guineas throughout the period, a *capitation grant* of seven guineas for each College boy from the Education Board, and a *capitation grant* from the Local Authority. Preston BC paid four to five guineas, while Lancashire County Council (CC) paid £5 for about half the county boys who attended the College. They would not pay for the remaining boys if they lived in an area where there was a non-Catholic County Secondary School. They would, therefore, pay a grant for a boy living in Longridge, where there was no such school, but not for one who lived in Higher Penwortham, as he lived nearer to Hutton Grammar School than Preston Catholic College.

This 'religious disability' continued until shortly before the Second World War, although about half of the College boys came from the County area. Preston BC, unlike Blackpool and Blackburn BCs, would not, until 1929, pay the fees of any Preston boy who won one of the free places that the College, as a Grant-aided school, was obliged to offer boys from Elementary Schools. In 1927 the College offered 27 free places. By 1939, 70 per cent of the College boys held scholarships or free places, and only 30 per cent paid the nine-guinea fee, almost an exact reversal of the position in 1909.

It was clear from the beginning of Fr Grafton's reign as College Headmaster that one of his chief concerns was the spiritual side of a boy's education, and their character formation. To create a Catholic atmosphere in the College, he laid great stress on formal Religious Instruction with no College boy in his time ever having less than three periods of Religious Doctrine weekly. In fact, it was quite usual for those in the Lower School to have four or five periods.

From September 1923, Fr Grafton brought the College week to an end by holding Benediction for the whole school in St Wilfrid's church. The Armistice Day Requiem Mass for the Old Boys killed in the War was continued, and High Mass was celebrated on many of the important Feast days. The School year commenced with a Spiritual Retreat for the Upper School and, in 1934, he started holding a Leavers' Retreat, at Stonyhurst or Rainhill, for all boys in their last school term.

Following the death of Fr Grafton in 1940, the College looked no further for a successor than his able deputy, Fr Bernard Malone, who, apart from two short breaks, had served continuously, acting as Headmaster during Fr Grafton's long illnesses. He kept everything Fr Grafton had instituted, distrusting in most new innovations, including ball-point pens, electric clocks, and evening masses. He even did a similar tour of the College on Sundays, when he could be alone to inspect the fabric of the buildings, armed with the huge bunch of keys that he always carried.

The majority of Fr Malone's Headmastership coincided with the war. After the initial impact and disturbance to routine had passed, College life resumed its even tenor with scant regard for external events, save perhaps for those sad notices which began to appear with increasing frequency on the College Notice Board, announcing the death of yet another Old Boy on active service. Joseph Bass, a regular soldier was the first fatality, killed at Dunkirk in June 1940, shortly followed by Harry Wrennall, a submariner whose submarine failed to return from patrol. There were about 700 Old College Boys known to have served with His Majesty's Forces, of whom 54 were killed. At home, the black-out had the biggest impact on College life, resulting in the curtailment of all after-school activities.

A great deal of excitement ensued on the 17 February 1944, with the destruction through fire of the Riverside Pavilion, the cause of which never became known. The fire started in the Masters' shed around 1 p.m., and as a result of a strong prevailing wind, set fire to the Pavilion at about 1.30 p.m., completely destroying the building and its contents; as a result, the boys had to change in the brick hut behind the Pavilion which had survived the blaze. Shortly after the fire, a fund was launched for a Memorial to perpetuate Fr Grafton's name, which the intention being for it to either take the form of a new Sports Pavilion, or a Sports Field; it had raised £1,000 by December 1946. A few years earlier, in 1940, a College Allotment Club was formed by Mr Gillow, an Old College Boy, to grow vegetables on the waste-ground behind the Riverside tennis courts, the arduous work being done on Wednesday and Saturday afternoons.

After the initial disturbances caused by staff changes due to the call-up of the younger lay staff and some Jesuits becoming Forces Chaplains, school routines soon returned to something resembling normality. However, in 1940, when the Winter War-time order was modified, a slightly shortened school-day was introduced. The College adopted a five-day week in 1942, with Wednesday becoming a normal school-day, and Saturday a whole holiday – a development which caused a lot of resentment when the traditional system returned in September 1946! Football was very much in the doldrums for a period, due largely to a lack of practice opportunities, with the College First XI frequently knowing the bitterness of heavy defeats, from which the credit for the subsequent revival must go to the young Scholastic Mr 'Johnny' Maher, who first served at the College from 1942-46.

During his time as Headmaster Fr Malone had two important decisions to make regarding the future role of the College. It had become clear to him by December 1942 that the two-stream Grammar School was inadequate to meet the rapidly growing needs of the Preston and District Catholics. He noted that while there were two Catholic Girls Grammar Schools, each having about 400 pupils, there was only the one Catholic Boys Grammar School. That year saw the College have 70 first form boys, with about 30 good applicants having to be reluctantly turned away. The only solution to the increasing demand was to build an extension to the school buildings.

In April 1943, when Fr Malone saw that the number of applicants for places had greatly increased, he decided to open a third first form, using the Demonstration Theatre as an ordinary classroom. As a result, the 400 mark was passed for the first time in September 1944, and the traditional holiday was granted in celebration. It had taken just 18 years for the numbers to rise from 300 to 400. June 1946 saw Fr Malone acquire No. 25 Winckley Square, in order to house the growing numbers, with two first form classes moving in seven months later and a third first form class in September 1947.

The other major decision was forced upon Fr Malone by the Government's 1944 Education Act. He applied on behalf of the College, in June 1945, to retain the Direct Grant status it had held since 1903. But Christmas Eve 1945 saw the two Preston Convent Schools and the Catholic College receiving notice that their applications for Direct Grant status had been refused, without a reason being given. In March 1947, at the Annual Prize Day in the Queen's Hall in Saul Street Baths, he reviewed the position. Fr Malone felt that the College compared very favourably with the other Direct Grant Schools in the neighbourhood whose status had already been confirmed, but 'wondered whether the Ministry had misinterpreted the attitude of Preston Education Authority towards us'.

A meeting took place between the three Catholic schools and the Preston Education Development Sub-Committee, who immediately passed a resolution, supporting the Catholic Schools Governors in their appeal against the Minister's decision. A deputation, headed by the Bishop of Lancaster, visited the Ministry on 7 May 1946. Here, for the first time, a Ministry spokesman gave the reason why the Schools could not retain their Direct Grant status. It was due to the fact, they explained, that each of them allotted more than 50 per cent of their places to Scholarship holders, and unless the number of fee-paying students exceeded 50 per cent of the total school roll, a school had no right to receive a Direct Grant. In response, the deputation pointed out that that this rule was completely at odds with the Minister's own regulations, which clearly stated that Direct Grant Schools could be obliged to take up to 50 per cent Scholarship holders if the Local Education Authority required them, but that they could exceed this percentage voluntarily at the request of the Local Education Authority. They also pointed out that, to their certain knowledge, a good number of schools that had their Direct Grant status confirmed had considerably more than 75 per cent Scholarship holders.

These arguments, however, proved in vain, although the two Convent Schools were able, by combining, to show they could meet all the new requirements, and were granted temporary Direct Grant status, reviewable after two years. The College Governors could give no such assurances, however, as to have done so would have meant that they would have to become a six-stream school by admitting 90 Free Place holders each year, as well as a similar number of fee-payers.

The choice facing the College Governors was thus to either accept Voluntary Aided status or to become an Independent School. Voluntary Aided status would mean that the College would have come under the control of Preston Education Authority, and thereby lose its independence, forfeiting the right to admit any boys except those that the Preston Authority directed. They therefore had little hesitation in resolving to make the College an Independent School, which would mean that it would receive no grants from either the Government or Local Authorities. The loss of the Government Grant immediately saw an increase in the fee from £24 to £42 per year for the fee-paying boys, while the Local Authorities would have to pay the new full fee of £42 for each Scholarship boy instead of the previous 60 per cent of the original £24 fee (£14.40, with the Government having paid the difference). This was, of course, a tremendous increase. But both of the main Local Authorities accepted the situation, which meant that for the next thirteen years the local ratepayers were the main losers, as there was no limit placed on the number of boys selected to be educated at the Catholic College. Time vindicated Fr Malone's policy, as the College was quickly accepted, with the Local Authorities' approval, to the Direct Grant list when it was re-opened by a later Government.

Fr John Duggan took over as Headmaster on 31 March 1947. He

inherited a school of 460 boys, which, in September of the same year, increased to slightly under 500. However, due to Lancashire Education Authority's demand for more places, he felt obliged to comply with their wishes and become a four-stream school from September 1948. He thus committed the College to grow by at least 150 boys over the next five years. The school rose to the challenge of the associated accommodation problem, with very few changes needing to be undertaken initially; instead, No. 27 Winckley Square, which had long been College property, was adapted for use by the four second forms in January 1950. Several features of the house were retained, including impressive plaster ceilings, ornate Victorian window valances, and a room with an open fire, while others had stoves. A flat for Mr Kinleside was fitted up on the top floor.

Due to stringent Government restrictions in the post-war era, there was no possibility of obtaining official sanction for any permanent building extension work for many years, and it was thought that it would be better to build a completely new College, away from the town centre. The College Governors viewed several possible sites around Preston, but there were many considerations to weigh-up, and no firm decision was ever made. Fr Duggan, meanwhile, was gradually paying-off the capital debt from Fr Grafton's pre-war building operations.

Fr Duggan decided he needed to offer some vocational training to open the door to valuable professional careers, and he introduced some Science subjects to the sixth form, the intake of which was slowly increasing. Shortly after his appointment he introduced Mathematics, and, in the following years, Physics and Chemistry. He still considered that a Classical formation was the best education, however, with modern subjects representing a very good second-best option. Similarly, in the Lower School he realised that an increasing number of the boys sent to the College by Preston Education Authority were, in his own words 'unsuitable for a grammar school education in the full sense of the word'. He therefore introduced a certain amount of practical work courses; woodwork under Mr Foulkes, held in a workshop fitted-up under the Gymnasium, and metalwork in February 1951, under Mr Caton, in a workshop in a small room in the basement of No. 27, which was considerably enlarged in 1955. The classes were renamed in 1954 from A, B, C, D, to Arts, Science, General, and Modern.

Fr Duggan's name will always be linked with the foundation of the War Memorial Library, which he had proposed as Chairman of the Catholic College Association during its Annual General Meeting in December 1948. He asked if a College War Memorial might be created, featuring an illuminated Roll of Honour containing the names of the 54 Old Boys who had lost their lives in the Second World War. It was commissioned by the CCA and hung in the College Hall, unveiled by the CCA President, Mr Frank Pyke, in June 1949. The CCA decided to launch an appeal for funds to create a permanent War Memorial akin to the Gallery, that had been erected during Fr Grafton's reign to commemorate those killed in the First World War. The appeal, launched in March 1949, raised £1,143. This amount had grown with interest by 1953 to some £1,200.

The decision was taken that the Memorial should take the form of a library for the use of Forms III, IV, and V, since the sixth form had the exclusive use of the Wright Memorial Library, and with Forms I and II already having their own libraries. The War Memorial Library was created by joining together two large front rooms on the first floor of No. 27 Winckley Square, re-flooring and then re-wiring them for lighting. The rooms, having proved very suitable for the purpose, cost very little to adapt, and the bulk of the money raised was spent on the oak Memorial Tablet, and the handsome bookcases, tables and chairs that filled the space, which could accommodate 48 boys.

It was envisaged that one day the sixth and second form libraries would be amalgamated with the War Memorial Library, (this was ultimately achieved under Fr Carty in 1959). Fr Rector formally opened and blessed the new Library in December 1953, which had by this point been stocked by a comprehensive selection of books thoughtfully purchased by the Senior English Master, Mr Lawson.

In June 1953 the Fr Grafton Memorial Fund was at last put to some good use with the purchase of 13 ½ acres of land at Factory Lane, Lower Penwortham, for a sum of £1,250. This provided seven football pitches and a cricket square, which were immediately brought into use, even before drains had been laid. The lease the school had on the 'Bull-field', adjacent to the Tram Road, was relinquished, and the huts and Old Boys' Cabin that had been used at Riverside since the Pavilion fire were transferred. However, the well-loved Riverside Field was retained, and each week buses were provided to take the First and second forms to games.

On launching the Grafton Memorial Fund in 1944 it was optimistically hoped that the monies raised would provide for both a pavilion as well as playing-fields, as it was thought that the insurance money for the old pavilion destroyed by fire would cover about half the cost of a similar building. By 1953 the stark fact was that there was only £1,750 in the fund, while a suitable pavilion would cost £4,000. A further appeal was made, chiefly to the parents of the boys then attending the College, and by the time that Fr Duggan left the College in 1956 almost all the money had been raised. Planning was applied for in Spring 1956, though building did not commence until Fr Carty became headmaster. The pavilion was opened at the end of 1957 at a cost of £8,000 due to the increased cost of labour and materials.

Fr Duggan will also be remembered for the formation of two Associations. One, a College Parents' Association (PCA), first suggested by him at the November 1953 Prize Day, was launched in 1954, and brought together, through a means of consultation and co-operation, both parents and staff. The PCA raised a considerable amount of money for the College through various enterprising ventures. The second Association was the formation of the Preston Catholic Grammar School Association, which was a joint venture of Preston Catholic College, and Lark Hill and Winckley Square Convent Schools. The first Annual General Meeting was held, with Fr Duggan as its Chairman, in the College Hall on 21 January 1949. There were quickly over 300 paid-up members who enjoyed a series of plays, concerts, and Gilbert and Sullivan Operas, all staged by the PCGSA in the College Hall. The profit from these ventures made a welcome contribution to the pavilion fund.

The College boys were re-arranged into six houses in September

1949 with the formation of the Arrowsmith and Southworth houses, which augmented Campion, Fisher, More, and Mayne. However, in October of the following year the College scouts suffered a tremendous blow with the death of Mr W.C. Park, who had spent almost 20 years on the Staff and 35 years in scouting. Mr Rigby took over the Loyola troop for a time, but it was combined with the Xavier troop under Mr Kinleside in 1954. At this time Mr Manbre first formed the senior scouts, but they did not flourish until his second attempt in 1957 under Fr Carty. Traditional College Camps abroad were replaced by visiting various parts of Europe in a series of continental journeys, while the second form spent Easter touring the North Wales castles.

At the Preston Guild Merchant in September 1952 the College played its part once again. The Madrigal Choir joined with the other schools in the massed Festival Choir, conducted by Mr Richard Iddon, while another group, attired in very striking costumes designed by Miss I. Bolton, appeared in the Children of Yesterday Pageant, representing the English Bowmen practising at the butts in 1459. The College Tumblers, trained by Mr Jimmy Flynn, took part in a 'Children of Today' item, and the Catholic College provided a tableau representing the Sacrament of Baptism, in the Catholic Procession. The Catholic Exhibition held in St Ignatius' Hall in the Guild Week had some displays designed by a few College Boys, directed by Miss Meagher.

Fr Duggan's health deteriorated in Spring 1956, resulting in Fr Brooks, who had returned to the College as Deputy headmaster the year before, standing in for him for about half a term. Fr Duggan returned after the Whitsun Break, but he clearly had not recovered fully and was replaced by Fr Robert Carty as Headmaster on 31 July 1956. By now, the College ranks had swelled to 620 boys.

Having served as a scholastic at the College for three years during the war, Fr Carty returned to the College in 1952 to teach Chemistry and Mathematics. His five-year tenure as Headmaster saw further developments at the College, where his outstanding administrative ability and seemingly limitless energy came to the fore. He possessed a prodigious memory and claimed to know each College boy's achievements and shortcomings, as well as where he resided. Knowing the workings of the College, he spent little time dwelling on what changes might be required, and immediately commenced with restoring the five-day week, with a whole afternoon of games provided for each class, along with a swimming period once a week. He also immediately embarked on a complete re-organisation, particularly with the sixth and Middle School curricula. With the departure of Mr Adrian Henri, Art was dropped from the School curriculum, and replaced, for the two lower streams, with Technical Drawing.

Specialisation in Arts or Science subjects was delayed until the sixth form, and, deciding that the syllabuses of the Associated Examining Board offered subjects and courses better suited to the G and M streams than those offered by the Joint Matriculation Board, Fr Carty changed to them in 1957 with considerable success. He also pioneered the organisation of a General Studies subject after it was made examinable by the Joint Matriculation Board, to counter the danger of having too narrow a specialisation in the sixth form.

In September 1959, having decided that blazers were not suitable garments for lower school wear, he introduced a green tweed jacket as the new school uniform. However, the sixth form continued to use the smart black blazer with the Gonzaga Eagle on the pocket, which had been introduced by Fr Duggan in 1954. Later, in Fr Wren's time, this became the uniform of the whole College, except for the sixth form.

Spring 1957 saw the commencement of pavilion building works, but over £2,000 had to be spent installing a water-supply and a sewerage system, prior to starting work on the building. September 1957 saw 'Grafton' pavilion put into use for the first time, although the official opening and blessing by the Vicar General, Monsignor Eaton, did not occur until Sports Day in May 1958.

The post-war 'bulge' in child population began to reach Secondary Schools in 1957, and the College authorities were obliged to provide more places for students to cope with the extra demand. A fifth stream, IR, was thus admitted to the College in September 1958. This decision increased the number of first form boys to 150, of which fewer than half now came from Preston BC. This ensured that no boy within the College's catchment area from Carnforth to Ormskirk, and from

Southport to Accrington, would be deprived of a Catholic grammar school education. The first form then occupied No. 25 Winckley Square, with the classroom of IR, (in which I was placed), on the first floor, overlooking Garden Street and Winckley Square. Winckley Square Convent School was then engaged in building a new extension to their School at No. 24 Winckley Square, which later became Heathcote's Restaurant.

For the first time in 20 years, major building works had to be undertaken in order to cater for the increased numbers, with the demolition and rebuilding of No. 28 Winckley Square, which, unlike No. 27, was unsuitable for use as classrooms. The work started in 1957, with the façade facing Winckley Square being rebuilt to look as similar as possible to the previous building, in order to comply with local planning regulations, sash windows and all, but with a considerable extension at the rear in a modern style. The new building consisted of six large classrooms with two smaller division rooms over a modern entrance hall, and extra toilets and cloakrooms in the basement. When No. 28 was being demolished, it was discovered that the adjoining No. 29, which had served as the Catholic Grammar School until its disposal in 1898, was in a very precarious state, with one wall being 15 inches out of true, and a stout buttress was erected to support the building. The new building cost £24,000 and was formally opened on 24 January 1959 by the Bishop of Lancaster.

The second phase of Fr Carty's alterations started immediately after, with the second form classes being moved into the new building to cater for these works. No. 27 was rebuilt internally, linking it up at each floor level with No. 28, in order to form a single unit. Further classroom and toilet facilities were provided in the basement, while on the ground floor two rooms were joined together to form a large Common Room, with the old staff room near the hall being freed to become an ordinary classroom. The War Memorial Library was greatly extended to encompass the whole of the first-floor area, including the blocked-up staircase-well, and, henceforth, the Sixth and Junior Libraries were all able to be accommodated in this room. This allowed the Wright Memorial Room to be converted into an ordinary classroom. Two more classrooms, together with Mr Kinleside's flat, comprised the top floor, while on the old coach-house site and air raid shelter, two new rooms were built, one to serve as a Music Room, and the other as a large Engineering Workshop. The Second and third forms were able to occupy the rooms by September 1959, while the first forms vacated No. 25 Winckley Square, where they had become isolated from mainstream College life, and moved into the former Middle School block.

Work commenced on the third phase of extensions in similarly swift fashion, with the construction of a completely new building on the side of Mount Street, which opened in September 1960. This adjoined the swimming bath block, and contained a spacious dining hall and kitchen on the ground floor. The old kitchen became an extra chemistry laboratory, with the old dining room being converted into an additional physics laboratory. Later more large laboratories, preparation rooms, and classrooms were completed on the two floors above the new dining hall.

Five years of almost ceaseless building activity had cost the College £90,000, which might explain why in May 1958, at the CCA's President Night, Fr Carty entreated, 'Gentlemen, I need your help!' The Catholic College Building and Development Fund was launched soon afterwards, and the weekly lotteries subsequently raised more than £10,000 from October 1958.

The re-opening of the Direct Grant Schools list by the Conservative government enabled the College to be re-accorded its former status from 1 August 1959, but only after more stringent conditions and detailed negotiations with the Ministry. This status change, after 13 years as an Independent School, did nothing to assist with the building costs, but it did bring an immediate reduction in the payable fees, to the benefit of both Local Authorities and fee-paying parents.

Although Fr Carty abolished several of the old institutions, such as the Lent Steeplechase, and the Christmas Concert, the Shakespeare Plays continued and went from strength to strength, with the Headmaster himself producing *Henry IV Part I* in 1958, and *Hamlet* in February 1959. He was assisted by Mr Arthur Malone, a Glaswegian

Scot who had recently joined the College staff in the English Department. Following Mr Malone's appointment, it was decided to transfer the Shrovetide Play to the November half-term holiday, with the new teacher producing a second play in 1959, *The Merchant of Venice*, and in 1960, *Macbeth*. After the 1958 Shrovetide a Drama Group inspired by Mr Malone was inaugurated, to give the boys the opportunity to produce plays as well as act in them.

The College Orchestra was less successful, owing mainly to a number of the outstandingly good players leaving the College shortly after the departure of Music Director Mr Smith in 1957. Mr Robson replaced him as Music Director, and expanded the Madrigal Society into a Junior Choir, which it was hoped would become the nucleus of a School Choral Society. Most of the old clubs and societies continued to flourish under Fr Carty, and new ones were added: the Fencing Club was formed in 1958, Railway Club in 1959, Rifle Club in 1960, and the Chess Club in 1960.

In the spring of 1961, Fr Carty was chosen (with very little notice) to become the Headmaster of St George's College, Salisbury, Southern Rhodesia. He was replaced by Fr Richard Wren, an old boy of St Francis Xavier College, Liverpool. Fr Carty returned to England in 1968 to become Headmaster of Wimbledon College, and, like Fr Duggan, maintained his contact with Preston and the College, which he had served for 12 years.

Fr Wren's tenure as Headmaster continued in the same vein as that of Fr Carty, with the College continuing to expand in both numbers of boys and in the accommodation needed to educate them. This was largely a result of the need to provide specialist rooms for the great number of new subjects and courses now being provided by the College.

No. 33 Winckley Square, adjacent to the College Main Entrance, was adapted in 1962 for use as sixth form classrooms, mostly for the Arts subjects. During the following year the basement of the block was enlarged to form a large cloakroom with toilet facilities for the use of the whole of the Upper School. At the same time, the large classrooms on the top floor of the new dining hall block were divided by sliding partitions to form smaller division rooms more suited to the needs of the Advanced Level Science and Mathematics students.

The following summer saw the Science Laboratories re-organised, with the objective of separating A level from O level work; at the same time, a projecting gallery was added to the first form block to afford separate access to the various classrooms. The Caretaker's Cottage was demolished in order to enlarge the Lower School playground and to give space to build a garage for the College minibus. That summer a large Language Laboratory was constructed in the former Governor' Room, which was the first of its size constructed in any secondary school in the district.

Summer 1965 saw the College hall transformed with the removal of the old partitions and the laying of a vinyl floor, and it was fitted out with upholstered tip-up seats containing retractable desk-lids. Stereophonic equipment and a television were also installed to supplement the film projector. The hall became a place for sixth form private study and General Studies courses involving the use of films, records, and television, as well as serving as an entertainment centre. However, it was no longer large enough to serve as the Examination Room for all the College candidates, which made it necessary for A level Examinations to be held in the modernised Roper Hall in Friargate.

In 1966, No. 26 Winckley Square was adapted to become another sixth form block for Arts students, with rooms for the Classics, English and History Departments. The adjacent No. 25B was also taken over three years later and reconstructed as a sixth form '*Palace of Mathematics*', as it came to be called, which linked up at each floor level with No. 26. These new sixth form rooms, despite being imaginatively decorated, retained the splendidly ornate nineteenth century plasterwork. The house basements of both premises were made into sixth form locker rooms as these boys no longer had their own classroom.

In 1970, No. 25 Winckley Square was re-occupied by the College. The ground floor, including the room which in 1865 must have been the original home of the Catholic Grammar School, was taken over by the Music Department, allowing the former Music Room to be converted into an A level Metalwork Shop, while the Upper Floors became Drawing Offices.

Finally, after almost 13 years of almost ceaseless building and reconstruction activity, an impressive new gymnasium, on the site of a row of Garden Street cottages, was built. The structure cost some £60,000, which was almost three times the cost of all Fr Grafton's buildings. The old gymnasium was then converted into an Art Studio, as Art had been restored to the College curriculum.

Since the end of the War the College had nearly doubled in size, with pupil numbers reaching 914 by 1970. Sixth form numbers had increased to nearly 300, with no sign of a reduction in the demand for places. The final years of the 60's saw the College offering some twenty different A level courses of both technical as well as academic subjects, allowing the sixth form students to choose a variety of combinations. In addition, a wide range of O level subjects were provided for sixth form boys. A degree of collaboration took place at this time with the Winckley Square Convent School. This included joint informal extra-curricular and social activities, and later combined the introduction of General Study courses. By the end of the 1960s more than 40 boys a year were going to University, as well as to many Further Education institutions. It was noticeable that two-thirds of the University places won by the College boys in 1970 went to those pupils who had been taking A level Science subjects.

A document was published on 22 April 1964 by Preston's Chief Education Officer Mr W.R. Tuson, entitled '*The Organisation of Secondary Education: A Re-appraisal.*' This was written in part as a response to the impetus of a change in Government, and the issue in July 1965 of the now famous Circular 10/65. Preston B C decided to implement the re-organisation scheme proposed originally in the *Re-appraisal.* The proposal recommended replacing existing Secondary Modern and Grammar Schools with Junior Comprehensive Schools, for children aged from 11 to 16 years of age, and a sixth form College, for those students wishing to continue full-time education, post 16. The Catholic authorities subsequently decided to re-organise their Preston schools accordingly. The two Convents and the College agreed to act as the 'Sixth Form College' for Catholic children.

As a result, after 1966, Preston Education Committee took up no places at the College for boys of 11 years of age. Consequently, the first form's annual intake was reduced to about 120 boys from September 1967. The College sixth form grew, however, with a greater number of boys transferring at 16 years of age from those Secondary Schools who had developed sixth forms.

Fr Wren began to inaugurate important administrative changes from 1962 onwards. The most significant of these was the separation of the sixth form, in March 1966, from the rest of the College, by the introduction of a partially elected sixth form Council, which replaced the Prefectorial System. This body's role was to regulate sixth form affairs, organise its various activities, and run the sixth form Centre, which was established in a large room made up of the former Art Room or combined with the adjacent classroom. The following summer it was the members themselves who decorated the room, equipping it with a hot-beverage dispenser and a soft-drinks bar, and furnishing it with coffee tables and upholstered seats. Prefectorial duties were then passed to the fifth form boys, who were at first called *Prefects*, but later became known as *Monitors.*

Fr Wren also introduced a 'clocking-in' system, with machines installed in the Main Entrance Hall, and later in No. 25B Winckley Square, for the sixth formers to record their presence and arrival time. Further changes were made to the College uniform, largely as a result of the difficulties brought about by the cost and durability of the tweed jacket, and a return was made to the traditional blazer, this time in black for the whole School. Forms I to V would have the silver Gonzaga Eagle on their breast pocket, but all the sixth form now had the full College coat of arms emblazoned on their jackets, which previously had been the exclusive privilege of the Prefects. Fr Wren also introduced a distinctive green sixth form tie, which contained a number of small silver eagles throughout its length.

At the end of Fr Wren's first College year, he introduced the Leavers' Dinner, at first in the College Dining Hall, and later in the more sumptuous surroundings of Roper Hall, for those boys who were leaving the College from both the Fifth and sixth forms. Also invited were Staff members and Old Boys' Association officials, who attended in order to try to win recruits for the CCA and players for its Football Club.

The Parents' Association continued to fulfil a useful role and arrange a wide variety of activities at the College. Under its direction, Parents' Form Nights, which enabled parents to discuss their son's progress with staff, had been systematized. In the College hall, fortnightly Musical Evenings for parents were instituted, presented by the Headmaster. The weekly Lottery continued to contribute substantial sums of money to the College Development Fund, and was renamed the 'Catholic College Club'.

During this period, life outside the College curriculum thrived, with a plethora of voluntary activities being available to students. There were 25 official Societies or Clubs in the College. A sixth form Society called *The Saturnalia,* was founded in 1964 to arrange various Saturday evening activities, presided over by the Headmaster, and to which sixth form girls from the two Convent Schools were invited. Activities included regular visits to Liverpool Philharmonic Hall concerts, as well as recorded musical and dramatic recitals, film presentations, and talks in the College Hall. Drama, especially the annual Shakespeare play, continued to be one of the most popular and successful of all the College activities. In addition, music at the College underwent a spectacular transformation after the appointment of Mr Harry Duckworth in 1966, and with the active encouragement of the Headmaster. 1967 saw the formation of the College Brass Band, and two years later the College Orchestra was reformed and began to play its part in the flourishing musical life of the College once again.

Sporting successes continued to come at the College, and were not only confined to the Football First XI. Several younger teams won local football competitions, including the Under 15 XI who became Lancashire Schools Champions in 1965, beating Openshaw Technical High School, Manchester, 2-1 on aggregate in the two-legged final. Hockey was introduced in September 1962 by Mr Sam Foulkes and

Mr Arthur Malone, proving a popular alternative to football from the third form upwards. In the summer of 1966, Mr Robson and Fr Middlehurst introduced Tennis as a competitive sport. And the Easter term of 1970 saw Rugby Union introduced by Mr N Hodgkinson with a Rugby pitch installed on the old Bull-field. The Swimming Club extended its activities to include Water Polo, while the Boxing Club was supplemented by a newly formed Judo Club. Cross-country running was also introduced as an alternative to the ball games on games afternoons, which revealed some outstanding talent, including one boy, J A Holden, who went on later to represent Great Britain.

The traditional Sports Day, however, was abandoned by Fr Wren at the end of his first year, although a smaller equivalent for the first three Forms only, was held at Riverside in July 1964 – Fr Wren felt that 'he did not like the casual garden party level it had settled into'. Another Grafton institution, House Competitions, also ended, with house matches no longer being played.

In Fr Carty's time the weekly Dialogue Mass was changed to 12.15 p.m. in order that the boys could receive Holy Communion. As the number of College boys in Fr Wren's time had grown too large to be accommodated all together in St Wilfrid's Church, he arranged for different Forms to have their own Mass on a particular weekday. Weekly School Benediction was abandoned in 1970.

The 1960's saw the deaths of several stalwart members of the College Staff. Mr Charles Kinleside, who had served the College devotedly from 1925 until his premature retirement after a series of heart attacks, died in Mount Street Hospital on 10 February 1963. A fortnight or so later the Senior English Master, Mr James Lawson, who had joined the Staff in 1942, died suddenly from pneumonia. May 1967 saw the College suffer another double blow when, on the same day, Mr Eric Craven and Mr Jimmy Flynn both suffered heart attacks. Mr Craven died within a fortnight. Although he managed to return to School for a time, Mr Flynn never fully recovered, and after a further stroke, he died in October 1968. 9 January 1969 saw the death of Mr Albert Clarkson, swimming instructor at the College since September 1936, but whose connections at the College went back to the earliest days of College scouting. There were also a couple of notable retirements during this period, with Mr Samuel Foulkes leaving on 11 July 1968 after 19 years of service, and Fr Mulvaney retiring in 1962 after 21 years of College service. Fr Mulvaney had founded the Q-Club during his tenure, and since 1949 he had also edited the College Magazine.

The departure of all of these College staff members left a gaping hole at the College to which they had given so much of their lives.

By now, the College had seen three people – one Staff member and two pupils – become Catholic Bishops, with two of them later becoming Archbishops. The first was the son of a British Consul, a Scholastic Staff member named Thomas d'Esterre Roberts, who taught at the School in two periods, from 1916-1922. He was ordained on 20 September 1925, and returned to teach at the College in 1929 until early 1935. He was appointed Archbishop of Bombay (Mumbai), India on 12 August 1937. He went on to become Archbishop of Sugdaea, Crimea, and Archbishop Emeritus of Bombay.

The second was a pupil who'd attended the College from 1947-1954; Brian Michael Noble was born on 11 April 1936, and, after studying for the priesthood at Ushaw College, was ordained on 11 June 1960. His first parish was St Ignatius', Preston from 1960-1968, where I often served his Mass. He was appointed Bishop of Shrewsbury on 23 June 1995, retiring on 1 October 2010, when he then became Bishop Emeritus of Shrewsbury. He died on 21 October 2019 in Wirral Hospital.

The other Bishop was Patrick Altham Kelly, who'd been a student of the College from 1949-1955. He was ordained on 18 February 1962 at the Venerable English College, Rome, and became Bishop of Salford on 9 March 1984, being appointed Archbishop of Liverpool on 21 May 1996 until his resignation on 27 February 2013, when he became Archbishop Emeritus of Liverpool.

Although the College had opened in 1865, Father Wren decreed that the centenary celebrations should take place in 1970. He decided to hold the centenary celebrations in 1970 because, owing to a lack of appropriate records, it had been quite impossible to pin-point the exact date of the foundation of the school. It seemed certain that it came into existence during the 1860's, and was definitely known to have been functioning by 1870. The College Centenary Thanksgiving Mass was held in St Walburge's Church on 23 September 1970; this was a spacious hall, without columns, and comfortably seated 1,300 people, all of whom had an uninterrupted view of the altar. The Church, built by the Society of Jesus Fathers in 1854, was chosen for this capacity. As St Wilfrid's Church could only seat 900 people and the number of College boys at that time was over 900, there would have been no room for the many parents, Old Boys, staff and friends of the College, who filled the Church to its capacity on this great occasion.

The Mass was concelebrated by Archbishop Roberts S.J., formerly Archbishop of Bombay, who had taught at the College for twelve years. He was flanked on one side by Frs. Francis Roberts, Robert Mills, and Thomas Middlehurst, all previous Rectors of St Wilfrid's, and on the other side by Frs. John Duggan, Robert Carty, and Richard Wren, all past and present headmasters. They celebrated the Mass in honour of St Ignatius of Loyola, founder of the Society of Jesus.

The occasion was graced with the presence of the Bishop of Lancaster, Bishop Brian Foley, who, following the entry procession, stood on the steps of the Sanctuary and summoned before him Mr Dennis Mather, the Centenary President of the Catholic College Association. Bishop Foley invested Mr Mather with the insignia of a Knight of the Order of St Gregory, which His Holiness Pope Paul VI had conferred on him, both as a personal honour for his work as a leading Catholic layman, and to the College he had been chosen to represent in its Centenary Year.

Mr Bernard Moulding, a staff member and Old Boy (who'd left the College in 1938), read the first lesson, while the Gospel was read by Dom Alban Crossley ('53), O.S.B., an Old Boy who was then at Ampleforth Abbey. One of the concelebrants, Fr Francis Roberts S.J., read the specially composed Bidding Prayers. The preacher for this special occasion was Fr Robert Brooks S.J. ('39), then the parish priest of Farm Street Church, Mayfair, London. Congratulations were given to the ninety strong choir, so ably conducted by the choirmaster, Mr

Harry Duckworth, with Mr G. N. Robson at the organ. They had hardly more than a week of the new scholastic year for rehearsal. Congratulations were also due to Mr D. Townshend S.J. and the dozen or so altar boys he had trained so carefully.

Within an hour of the end of the Centenary Mass, the Centenary Old Boys' Dinner was held in the Top Rank Ballroom with 291 Old Boys' and guests in attendance and Mr Denis Mather K.S.G. presiding. The Chief Guest was Lord Craigmyle, who gave a heartening, eloquent speech. Many old friendships were renewed by Old Boys who had not seen each other for many years, and I attended with my father.

The College Centenary Ball was held at the Top Rank Suite on the 17 February 1971. The Ball was a joint effort organised by the Catholic College Association and the College Parent Teachers Association, a splendid event which was thoroughly enjoyed by all who attended.

The evening of 27 June 1971 saw the official closure of the College's Centenary Year with a concelebrated Mass in St Mary's Church, Friargate. This Mass contrasted starkly with the Solemn High Mass sung in St Walburge's Church to commemorate the start of the Centenary. There was no great congregation of people, no choir and no clouds of incense. Instead, in the oldest Catholic church in Preston, where according to tradition, the Jesuit Fathers had served since 1605, the English Jesuit Provincial, the Very Rev. Fr. Bernard Hall S.J. concelebrated Mass together with 30 priests who were also Old Boys of the College. The congregation was made up of then present and retired staff members, and other friends of the College. Mr Townshend S.J. acted as M.C. and Fr Wren preached the sermon and observed how fitting it was that the closure event should be held in St Mary's Church, with its long history with the Jesuit Fathers. Following the service, a splendid buffet was served in Roper Hall, where a most enjoyable evening followed with a meeting of old friends, again led by Mr Herbert Bolton, who at 92 was the oldest old Boy and Master of them all.

Fittingly the College's Centenary Year ended with the ordination of Fr Bernard Walker S.J. ('56) by His Lordship Bishop Brian Foley in St Wilfrid's Church on Saturday 4 July, 1970. He was, as far as was known, the 142nd Old Boy to be ordained a priest. Saturday, 6 March 1971, saw the ordination of my old classmate Fr Edward Gannon ('65) to the priesthood at the Church of Our Lady and St Edward, Fulwood by the Auxiliary Bishop of Lancaster, Mgr. Thomas Pearson (Edward was the second of my classmates to be ordained, the other being Fr Chris Moss). The occasion was enhanced by the singing of the College Choir. Sunday, 27 June 1971, at St Wilfrid's Church, saw the ordination to the priesthood of Fr David Gould by the Bishop of Lancaster, Brian Foley. He became the 156th Old Boy to be ordained, since the foundation of the College by Fr Cobb one hundred years before. 15 May 1970 saw the College Groundsman, Mr Bill Cross, retiring to St Annes after 20 years' service with the College, with Fr Robert Monk also retiring on 10 July to St Wilfrid's Parish staff. Fr Peter Whittall left the College after 12 years' service for Farm Street Church, Mayfair, London on 9 July 1971, with Mr Tom Smith leaving after 14 years' service, in July 1972, to become Head of the History Department, and later Deputy Headmaster, of St, Cuthbert Mayne School.

In December 1972, a presentation was made on behalf of the College Boys to Fr Richard Wren in the School Hall by the College Captain, on his leaving for Rhodesia after 11 years' service. Fr Wren later addressed the College Boys at Benediction in St Wilfrid's Church, and, on the last day of term, he presided at the Carol Service in St Wilfrid's, following which, at the Staff's sherry party, a farewell presentation from them was made to him. He was replaced as Head Master by Fr Peter Hackett. Fr Wren's last Head Master's Report was chiefly a survey of the great stride in Scholastic Achievements that had been achieved at the College from 1961-1972, while he was the Head Master.

The death of the Mathematics teacher, Mr John 'Jack' Radcliffe, occurred suddenly, on 10 April 1973. Mr Radcliffe was a former College Captain who joined the Catholic Day College as a pupil in 1915. A former pupil of St Ignatius' Primary and Higher-Grade Schools, he had, been the St Ignatius' Boys School Headmaster since the late 1940's; he'd retired from that role in 1968 and had taken a teaching post at the College following his wife's death in 1969.

The Summer of 1973 saw the enactment of plans to refurbish the College, with 19 firms being commissioned for goods and services to both smarten and provide it with better facilities. The College Hall and Attica were supplied with furniture that looked new, with either new or refurbished notice boards placed on the walls. No. 28 Winckley Square had been redecorated throughout, with the ground floor Staff Room extended to accommodate extra staff. The Ladies Staff Room was redecorated and carpeted throughout, while the sixth form had their classrooms adjoining the Science Wing redecorated and supplied with new furniture. No. 33 Winckley Square had new, much more suitable carpets laid, with the sixth form rooms given more new chairs and tables. A new and more spacious College van had also been purchased.

A 'Declaration of Intent' had been produced in 1965 by a Catholic Body, proposing the Reorganisation of Secondary Education in the Preston Area along comprehensive lines. Two elements of the proposals that chiefly affected the College were that sixth form education largely became the province of Direct Grant Schools, and that Winckley Square Convent School and the Catholic College should begin to co-operate more closely. The declaration had been due for revision in 1972, but a 'working party' was only convened in 1973 to review the position. Governors, Staff, and Parents of the affected schools were represented, which stimulated the three Direct Grant Schools (now including Lark Hill Convent School), to meet, encouraged by the working partners' general conclusions. There was a wish that the Catholic Body still wanted the Schools' religious orders to be involved to continue their Catholic Education concern. Although noting that there was still much work required before a satisfactory plan could be reached for the area, the College's governing body accepted the principle of a parallel timetable between the Catholic College and Winckley Square Convent School for the sixth form, with immediate benefits chiefly arising from the inter-availability of courses.

On 12 July 1974 Fr Richard Birch left the College, where he had been teaching since 1954, to go to Barlborough Hall School, Mount St Mary's, Nr. Chesterfield, while Fr David Townshend had been appointed as a School Counsellor for both Winckley Square Convent School and the Catholic College.

Fr Hackett's Head Master's Report mentioned the decline in pupil numbers from 914 to 874 in 1972/3, to 814 in September 1974, to an expected population of approximately 790 in September 1975. Meanwhile the parallel timetable between the Catholic College and Winckley Square Convent School at sixth form level, which had been running for one term, brought the two institutions closer together in as much as joint O level, and General Studies Courses had been implemented, although integration was still only minimal at A level. Following a statement by the Secretary of State for Education and Science in the House of Commons on the 11 March 1975 concerning the future of Direct Grant Schools, it was clear that the Catholic College Governors, while having not yet formally applied for acceptance as a voluntary aided school, wished to remain within the mainstream of Catholic Education in the Area, particularly in sixth form Education.

Winckley Square Convent School celebrated its Centenary on Sunday afternoon, 20 April 1975, with an 'At Home' event in the School. The exhibition featured a general section showing the historical background of the century; pictures, maps and plans to illustrate development of school buildings; a display of school uniforms (in both drawings and reality) and of badges, medals, prizes etc., and a 'Rogues Gallery' of photographs from 1900 to 1975. The following evening saw the Guild Hall filled for a Concert and Mass. The Orchestra opened the Concert with a Farandole by Bizet; the Lower School Choir sang Rowley's *Robin Hood,* with 1A and 1P classes miming the story; the Senior Choir sang a madrigal and two-part songs. Next, a fascinating display of Gymnastics and Dance linked past and present: first came old-fashioned 'drill', performed in black leotards and to rousing music; then Greek dancing; then modern Gymnastics and Dance, a revelation to many in controlled agility, precision and gracefulness. Two final songs involved the whole school, as well as the Choirs and Orchestra. There followed two short speeches by Bishop Foley, with a vote of thanks from the Head Girl.

The culmination, and most memorable part of the Centenary, was the Concelebrated Mass, said by Bishop Foley with 22 priests concelebrating. A special school choir sang the Kyrie, Sanctus, Gloria, Agnus Dei from the English Mass in D by P.V. Ollis. After the recessional hymn, Mass ended with the School Hymn *Let Folly Praise,* followed by over 1,000 people returning to Winckley Square for light refreshments, and another opportunity to enjoy the exhibition.

The College provided volunteer photographers, Orchestra members, and Altar Boys, with Mr Leo Warren organising the whole of the Mass. There had been a precedent to this occasion; at the Convent's 50th Birthday Celebrations in 1925, the High Mass in St Wilfrid's, was sung by a combined choir from the Convent and College.

Mr John Cocker left the College on 30 April 1975 to go to Walton-le-Dale High School as Head of its Mathematics Department. He had joined the College in September 1970 from Christ the King High School, and was greatly missed by the Badminton Club, whose players benefited from his coaching, and watching and playing with and against him. In 1974, he won two Lancashire County titles, the men's and mixed doubles, and the men's doubles title in the London Open. He had also apparently held a match point against the England No. 3 player at a tournament in Worcester.

Mr Herbert 'Big Ben' Bolton died on 26 June 1975 at the age of 95. He had attended the Catholic Grammar School in the 1880's when Fr Payne was Headmaster, before leaving to go to Mount St. Mary's School, then returning in 1900 having been appointed to the College Staff to teach English by Fr Flynn. He remained at the College – apart from the years 1908-1913 when he was in Portugal – until his retirement in 1947. He produced the Shakespeare plays for many years, and ran the Glee Club with great success. After retiring he remained remarkably active, appearing regularly at Sports Days to announce, with his tremendous voice, the results as recorded by his great friend Mr J Lawson, who had succeeded him as Head of the English Department. (Ralph Cooper – 'I remember his booming voice announcing them at the College Sports Day in 1959, and he continued to take private pupils until he was 94.')

Mr G N Robson, the Music Teacher, had retired in July 1975 after 18 years' service, latterly as Head of the Spanish Department. He was remembered particularly for beginning the carol service at St Wilfrid's with Fr Wren, on 21 December 1962, which was recorded as the finest within a memory that went back twenty-two years.

Fr Peter Whittall died on 10 August 1975. He joined the College Staff in September 1959, becoming the third member of the famous trio known as 'Birch, Whackett and Hittall', to teach Mathematics and Religious Doctrine. He wore many hats, often at the same time: including sixth form Chaplain, hockey umpire, wrecking squad leader, director of the repair squad, master of the Mars bars, lord of the slab cakes, and coiner of phrases such as 'order a dozen'. Fr Whittall could be formidable when roused, and at times quite impossible, but would be remembered for his kindness. No one ever came to him for help and did not receive it. He was down-to-earth and practically minded especially when individual boys had difficulties, and was always happiest doing what priests can do, saying Mass 'decorum with dispatch', and giving absolution. His health had begun to fail before he left Preston in 1971, but, despite further setbacks he was able to do some teaching at Wimbledon College, under his great friend Fr Carty.

Fr Hackett's Head Master's Report, prior to his leaving the College, after a further three years' service, to replace Fr Carty at Wimbledon College, on 19 December 1975, reported with some frustration that the years of his tenure had seen Committee Meeting after Committee Meeting involving the three Direct Grant Grammar Schools in reorganising their sixth forms to form one Voluntary Aided Catholic Sixth Form College administered by the Lancaster Diocese. By the time of his departure, all the schools who might be expected to send pupils to it were committed to doing so, with one exception, and the declaration of intent had been signed, with both the Local Education Authority and H.M. Inspectorate actively helping in the problems involved. The schools were, however, still lacking the official go-ahead; an agreed timescale in terms of which proper planning could take place; a final decision as to which buildings will be involved; and a clear picture of the proposals for further reorganisation in the 11-16 age group.

Following the appearance of strange, damp stains on the floor of the College Gymnasium from 16 September 1975 onwards, it began to buckle. Within a week, a large hump appeared in the middle, extending along the length of the building over just two days, before cracking open to reveal a mass of water underneath. The College Gymnasium was only back in full use from 20 January 1976, having had a completely new floor fitted.

Out of necessity, negotiations had progressed slowly between the Direct Grant Schools, the Dioceses, and the LEA, but after a detailed investigation, the parties concluded that a purpose-built College on a campus site had no immediate and little long-term possibility of implementation. It was decided that the only realistic alternative was the adaptation and extension of one of the Direct Grant Schools, and that the Lark Hill House site offered the best scope to achieve this end. Having decided on the College site, the Public Notice about the intention to establish the Sixth Form College was published in the Autumn of 1976, with the appointment of the Principal Designate made in early 1977. The three Direct Grant Schools sites continued until August 1978, with Form 1 pupils being admitted in September 1976 and September 1977.

The Voluntary Aided Catholic Sixth Form College gradually moved from three to two sites at the Catholic College and Lark Hill, until finally relocating at the Lark Hill Site. The Catholic College Games Hall and the Swimming Baths remained in use for a longer period, until the St Augustine's New Avenham Centre was purchased, and the Swimming Baths building had been sold. Pupils in Forms 1-5 continued to be educated by Staff at the three former Direct Grant Schools' sites, with no alteration to their single-sex pattern of education.

Fr Wren had taken over as headmaster from Fr Hackett in January, 1976. In his Head Master's Report in that year he informed readers that a Tutorial System had been established to help to integrate boys – particularly those from the various feeder schools – to the College sixth form system by placing them in small groups in which they remained during their two year course. This development, along with regular meetings with their Tutors, allowed them to make personal contact with at least one staff member, and they thereby received help and guidance in their studies. The Tutorial System was amended to allow each group to meet its tutor at the start of each school morning for the daily prayer and registration, which helped the group to integrate with each other quicker, and provided an opportunity for any sixth form news and notices to be personally communicated. The amalgamation of the Catholic College and Winckley Square Convent sixth forms had continued, with the pupil numbers interchanging between the two establishments steadily increasing. Two further meetings had taken place of the Negotiating Body concerned with the formation of the Catholic Sixth Form on the Lark Hill site, which had determined that there would have to be a new building at Lark Hill for teaching Science. The number of pupils at the College was 830 at this time, made-up of 492 students in Forms 1-5, with the sixth form having 338. Full-time Staff numbered 54, with five part-time teachers.

Fr Wren's Head Master's Report in 1977 stated that the Governing Body for the new Sixth Form College had been appointed that summer, and at its first meeting on 14 July it had appointed Fr Wren as the Principal Designate of the new College, which, from September 1978, would be known as Newman College. The September meeting of the College Governors saw the appointment of three Vice-Principals: Sr Gabriel from Lark Hill Convent, Miss M Roberts from Winckley Square Convent, and Mr J P Newsome, from the Catholic College, with Miss B Green from Lark Hill Convent being appointed Director of Studies. Sr Catherine, Winckley Square Convent's Headmistress, had earlier informed the Governors that she would not be seeking a post at Newman College.

The next year's report from Fr Wren went on to explain that from September that year Winckley Square Convent, Lark Hill Convent and the Catholic College would become a Voluntary Aided Sixth Form College, Newman College, under the Trusteeship of the Lancaster Diocese, in collaboration with the Liverpool Archdiocese and the

Salford Diocese. Pupils in Forms 1-5 would complete their studies, on the three sites, until taking their O levels. The total school population across all sites would be approximately 1,200 pupils under 16 years of age and 860 sixth formers, with the three Vice-Principals having responsibilities for their respective sites. The administrative arrangements for Newman College included three Consultative Boards for its Academic, Pastoral, and Administrative affairs.

However, as academic life carried on, College sporting accomplishments had suffered a jolt by the time the Sixth Form Colleges merged. The Catholic College had started entering the Preston School Cups in Season 1962/3, when the U'16 XI drew 0-0 against St John Southworth School in the Lucas Shield Trophy Final at Deepdale. There were only three Preston cups initially, but the U'13 Cup was added in 1967, and to complete the picture, the U'12 Cup in 1976, with the Catholic College team the first team to win it.

In 1977 the school had three teams at Deepdale; the U'13's won the LFA Cup, the U'15's were joint-winners of the Ord Cup, while the U'16's won the Lucas Shield Trophy. In the fifteen seasons up to and including 1977/8, the College had entered a total of 57 cups, reaching 28 finals, of which only three had been lost. But in 1978, for the first time since joining the Preston Schools' Cups, the College had alas no teams in the green College shirts in the Finals. The U'12 XI had lost 1-3 to St Edmund Campion in the Semi-Final, while the U'14 XI lost 2-3 to a Combined Longridge and St Cecilia's Schools' team.

The next year, however, saw the College U'13's win the Jack May Trophy, beating St Cuthbert Mayne 1-0, at Deepdale, with Peter Cooper the scorer; the U'15 XI won the Ord Cup on the same evening, once again by beating St Cuthbert Mayne 3-0, this time with Andy Cooper scoring a hat-trick. Tom Smith, St Cuthbert Mayne School's Deputy Head Master and a former captain of the College team himself, who had also returned to teach History in 1958, was heard to say in the Deepdale Main Stand after the games that 'they had been done by the Coopers', knowing that my father and I were sat in the row behind him.

It is clear that from the inception of the Catholic Grammar School in September 1865, through to its closure as the Preston Catholic College, in August 1978, that the Jesuit Fathers played a very important, and significant role in the governance and teaching of Catholic Education to their pupils from both Preston and the surrounding Lancashire Area, providing them with as sound an education to both O level and A level in many subjects, that could be found anywhere in the country. This remarkable success story was often achieved only with great sacrifices, and in the face of considerable odds, on the part of the Jesuit Fathers and their assistants. The leadership shown from the beginning by Frs Cobb, Martin, de Lapasture and Payne, through the years between the World Wars by Fr Grafton, to the post-war years involving Frs, Duggan, Carty, Hackett, and Wren, was exceptional, and they can only be afforded our highest praise. They were also aided by many long-serving Staff members, both Jesuit Fathers, and Lay Staff, many of whom had previously been pupils at the College.

It is perhaps also fitting that now, in what would have been the College's one hundred and fiftieth anniversary, the lives of the last first form College pupils who attended the School in September 1977, should be portrayed in this book, and that we should have the chance to read about their escapades while they were in attendance at the Catholic College, and their lives after leaving for the wide world.

I would like to thank my old History teacher, Alban Hindle, who compiled the book 'A Centenary History of the Catholic College Preston', which he published when he was Head of the College History Department on 30th April, 1971. The book was extremely useful in enabling me to piece together the first 100 years of the College, before gleaning much information from the College Magazines regarding the period from the Centenary until the College's closure at the end of August 1978.

I would expect many ex-Catholic College Old Boys will be interested in reading the book.

JOHN GARLINGTON: OLD BOY 1963-1971, AND TEACHER (1979-1980)

I was employed on a year's contract at the College from 1979-80, spending some time at Winckley Square, mostly in the afternoons. The school I returned to after nine years was a bit different from the one I had left as a pupil. For a start, its name was officially Newman College – Winckley Square (Boys). My Dad, who'd attended the College from 1938-43, almost threw up when I told him.

There were signs of wear and tear all over the place, which Lancashire County Council had patched up in a way that the school would not have countenanced when it ran its own finances. For instance, the beautifully decorated Hall with its burgundy ceiling was wounded with a large, ugly patch of white plaster that had clearly been used to patch up a problem. No attempt had been made to blend it in to its surroundings. The central heating system at Number 33, Winckley Square was poor, because the system that had been installed in 1964 with money from Mr Kinleside's will was failing, but Lancashire would not fund repairs or a replacement. Another thing they'd done was to switch out the lights at the side of the War Memorial in the Hall; these had been lit since 1921 without a break, because they were supposed to be on 'in perpetuity'. The reasons given were health and safety and finance. Former pupils of the College, like John Whelan and Dick Palmi who were in my year, occasionally wanted to have a look around, but I put them off because I wanted them to preserve their own memories of the place.

Some of the staff had gone, such as Dr Brosche and Arthur Culshaw, both of whom I had been looking forward to seeing again. Arthur Malone was welcoming, as were Leo Warren and Fr Magill. Also, the school secretary, Mrs White, and her assistant Mrs Howson, were both still working in the Office. Mrs White turned out to be a revelation, because when I was a pupil I always thought she was rather distant, but she turned out to be very friendly and very funny. I used to drop in to talk to them when I could.

Jack McCann had taught at English Martyrs' Boys School, where I was taught before the College, so I knew him well. One lunchtime a group of sixth formers were milling round the street door of No. 28 so I did my Jack impersonation, barking "Excuse me, boys," in that higher pitched register he used to use. You should have seen them scatter!

On my first morning in September 1979, Arthur Bunce, who had arrived in 1967/8 and was also an Old Boy, said "Come and sit by me", and for the next three terms I had the time of my life. He was so welcoming, friendly and funny.

I can't say that I was particularly enamoured of the classes I actually taught, but I did find an affinity with a bunch of the youngest boys, who were then third formers, who I talked to about television, football and cricket. Perhaps we were in similarly isolated positions.

Would I do it again? Yes, because of Leo Warren and the two Arthurs, Malone and Bunce, and the lovely chats I had with Mrs White and Mrs Howson.

MARTIN AINSWORTH: TEACHER (1976-1979)

A View from the front of the Classroom

Reading the varied and moving accounts of the Boys of 1977, I was transported back in time to my first teaching post at the College after leaving University. I had forgotten so much, so the students' stories retrieved wonderful memories and brought considerable pleasure.

Many of the accounts reflect on what it meant and what it was like to gain a place at Preston Catholic College. I was also a "New Boy" when I took up my post, and I experienced much of the same mixture of apprehension and excitement as the students. Some of the formidable and idiosyncratic teachers they were facing were equally scary to me!

The College was a labyrinth, both physically and culturally. Many of the staff were 'lifers'; having attended PCC as scholars, they had returned there to ply their craft. The school buildings were squeezed amongst various offices and businesses. I half expected to open the wrong door and end up in a Solicitor's briefing instead of 4S for English Lit. The main entrance was a burrow of a gothic arch from which you tunnelled into the warren of PCC, finding fellowship, challenge and learning on the other side.

After a year of being on probation I was entrusted with the very last first year football team in my second year. It was considered a big honour to manage a PCC football team, and there was an expectation your side would not let down the proud track record of the College. In 40 years of teaching, I have managed many school football teams. This PCC team was the best I cared for. When we won the Jack May Cup at Deepdale I perhaps should have quit while we were ahead!

That side was particularly good because its composite parts were better than any one individual. The players slotted into their positions comfortably, and they did their jobs well for boys of their age and experience. We tried to foster a positive mantra of helping each other, especially during a match. None of the team, as far as I know, went on to play professionally. I have been privileged to coach and play with youngsters who did 'make it'. Most of these individuals knew that to progress they had to look after 'number one' and sometimes this meant they were not the best or most unselfish team members. The whole squad at PCC loved playing for the School and each other. We were supported brilliantly by a faithful band of parents and assorted brothers and sisters. They kicked and headed every ball through rain, wind and snow.

The Cath Coll was probably the most successful footballing school in the greater Preston area. The backroom team contained gifted and experienced individuals. The best coach was Eddie Brown, an ex-PNE and Birmingham City player, who by day masqueraded as a French teacher but on 'Games afternoons' and Saturday mornings was the all-seeing expert eye and the source of real footballing nous. I was happy to learn at the 'master's knee' and throughout my career used his tactics, tips and sayings: 'Get your feet off the floor' for headers, and 'Stay on your feet', for marking, blocking and tackling. If Eddie was Alex Ferguson, then Father Spencer was the scheming, Machiavellian Don Revie. Winning at all costs mattered greatly to this cleric and he wasn't above taking advantage of his priestly status when it came to the odd outrageous penalty award to PCC in the last few minutes of a game. As a result of his career of chicanery PCC were not greatly loved by neighbouring schools, so when my band of innocents proudly ran onto the hallowed turf of Deepdale for the Schools final we were greeted by a chorus of boos. Unperturbed, we honestly and courageously battled through a quagmire to win 1-0!

Sadly, the school was shrinking during my time there, resulting in less teachers being required. The rule of thumb applied was 'last in, first out', so I had to move on. I joined Broughton High School and went on to become Head of English at St Mary's in Leyland, Deputy Head at Hodgson High School, Poulton, and then Head of Wellfield High School, also in Leyland. I finished my career working for the Ministry of Defence, leading their two secondary schools on the Sovereign Bases in Cyprus.

Meeting the class of '77 in 2016 was a thrill. It was fantastic to hear of the experiences of these 50-plus men. It reminded me why teaching is one of the most important and rewarding careers in the world. We don't change the lives of those we teach, but we do open doors and point them in positive directions they can choose to follow and explore. Well done to Jimmy Clune for pulling the threads together. May I finish by expressing the honour it has been to know these boys and men.

Correspondence received by students prior to beginning their life at Preston Catholic College:

Lancashire
County Council

Education Offices, Joint Divisional Buildings, East Cliff, Preston, PR1 3EU Telephone 54868
J. C. D. Rainbow, M.A., Chief Education Officer
T. C. R. Newhouse, M.A., District Education Officer

Extension 6371
Please ask for Miss Bowcott
Your reference
Our reference BB/KK
Date 6th May, 1977

Dear Parent,

Admissions to Secondary Schools 1977

I have to inform you that the District Assessment Panel have decided, after taking account of all the evidence available, that the most appropriate course of Secondary Education for your child would be a course of a type such as that provided in a grammar school.

A place is available for him/her at the Catholic College School, and provided you accept the conditions set out in Section 1 of Form ADM.308 enclosed herewith, the Lancashire Education Committee will pay tuition fees in respect of the child's attendance at that school. If you have not already done so, you may expect to hear from the School Authorities in due course.

Form ADM.308 sets out the conditions under which travelling expenses are refunded and gives information about other assistance provided by the Committee in necessitous cases.

If you wish to appeal against the decision of the District Assessment Panel you should do so by writing to me at the above address by 20th May 1977.

Yours sincerely,

District Education Officer

To: The Parent or Guardian of:
Adrian G. Jones

CATHOLIC COLLEGE,
WINCKLEY SQUARE,
PRESTON, PR1 3HH.

I have been informed by the Lancashire Education Authority that your son has qualified for Grammar School education. I am pleased to be able to inform you that the Governors of the College have offered a place to him at the Catholic College for next September.

I enclose an Application Form which should be completed and returned to the College as soon as possible, and not later than June 21st. Should you not wish to take up the place that has been offered, would you please inform us immediately as there are other applicants on a waiting list.

Also enclosed are some circulars giving general instructions for the new school year and details of the Parents' Night for New Entrants on Thursday, June 23rd. at 7.30 p.m. in the College Dining Hall.

R. Wren, S.J.
Head Master

The Society of Jesus

The Order was founded by St. Ignatius Loyola in the early 16th. Century. Its primary apostolic aim is to seek and serve the more urgent needs of the Church. Secondary education is but one of these needs, though the Society has long been associated with this type of work. Its association with English education goes back to the 16th. Century, but its present commitment is largely the development of a large expansion in the 19th. Century. We have to see ourselves against the background of history, and as part of an Order with word-wide interest.

The Catholic College

The school was opened over a century ago. It has evolved through the years according to the changing educational pattern of the country, and the changing needs of catholics. Its teaching is, therefore, coloured by the educational practice of the time. As a grammar school it still emphasises the academic and technical, as a grammar school, too, its teaching tends to be formal. We are not insensitive, however, to modern educational ideals, particularly that of the second Vatican Council which says that christian schools should be noted for their spirit of "freedom and charity".

On a more down to earth note, the College has moved towards the present needs of catholics by greatly developing its Sixth Form (some 340 boys). It is the normal Sixth Form, not only for boys at this school, but also for the 11-16 schools of the area. It has a parallel time-table with Winckley Square Convent school.

One thing remains constant, expressed by the words A.M.D.G. - ad maiorem dei gloriam: to the greater glory of God.

Direct Grant Status

The College is a direct grant school. The money for its running costs, and I emphasise running costs, comes partly from a grant from the Department of Education and Science, and partly from fees, sometimes undertaken by the Local Education Authority.

All capital expenditure (and in the past few years some £150,000 has been spent) has to be found by the trustees. Neither government nor diocese contributes. The almost total source of income is the difference between Jesuit salaries and their living expenses. One practical way of helping is to join the Catholic College Club, details of which will be made available.

The College has declared its intentinn of seeking Voluntary Aided status in the near future, and this may take place in September 1978.

Parents' Association

We have a Parents' Association which promotes many activities during the year: Parents' Evenings when parents can meet the staff about the progress of their sons, music sessions, dances and discussion groups. The aims are social and educational. All parents are members. There is no fee, but on parents' evenings a collection is made, partly to pay for activities of the Parents' Association, e.g. supporting voluntary work done by the boys, priests etc., partly to pay for the tea and biscuits.

Some points of Importance and Information

1. Mr. J. McCann has pastoral care of the First Forms. Their academic progress is in the hands of Miss Almond and Miss Mangan. All three will be grateful for any informatinn you can give.

2. For the first two years the education of all boys is general. Homework is set according to a fixed timetable each night, and consists of both written and learning work. This homework is obligatory; it is NOT optional. A boy can be excused for a valid reason, but only by means of a written note from the parent. Each form has its own homework timetable; and each boy has a homework notebook, which should contain the timetable and work set for each particular day. For a Form I boy homework should take about an hour each day. Some of this work may have been done on certain days at school.

3. Every fortnight during term a Report Card is sent home by means of the boy to the parents, indicating the standard of achievement and work reached during the preceding fortnight. It has to be signed by the parent and returned to the College via the boy.

4. On entry boys are arranged alphabetically in classes. Rearrangement takes place as soon as it becomes desirable for the good of the boys.

5. Games are on Friday afternoon and the boys are taken to and from the Playing fields by coaches. Football boots and white shorts are required for games. The College supplies football jerseys (one white and one of the House colour) at ordinary prices.

6. All boys require white gym shoes, white gym vests, navy blue gym shorts, swimming trunks and a towel.

7. All clothing should be clearly marked with boy's name and class. This includes raincoats, caps, scarves etc., as well as P.E. and games equipment.
One of the College regulations is: "No money or valuables should be left in cloakrooms, changing-rooms or classrooms."
The College cannot be responsible for the loss of, or damage to, any article of clothing.

9. All who cannot get home for a hot meal in the middle of the day are encouraged to attend College dinners. The cost of the school dinner is 15p per day, paid daily.

10. There is no charge for ordinary school text books, stationery games etc.; extra personal stationery, geometry sets etc. (which are retained by the boy for his own personal use throughout his school career) are to be paid for, and also anything damaged or lost through his own fault.
Boys are, too, expected to buy a copy of the Jerusalem Bible New Testament by Christmas.
In order to prevent too much buying and selling we collect £1.00 at the beginning of the year to cover the cost of two magazines and the school calender. Boys with older brothers or fathers in the Old Boys' Association pay 25p only - the cost of the calender.

11. We do not think that the satchel is a good piece of school equipment. We think it is better to provide a boy with either a small case or a brief case, and also a duffle bag for his P.E., swimming and games equipment.

N.B. All notes of exemption should be addressed to Mr. J. McCann.

PARENTS' NIGHT: Thursday, June 23rd. 1977 in the School Dining Hall.

Please bring these sheets with you.

College Badges will be on sale.

GENERAL INSTRUCTIONS FOR THE SCHOOL YEAR 1977-8

The Beginning of Term:

a) Form I boys only: Monday 5th. September; schools end mid-day.

b) Forms II, III, IV, V: Tuesday 6th. September; schools end mid-day.

c) Sixth Form
2nd. and 3rd. Years : Tuesday 6th. September at 10.00 a.m. schools end mid-day.
1st. Year : Thursday 8th. September at 9.30 a.m.

The Daily Timetable

The morning session begins at 9.00 a.m. and ends at 12.40 p.m.

The afternoon session begins at 2.00 p.m. and ends at 4.00 p.m.

No boy will be allowed to leave school any earlier than 4.00 p.m. to catch a train or bus. Any boy may stay at school and do some homework in a classroom if he has to wait for a later train or bus.

Terminal Dates

Autumn Term:	September 5/6 to	December 21st.
Half Term:	October 31st to	November 4th. inclusive
Spring Term:	January 9th to	March 22nd.
Half Term:	February 6th to	February 10th. inclusive
Summer Term:	April 10th to	July 14th
Half Term:	May 29th to	June 2nd inclusive

These terminal dates are given to enable parents to make satisfactory arrangements for family holidays. It is hoped that parents will do their best to make their arrangements in accordance with these terminal dates, is so far as this is possible.

School Uniform

School uniform is to be worn on all school occasions and at all College functions. Temporary exemption from any particular part of the uniform will be granted for sufficient reason, provided that permission has been correctly asked for from the Head Master.

FORMS I TO V

a) Black blazer (which may be bought from any outfitters)
b) White Eagle Pocket Crest (from the College, price 30p)
c) College tie (from Lingard's, Fishergate)
d) Grey or white shirt
e) Grey shorts or grey sports trousers
f) Grey pullover; quiet socks.

Notes on Uniform

a) Overcoats and raincoats should be worn whenever the weather requires them.

b) Attention is drawn to the need for marking personal belongings.

c) A satisfactory haircut for a College boy in Forms I to V is that the hair is not to touch the collar of the shirt or coat. The hair should be clean, well brushed or combed and tidy. Many boys have unsatisfactory haircuts. Parents are asked to co-operate. The shorter the hair the easier it is to keep tidy.

General Information

1. Except in the case of sickness no boy may be absent from school without permission, which can be granted only for serious reasons on receipt of written application from the parents or guardian.

2. If a boy has been absent he must, on his return, bring written notification of the dates of his absence and the reason for it.

3. All are reminded of the necessity of punctuality in arriving at school.

4. Any complaint (e.g. against punishment) should be made within 24 (school day) hours to the master in charge of the section of the school to which the complainant belongs:

   Forms I - III: Mr. J. McCann
   Forms IV & V : Mr. Bamber

   Failing a satisfactory settlement the Head Master should be approached immediately.

5. All boys are required to take part in games and physical education organised by the College, unless personal exemption has been granted after written application from parents or guardian. Application for a particular occasion should usually be made, if possible, a day beforehand.

6. Permission to come to school by bicycle and to use the bicycle shed must be obtained from Mr. Bamber by means of a written note and should include acknowledgement that the College will not be held responsible for damage or loss.

7. Parents must inform the College of any change of address that takes place during the school year. If this change of address also involves a change of Local Authority then they should also inform the Local Authority of the change.

8. Information concerning railway or bus contracts, and all enquiries concerning the payment of travelling expenses, clothing and school meals and maintenance allowances, should be made at the Local Education Authority's offices, not at the College.

THE LAST INTAKE

PAUL ALLISON: FORM 1A

Preston Catholic College was a whole new world from St Anne's Junior School in Leyland. Greek mythology, briefcases, free scones in the afternoon, the ferula and lots of Mass. I did feel out of my depth. I am one of eight children, and my parents really struggled to pay the £17 per term. I was given textbooks, an old briefcase and helped with uniform. Our form teacher, a woman whose name I can't remember, was really kind and discreet. I enjoyed studying and found the strict teaching style suited my own desire for learning. I remember the famous weekly Report Cards, and looking back now I realise how tightly governed everything was, from behaviour to homework. I remember Father Wareing talking to Franco Mastrobouni in Italian, especially, constantly having to say 'Silencio, Franco, silencio!' Shaun Daly was the other person from my Primary School who went to PCC.

I remember being taken to the sports fields where it just seemed to rain all the time. Football was a great memory, because we had a fantastic team; it was such a pleasure meeting up with them and with everyone else in October 2016. I think I was on the periphery of the team and wasn't always first choice defender. I didn't mind, because I was quite small and being part of a football team brought other financial pressures for my family. We nearly played at Deepdale, but I think we were beaten by Edmund Campion school in the semi-final. I do remember Neil Slater shouting 'Come on lads, let's break their legs' at a game against a school in Blackpool, after a rousing half time team talk by Mr Ainsworth! St Kevin's Kirkby were probably the roughest team we played; they smashed some milk bottles in our goal mouth, resulting in our keeper cutting his knees and having to come off.

Our singing auditions were a life-scarring moment. We were told how great the PCC Choir were, and that they 'compete in Rome' etc. The music teacher sat at the piano and we had to stand up one by one and sing a few lines. Good singers lasted maybe 20 seconds; I lasted about three. Mark Beattie was the best singer, and I think he went on to be a priest.

I was only at PCC for two terms, and often wonder what I would have done for a career had I stayed at the College. My dad was a printer/journalist and had a new job at The Ormskirk Advertiser so we moved from Farrington Moss. I could have travelled to Preston every morning, but the expense of the train journey and the school fees was too much. (I only found out at the reunion that the College scrapped the fees after the first year). Reluctantly, I made the decision to leave PCC and start at St Bede's School in Ormskirk. However, God decides these things, and I met my beautiful wife of 25 years at my new school.

Leaving the College allows me to compare PCC with a 1970s comprehensive school. There was an enormous difference in quality of teachers, classroom discipline and intellect. At St Bede's there was a clear demarcation between the top and lower sets. There were nearly 200 people in my year, with six or seven different classes. PCC felt very small and controlled compared to the sheer chaos of a secondary high school.

The Catholic ethos at St Bede's was like the elephant in the room, whereas at PCC the elephant was stood out the front wearing a collar! Things were definitely tougher at St Bede's, with a lot of fighting and daily use of the cane. At PCC the discipline felt a little darker somehow, almost as if justice was exacted in a cupboard! We didn't have an 'Eddie Brown' at St Bede's, and sport was generally seen as an inferior activity to studying. Consequently, those in the lower sets tended to be picked for the teams, and because we played all the Skelmersdale schools, most games ended in mass brawls with people getting sent off.

At 18 years old I joined the Royal Air Force as an Engineering Apprentice in Airframes and Propulsion Systems. I was commissioned as an Engineering Officer and sent to Royal Military College to do a BEng in AeroSystems Engineering. I went on to complete the Initial Officer Training and spent some time as a Flying Officer, working for the Ministry of Defence in Whitehall – which was a fantastic job!

I went on to complete professional Engineering Training, and became a Junior Engineering Officer (JEngO) Flight Lieutenant on 25 Fighter Squadron Tornado F3. I did lots of travelling around the world, including operations in support of the Balkans War. My next posting after that was RAF Coltishall in Norfolk, in Engineering Support of Jaguar aircraft (including some flying). I was then sent to HQ Strike Command in north London and promoted to Squadron Leader at 31 years old. I was the Staff Officer for the introduction of Typhoon aircraft into RAF service.

My final posting before leaving the RAF was as Officer Commanding the United Kingdom International Air Forces Field Team (UKIAFFT). This job was fantastic, as I had junior officers and SNCOs working for me in Italy, Spain and Germany.

My wife Shelly and I were married in 1994, and as an artist she hated the life of an Officer in the Military. I retrained as a Chiropractor and have run my own clinic (St Jude's Chiropractic Clinic) for the last 18 years. I also spend some time in London working for my governing body, the General Chiropractic Council, on three Professional committees, including Professional Conduct, Health and Test of Competence.

I started karate at the age of 17, and 37 years later I am still training hard as a sixth dan in Shotokan. I represented Great Britain in four World Championships and various other European competitions. My greatest achievement (besides our two boys) was winning a bronze medal in the 1995 WSKF World Championships in Mexico.

I spent time in Africa on a Catholic mission 1990, which was life-changing. I still go to mass regularly. I am a Pastoral Outreach Coordinator and Eucharistic minister at Our Lady's Church in Tarleton. I have competed in lots of ultra-events (seven marathons in seven days – ran 100 miles in a weekend – ran in a team of six from St David's to Great Yarmouth) to raise money for different charities. I received an MBE in 2003.

STEVE BARROW:
FORMS 1C, 2B, 3A 4A AND 5A

First impressions

Some memories are still vivid, even those from as far back as September 1977. Like most kids from my cohort, I came from a small primary school (which in those days meant one with no school uniform, nor any homework), so my first day was quite daunting, particularly when I encountered about 90 other kids that I didn't know and only four that came from the same primary school as me. I remember shopping for the regulatory uniform with mandatory briefcase and sports bag in the days before I started at school, along with getting a haircut short enough to not touch my collar! I think there was a choice of grey or white shirt, and long and short trousers . . . one kid did turn up one in shorts on day one; I can't remember who it was, but he sure got some stick. By day two he was in long trousers!

My Dad had gone to Preston Catholic College and was keen for me to attend, too; as this was the last intake, I didn't qualify to sit the 11 Plus; I had to sit an entrance exam instead, which I somehow managed to pass so skipped junior 4 (year 6 in new money).

Armed with a bus pass and dinner money off I went in my uniform and briefcase for the journey that lasted seven years (five at Catholic College and two at Newman College): through the bus station, across the flagged market, down Cheapside, Fishergate and Winckley Square, to arrive at the school gates. It took about 15 minutes to walk, and about six minutes if you were late and needed to run. I remember we were allocated to one of three classes, and I was in 1C. You sat in alphabetical order . . . surname first, of course. I don't think anybody ever got called by their first name, and all teachers were Mr, Mrs or Miss – well, at least officially. It was made very clear to us that we were privileged to be pupils at the school and would be expected to work long and hard; in some ways I think it stood you in good stead for your working life. Many teachers wore gowns, looked very serious and generally took no nonsense so first impressions were that it was strict and regimented, and that secondary education wasn't going to be anything other than hard work.

The Football Team

I thought I was a reasonably good footballer until I turned up at football trials, where I realised that I was just very average. Football trials weren't mandatory so the kids that turned up all wanted to play which was unfortunate as there were some very good footballers, so the level was very high. I managed to get into the second XI, and turned up religiously at Grafton on a Saturday morning in the wind, rain and occasional sun. I don't really remember that much about the games for the second XI, but strangely I remember one game for the First XI more than the others.

My best position was striker. One week when Pete 'Coops' Cooper was unavailable for the First XI, I got the nod. I fail to remember the school we played against, but I played up front with Jimmy Clune and I had the perfect game. Everything I did seemed to work or hit the back of the net, so we won convincingly, and I scored six . . . yes, a double hat-trick. Never done that before or after. Obviously, I couldn't wait for the next match, but I had to wait ages. Why? Because I got dropped in favour of Cooper! I'm not sure many people score a double hat-trick and get dropped. But to be fair, Coops was a much better footballer than me!

In all honesty the school team was good, and went on to win the Preston schools trophy, in a fixture played at Deepdale.

The Cricket Team

We weren't a cricketing school; although there were some decent cricketers, it wasn't a sport we excelled at. I couldn't take to cricket – too much hanging around unless you're good with bat and ball – so I didn't take much interest. However, for some reason I played one day; presumably all the other choices weren't available or couldn't be bothered, so I was called up. We played Hutton Grammar, who *were* a cricketing school. I remember we got battered; I fielded at third man (the position they usually put the worst player in), I didn't bowl (probably because I couldn't), and I scored nought (you can guess why).

The Swimming Pool

It was unusual for a school to have a swimming pool but we had one, situated in the lower playground. One year, I can't remember which one, swimming was the first lesson on a Monday morning. Mr Bradley was the teacher, and he took great delight in making all the kids stand on the side in the cold until he said jump in. As the heating only got switched on at the start of the lesson the water was Artic-like but you weren't allowed out until you'd turned blue. Mr Bradley had played water polo, so that was popular in lessons and lunchtime sessions, unless you ended up in the goals and your head became target practice for him. I remember Paul 'Ritchie' Richardson seemed to be one student Mr Bradley picked on . . even though we weren't that matey at school, we have become firm friends and meet up regularly with Micky Wilson. We always end up mentioning some memory of school.

School pranks

Every kid has an element of mischief, or sometimes malice, in them, and sure there were many pranks that I'm not aware of. But there are two that I remember. Both were probably around Form 3: one involved a fishing line, and one involved washing up liquid . . .

Somebody had the bright idea of tying a fishing line around the board duster and then feeding the line around the pipes in the corners of the room. The idea was that the board duster would then move along the shelf under the blackboard, behind the teacher's back, confusing them as it would always end up in a different place to where it was left. It worked, and everybody thought it was hilarious, but unsurprisingly the teacher eventually realised what was going on and instead of gently using the duster pulled it viciously. The culprit was revealed when he screamed as the fishing line dug into his fingers!

The washing up liquid was much simpler; we simply poured the said liquid on the round brass doorknob after the teacher entered the room so they couldn't open the door after the lesson had finished. It worked, and it was worth the whole class getting additional homework as a result, probably!

I don't know why this comes to mind, but I do also remember some kids putting Michael Kellet in a shopping trolley and pushing it down the hill in Avenham Park! He survived, although looking back it was cruel.

Nicknames

There were dozens of nicknames for kids and teachers alike, and I'll name a few. It's only afterwards that you realise that all nicknames tended to end in the letter s, o, z or y!

'Suds', 'Goz', 'Huggy', 'Higgy', 'Ashy', 'Harry', 'Hendo', 'Conno', 'Crooky', Moz . . . you get the drift.

There were a few others that didn't end in said letters, but to this day I still don't know why or how they came about. A couple of the stranger examples I can remember were Biff and Pig – answers on a postcard! 'Fat Jack', 'Pop', 'Bunny' and 'Granny' were some of the most endearing for the teachers. As it was a Jesuit School, many teachers were priests, so it seemed fitting that God was the headmaster's nickname. In case you're wondering, mine was 'Baz'.

School Yard Games

Generally, there were just two of these –football, and cricket (of sorts). Football was the favoured option, but both were played with a tennis ball for some reason. Football would end up being a match between two teams consisting of about 25 players a side or as an individual variation, with you against 50 others. It seemed fun at the time, although you could go a whole game without touching the ball.

Our version of cricket was for somebody to stand at the top of the yard and whack the ball as high as they could; the kid who caught it could then have a go with the bat. It seems pointless now, but it did pass a few hours. The other school yard event was the occasional scrap between a couple of kids, probably over something and nothing.

It wasn't so much a school game, but in the early years you weren't allowed out of the school at break times. I'm not sure whether or not the teachers knew this, but there was a way to escape, if you ran up the back of the bike shed roof and jumped over the school wall into Mount Street, then nipping through St Joseph's Hospital into Theatre Street. That was the easy bit. Getting back into school proved more of a challenge.

The Fire Extinguisher

I generally didn't get into that much trouble, probably because I never did anything really bad or was just fortunate that I didn't get caught. Yes, I got several lines, detentions, and the odd whack across the palms of my hand with the ferula (a whalebone wrapped in leather), but no more than a few others, and a lot less than many others. It was probably for the usual stuff: late homework, talking, fishing line (oops, I've exposed the culprit). But the worst punishment I got was being banned from the gym for a couple of weeks, when I'd let the fire extinguisher off. I maintain to this day it was an accident. I was innocently bouncing the basketball in the gym storeroom, in a space in the corner, when it accidently caught the handle of the fire extinguisher, resulting in the entire contents of the water-filled container dispersing itself all over the gym wall. The PE lesson was abandoned while I had to mop up said water, and I landed myself a two-week ban. It's only writing this now that I realise that in accordance with health and safety regulations, the extinguisher should have been fixed to a wall, not propping open a door, but I'm 40 years too late to make the point in my defence.

School Trips

The best school trips were those enjoyed by the choir, who went to places as varied as Wales, Italy and New York. The school choir was the pride of a certain Mr Duckworth, but on the basis that I couldn't sing, I wasn't picked, and so I missed out. I couldn't draw either, by the way, so Art was a subject that didn't last long, although as an accountant you learn to be creative sometimes!

I did get to go on school trips to Castlerigg in Keswick, a popular venue for many schools, as well as Betws y Coed, and St Johann in Austria. We were all of an age where you weren't supposed to drink of course, but hey, it's part of your life education and growing up, so the aim of the game on all of these excursions was to smuggle alcohol into your rooms and get drunk. A great idea until the morning after! I'm sure the teachers knew what was going on but turned a blind eye. I think they enjoyed the challenge of the hunt, especially as they probably drunk what they found!

While Castlerigg and Betws y Coed were outdoor, walking-type trips, St Johann was the ski trip. That provided some great memories, as it was a joint trip with Winckley Square Girls school; maybe others will share stories about that (I'm not sure where the photograph is!), but most importantly it gave me my first taste of skiing, which is something that I've continued to do. I'm fortunate to have regular ski holidays still, and have been to some fantastic places.

Good Friends

You can't keep in touch with everybody, although I still see a few lads knocking around town or out and about. But the friendships formed at school are long lasting, and I still see, on a regular basis, Mark Connolly (Conno), Paul Richardson (Ritchie) and Mick Wilson (Micky – I'm not sure why his nickname wasn't Willy or Willo – the exception to the rule, perhaps).

Lasting Impressions

Looking back, I thought Preston Catholic College was a good school, educationally and holistically. Not everybody likes school, but on reflection I took more good than bad memories away from it, and hopefully it set many lads up for the future and their careers. It was a typical grammar school, you certainly knew where you stood, but that was no bad thing. I think my school report would have said 'could have done better educationally', but it's too late now; nevertheless, I consider myself lucky to have attended and benefitted from the experience. Hopefully I'll see many colleagues again at the book launch or perhaps another reunion . . . if we recognise each other, that is!

Unsure of what I wanted to do after O levels, I remained at the now called Newman College to study Maths, Physics and Chemistry, and considered many options, including university, the police force, and the royal navy. But one day I abruptly realised that physics and chemistry weren't for me, so I turned down a place at Cardiff University to study engineering. The last career I wanted was a 'desk' job. I wanted to be active, and out and about, so after much deliberation decided on my career. In accountancy.

Having studied two subjects that don't lend themselves to accounting, I managed to get a job in the finance function of the NHS, that offered study facilities. So, after more studying, by now thinking it would never end, I completed a diploma in business studies and my accountancy exams to become a Chartered Management Accountant. I realised the NHS offered many opportunities and was, as a topic, quite interesting and varied. Thirty-seven years later, I'm still in the NHS, and thinking about my pension. I've worked in many places throughout the North West of England, but always remained loyal to my Preston roots.

The usual life pattern followed: girlfriend, fiancé, wife, kids. Of these, I still have the kids (well, young men now), and I'm extremely proud of them both; one is at university studying sports development and management, while the other is a qualified . . . yes, accountant. But I now have another lovely lady in my life!

Outside work I remained relatively sporty, and still am I suppose, although the sports have changed with age! I played football for Preston Catholic College Old Boys (now Newman College); Micky Suthers and Pete Cooper played, too (and Coops was still better than me!). I continued with badminton (you may not know this, but I was Preston Schools Champion back in 1983). I've also completed several half marathons and sprint triathlons (the word sprint is a misnomer, by the way) and a parachute jump! Nowadays I settle for squash, golf, cycling and skiing. I'm not great at these either. Apparently 'it's the taking part that counts' – but I don't buy into that!

I see a few old school mates regularly, namely Mick Wilson, Paul Richardson and Mark Connolly, and we talk about old times over a beer or at the occasional dinner party (it's really beer and food at someone's house). Despite knowing the stories and the outcome, they still make us laugh, while our wives and partners despair at hearing the same stories for the umpteenth time.

MAURICE (MOZ) GEORGES BLACK: FORMS 1C, 2A, 3S, 4S AND 5S

I arrived at the College in September '77 – the year of The Clash, Damned, Pistols and Punk. I was ten years old, and one of the youngest boys to be part of that final Preston Catholic College intake.

Rebellious in nature, mischievous, and somewhat less than studious. Hated Latin, German and Chemistry but excelled in Art, English and Maths. School reports generally said: 'Maurice has the capabilities to do better, if only he put his mind to it…'

Getting into trouble was a regular occurrence. Not for anything nasty, mainly getting caught 'nicking out of school' at lunchtimes. In fact, a claim to infamy I hold is being the last boy in the school's history to receive corporal punishment: three ferulas for 'nicking out of school', and three more for refusing to say who was with me . . .

School team sports weren't really my thing. I much preferred skiing, cycling and climbing, more solitary pursuits in nature and not part of the school curriculum. I suppose even at that age I was quite independent, due to family upheavals, although I did have plenty of friends, both in school and in the College scouts, which I was part of throughout and beyond my tenure.

The main memories I have of PCC all seem to centre around music. Seeing The Clash in '79 at The King Georges, the *Bat Out Of Hell* 12-

inch release on blood red vinyl, *Cranked Up Really High* by Slaughter And The Dogs, *She's Not There* and *Warhead* by the UK Subs are all standout memories. I recall doing an English class project with Matt Iddon on Sham 69 and The Pistols, and although we were lauded for our presentation, we were somewhat reprimanded for the swearing that featured on the song tape we played to the class. Which also reminds me of the time we submitted the Pistols *Friggin' In The Riggin'* single to be played in music class on the 'bring your own music to school' day. The words of the music teacher still ring in my ears: "Now, class, who actually enjoyed that . . . ", Not many had the courage to raise their hands!

I did well in my O levels and went on to Newman College with predominantly mathematical subject choices. Following sixth form, I spent a couple of years in jobs where I felt I was wasted, in more ways than one! I wanted adventure, to get away, so I sold my pride and joy, my Kawasaki GPZ, stuck out my thumb and went on an overseas journey that was to last 'nigh on' 20 years. A journey that took me from the American Rockies to the Antipodes, from the frozen glaciers of the Alps to the party beaches of the Mediterranean. Club 18-30 Rep, Ski Guide, Wine Tutor, Cabaret Entertainer and Excursion Host were just some of my roles before taking up more mainstream Tourism Management.

However, fate took an unexpected turn in 2006 with the diagnosis of my spouse's hearing loss. I left my life of travel, and studied to become an Audiologist, a job which I still fulfil to this day and one whose terminology is steeped in Latin, so maybe those lessons did serve a purpose after all. It's been a rewarding career so far, genuinely changing people's lives for the better.

My passion is still travelling the globe, but now I go as a tourist. I also really enjoy cooking, and music is still a very important part of my life. I go on a yearly pilgrimage to Blackpool for the Rebellion Punk Festival, and even took up the guitar aged 40, but don't expect any chart releases any time soon . . .

Likes: Mojitos, Sausages, Punk Rock, Snow and Ice
Dislikes: Cancer, Cultural Religion, City, Remainers
Fav All-time Band: Sisters of Mercy
Fav Current Band: System of Hate
Fav Song: *Homicide* by 999
Fav Film: *The Good, The Bad and The Ugly*
Fav Team: United, of course (cut me I'll always bleed RED)
Fav Places: Val d'Isère, French Alps / Koh Samui, Thailand / Jasper, Canada / Riviera Maya, Mexico
Highlights: Bungee Jumping, Parapenting, Off-Piste Skiing, The Sisters Leeds '04, Albertville '92, Italia '90, France '98 and '16, a season with the Elk in Jasper National Park, a desert island in New Zealand, the madness of Dubai and surprisingly, a short stay in Edmonton Penitentiary . . . are just a few.
Best Advice: Always be Honest, no matter the consequence.

My life certainly has been an adventure, with some lows, certainly, but mainly with highs, of all kinds. But to have experienced such a myriad of sights, sounds, cultures, in so many different destinations – that has been the best thrill of all.

JIM CLUNE:
FORMS 1A, 2B, 3M, 4M AND 5M

Prior to starting at Preston Catholic College, I went uniform shopping with my mum, Betty Clune (nee Birtwistle). I was one of six children. Money was tight back then, and mum and dad would always have to search for bargains when hand-me-downs had worn out! Everything was going fine until it came to my shoes. We headed straight to the renowned shoe shop, our first and only port of call – 'Tommy Balls'. If I remember correctly, they cost 69p. Mum's idea of a consultation was "you're having them", despite my desperate protests! My siblings, being the supportive lot that they were, decided with great glee and merriment, to nickname them 'daggers' due to their pointy toes!

Although I knew we were the last intake into the Cath Coll, it didn't register that much, apart from the need to pass the entrance exam, as there would be no further opportunity to do so. I remember being the last of the pupils at my primary school to find out I had passed. I can still remember my dad walking into the playground with a big smile on his face, giving me the thumbs up. I was so pleased and relieved!

Us 89 first formers made history as the last ever intake, crossing the threshold into the Cath Coll for the first time on 5 September 1977. The recently deceased Elvis Presley was at number one in the charts with *Way Down*, James Callaghan was Prime Minister, and Liverpool had won the European Cup for the first time. The Clune/Birtwistle family had 'previous' with the Cath Coll and Winckley Square Convent School, situated on the other side of Garden Street from the College. Mum, some of her sisters, her mum, and my sisters Mary and Elizabeth, all went to the convent school. My brothers, Richard and Francis and my uncles 'Pip' and Eddie all went to the Cath Coll, too. My cousin, Andy Hammond, was one of eight sixth formers at the College who were successful in passing the Oxford University Entrance Examinations in 1977, as well. My great uncle Wilfrid Holden also attended the school. His name is amongst those listed on the First World War memorial, which is now on display at Newman College, based on the former Lark Hill Convent site.

On what if any basis we were placed into classes I don't know, but I ended up in 1A – the other classes being 1B and 1C. My initial memories of school are that it was quite austere and disciplined. The top yard was on a slope, with an office halfway down on the left-hand side, known as the 'Wendy House'. There was a path that connected the top and bottom yards (which was lethal during the wintertime, especially if there had been snow). Some of the teachers dressed in gowns. My primary school headteacher at St Wilfrid's in Fox Street, Sister Canisius, was a nun, so seeing priests at secondary school didn't look too unusual. Classes were arranged in rows of individual wooden desks, one behind the other, each with its own ink well. We were addressed by our surnames. We had to start every piece of work with the letters 'AMDG' – 'To the greater glory of God' – written in the left-hand column. Attending Mass at St Wilfrid's Church, once a week, was a part of the timetable. We had to stand up, as a mark of respect whenever a teacher entered the room. I'd gone to football trials down at 'Grafton', the school playing fields off Factory Lane (named after a priest who had been a headmaster at the school), during that summer, and got picked to play for the first team, as centre forward. I played in that position throughout my time at the school. We had something called a Betamax video recorder at the school as well . . . very technologically advanced at the time!

One term that struck fear into the hearts of pupils was receiving 'cracks', the colloquial name for receiving the ferula, the College's form of corporal punishment. The first person I saw being told they would get the ferula was Franco Mastrobuoni. I can't remember what he'd done, but he was told that he would be getting one 'crack' by Father Wareing – aka 'Wez' – in an English class in 1A. Cracks would be administered by 'Jack' McCann, 'Pop' Moulding (whose favourite saying to quieten the class was 'In the words of the immortal bard, shut yer gob'), or Graham Billington (who sadly passed away during the process of writing and editing this book, RIP). The most you could receive at any one time was 'six of the best'. I received two separate amounts of 'cracks': a 'two', and a 'four'. They were administered across the open palm of each hand and really stung. I remember getting the first two for being cheeky in a music class we had at Winckley Square Convent, in the third year!

Academically, I found life a struggle in that first year at the school. Expectations were high, and tolerance low. I found my level from the second year onwards, as I was placed in the bottom class (2C, and subsequently 3M, 4M and 5M) for everything! My lifeline in that first year was the football. I remember our first game, at Grafton, wearing my brother's hand-me-down boots. We beat Cuthbert Mayne 13-3! I remember scoring my first ever hat-trick in a town cup game against Tulketh High School. It was on one of those classic freezing cold winter mornings when the sun was shining brightly and the playing surface was rock-hard. Mr Ainsworth, our manager, described our football, in the school magazine as follows: 'In treacherous conditions, beautifully simple, ruthlessly efficient football, tinged with suitable flair, resulted in a 7-0 victory.' We had a great team and went on to win the town cup at Deepdale in the second year, when we beat Cuthbert Mayne 1-0 in the final. I laid on the only goal of the game for Pete Cooper at the Kop end. For the first two years we were managed by Martin Ainsworth, who then left to teach at another school. Martin was a great manager. He was clear that he only wanted to hear words of encouragement on the pitch, not criticism.

At the start of the second year the school was renamed Cardinal Newman College, along with Winckley and Lark Hill Convents. From that second year onwards, the number of pupils decreased, while the number of sixth formers increased. By the time we reached the fifth year in 1981-82 we were the last pupils left at the school. We were playing less football matches as we could no longer offer other schools five teams to play against. Our manager for the games that we did play, in the fourth and fifth years, was Pete Singleton. He was a very well-respected teacher and manager who unfortunately is no longer with us. One game we did play in the final year was against Edmund Campion School who had beaten us in the semi-finals of the town cup in the first year. We beat them something like 10-1, therefore getting some measure of belated revenge! I managed to score four in that game. I also remember a game we played at home, again in the town cup, in our third year, when Fr Spencer was our manager. We were drawn against St. Thomas More School. There was an added edge to the game as my next-door neighbour, Paul Brown, went to 'Tommy Mores', and he was sure that they would beat us. In atrocious conditions again, this time at Grafton, we played some amazing football and won 8-2. I managed to score twice in the game, one of which was a header off a great cross from the left by Mick Suthers.

Now, I have consulted Pete Cooper about this, and I would like to claim the honour of having scored the last ever goal for the school. I remember us playing an away game in the fifth year, in the 'Lancashire Schools Cup' (or similar), to a school from the Blackpool area. I was sub in the first half as I had been ill and hadn't been able to play in the previous game. I remember coming on for the second half and scoring with my weaker left foot. I don't remember there being another school game after that. Mind you, I remember a cross coming in from the right after I scored that goal, and Pete shouting at me to leave it; thinking I could score, I headed it, but the goalie saved it. I'll admit that I should have left it to Pete, but he can't argue too much, as I did lay on the goal for him in the final at Deepdale! It would be remiss of me not to leave the last word to Pete, though, who told me "You could claim the last ever goal . . . or be remembered for not letting *me* score the last ever goal . . . "

Teachers had left the school as numbers became demonstrably smaller. Fr Wren had written in the College magazine notes that no pupils from the Cath Coll, Winckley Square or Lark Hill schools would be taught on any other site but their own. This did not happen though, as Lark Hill girls transferred to Winckley Square and then the Winckley Square girls transferred to Lark Hill for their fifth year, as their school closed in July 1981.

We lost two pupils during my time at the school. In the third year, Michael Watterson died while riding his bike and colliding with a vehicle. During half term in October/ November of our fifth year, Anthony 'Joey' Royle also died while riding his bike. I remember hearing a report of a 15-year-old boy being killed on a bike in Salmesbury on the local radio news, and for some reason having a sense of foreboding that it might be Joey. My worst fears were confirmed later that day in a newspaper report in the Lancashire Evening Post. I remember ringing John Bradley that night and breaking the news to him. Although we weren't close, I remember doing a collection for a wreath for Joey's funeral, which I picked up from the shop I worked in (Hills – more about my time working there later), on the day of the funeral. May they both rest in peace.

I have a lot of fantastic memories of my time at the Cath Coll: of characters like Len Rogerson and his unmissable guttural Lancashire pronunciation of 'Bonjour' in French lessons (and subsequent laugh!), of Form 1B getting severely told off by Miss Mangan in the first year for slamming their desk lids up and down in unison to tune of the 'Floral Dance' by Terry Wogan, and of the loyal parents who'd come to support us playing football, home and away in all weathers, including Mr and Mrs Slater, Mr Henderson, Mr Suddick and my dad, George. I always found the teachers to be hard but fair, and approachable. My lasting memories are that we had great laughs in class, but knew when we had to draw the line, stop and work.

Our last day at the school was on Friday 28 May, 1982. Apart from messages of good luck for our impending O levels, there was no fuss, and no fanfare. Number 1 in the charts was *House of Fun* by Madness. The Falklands war was raging, and dog licenses were still mandatory! To this day I keep in touch with great friends I made at the school and sixth form, including Damian 'Wammer' Walmsley, John Bradley, Paddy Gardner (who I first met at St. Wilfrid's primary school) and Pete Baldwin, whose brother Andy also went to the Cath Coll. I have also met up for an occasional pint or two with Simon Cuerden and Matt Iddon, in London.

Between 1980 and 1984 I worked at Hills Fish and Poultry shop at the junction of Adelphi Street and Moorbrook Street. I carried on the line of Clune brothers working at the shop, in my case on Saturdays and during the holidays. As always there was a strong link to the Cath Coll as the shop was run by the Hills family, of whom Peter, Bernard and John all went to the College. I'll be honest and say that I wasn't overly keen to work there initially, but I grew to really enjoy it. It was a superbly run and down to earth northern corner shop, which is sadly long since gone!

I stayed on at sixth form College, on the Cath Coll site. Armed with two A levels, I joined the Metropolitan Police Cadets in August 1984. I successfully completed all my training and in February 1986 was posted to Kings Cross Road Police Station. I really enjoyed my 31 years in the Met, but you can't ever beat your first posting, can you? I loved it at the 'Cross', working with many superb characters, having some great laughs and dealing with all types of incidents. For example, in 1988, while dealing with a fatal road traffic accident in Upper Street, Islington, we were having real difficulty identifying the deceased lady. In the mortuary at Bart's hospital, I immediately declared that she was a nun, as she was wearing a necklace with the letters 'SHCJ' on. Winckley Square Convent School was run by an order of nuns from the 'Society of the Holy Child Jesus' and I recognised the initials from my sister's schoolbooks. After contacting a local Catholic church in Islington, we were able to confirm that the lady was indeed a nun and lived in the area. A week or so later I had to attend the nun's convent house to take a further statement. While I introduced myself, I heard a familiar booming voice from inside the building. It was my primary school head, Sister Canisius, who had travelled down from Preston and knew all about the incident.

During my time in the Met I was also posted to 'One Area' Territorial Support Group (public order and surveillance), and the Diplomatic Protection Group (looking after government buildings and embassies and carrying a firearm). I also worked at Haringey Borough (both as a constable and on promotion to sergeant), working in Tottenham and Wood Green on response team (24-hour shift patterns), in the custody offices, and for the schools unit. I also worked in Enfield Borough (on promotion to inspector) in a variety of different roles, including being in charge of response teams providing the initial and critical response to murders, rapes, domestic violence and gang fights, for example.

While at Enfield Borough I met Police Sergeant Paul Rigby. During our conversations he told me he had been taught by Jesuits in Blackpool. I said that I had been taught by Jesuits in Preston. Paul said that his brother had been, too. I then uttered the immortal words, "His name's not Dave by any chance, is it?" It was clear that it was the same Dave Rigby that had been in the last intake with me! I managed to have a conversation with Dave on the phone. I was aware that he hadn't been well, but it still came as a massive shock to be informed by Paul afterwards that he had passed away. May he also rest in peace.

One of my numerous highlights in the Met was leading the Haringey Police Cadets to victory in the Met Police Cadet Championships in 2006. This was a competition that took place over the course of a weekend at the Hendon Police Training school between cadet units from across the thirty-two boroughs of London, and included problem solving scenarios, fitness challenges and marching. It's amazing what young people can achieve through hard work and self-belief! During those 30 years on the beat I appeared on the front pages of the *Independent on Sunday* and *Daily Mirror* newspapers as well as in the *Sunday Express* and several local papers! I was assaulted in Kings Cross in December 1989, and my nose was broken. The three suspects were arrested at the scene but were found not guilty by a jury at Southwark Crown Court. I broke my jaw playing football for a TSG side and then broke ribs trying to save a person's life while I was at Haringey! I am proud to say that I worked in the Met alongside colleagues whose bravery, work ethic and willingness to deal with all that society can throw at them, still never ceases to amaze me, even though I retired in 2015.

Since November 2015 I have been working at a local school, which is now called Goffs-Churchgate Academy. It is a great place to work, with committed, friendly and supportive staff and great pupils. I initially went there to volunteer to do some life coaching and they offered me a job. I have worked in the Student Support Team and been the Director of Learning for Years 9 and 10. I am now the Mental Health Lead, working to support the pupils, their families and school staff to have better access to mental health information and services.

On Friday 1 July 1988, while minding my own business, in the Friend at Hand public house in Russell Square, WC1, I met my future wife, Lesley, who funnily enough hails from the north west too, in this instance, Manchester. Lesley runs her own successful podiatry practice. We married in May '94 and settled in Goffs Oak in Hertfordshire. We have two fantastic grown-up children, Harry and Grace. I am a very lucky man! Harry has moved to Canada on a working visa. He is currently living in Toronto and works for Treetop Marketing and Promotion – a company founded by my brother, Richard. Grace, who has a real affinity for the north west, has moved to Preston to live. She worked for TUI travel agents, based in Deepdale, for some time, and is now a teaching assistant at Ashton Community Science College, also in Preston.

While writing this biography, my family suffered the awful news of the completely unexpected death of my younger brother John, on 4 June 2019. He was only 48. John went to St. Cecilia's School in Longridge. After a successful career in the army John worked in the risk management industry, most recently for a company called Jacobs, based in London. His funeral service was packed to the rafters with mourners. Friends and colleagues literally travelled the world to be there. One colleague had travelled from Brisbane, Australia. What a fitting tribute to an amazing man. It was and still is an honour to call him my brother. May he rest in peace.

There have been two school reunions, the first of which took place in 1988 and was organised by Shaun Daly (who sadly passed away while this book was being put together). Pete Cooper and I organised a second reunion which took place in 2016. While organising the event I became aware that at least four more old boys had passed away – Miles 'Jam' Hartland, Andrew Dixon, Ronan 'Rex' Sargeant and Michael Browne; may they rest in peace. Forty-seven old boys, and four teachers attended. It was a great evening, full of laughter and stories about our times, experiences and diverse lives since we left the school.

Although I understood why the Cath Coll was closing, I didn't agree with the decision. It didn't make sense to me that a school as good as ours, with its history, academic and sporting success, not to mention our internationally acclaimed choir, was being closed, while other less well-run and successful schools were staying open across the county. Mum and dad made massive sacrifices to send five of the six of us to grammar schools, an option not available to my brother John. I certainly had a keen sense of our school history and the opportunities being lost to the people of Preston. Are grammar schools elitist? Possibly academically, but certainly not from a class perspective, and certainly not at the Cath Coll. I can only imagine what their closures have done to social mobility for working class people across the whole country. I am proud to say that I went to the Cath Coll.

PETE COOPER:
FORMS 1B, 2C, 3M, 4M AND 5M

I remember my last year at St. Augustine's junior school being a big one as Miss Whitehead began her task of preparing six of her pupils, Anthony Rawlinson, Alec Crook, Paul Richardson, Simon Cuerden, Bernard Moon and yours truly for the Entrance Exam to the Preston Catholic College; PCC for short, or 'Preston Concentration Camp' as a few of the past pupils referred to it!

I must admit I didn't relish the thought of the additional homework that year, as it would definitely get in the way of my favourite activity of playing football at any given opportunity! Three of my siblings and my mum, Margaret, and dad, Ralph, had attended either the Cath Coll, Winkley Square Convent or Larkhill Convent, so I didn't think I had much choice about going, unless I failed the exam! Before I knew it the day of the exam arrived, and we were ushered in to do our best.

Unfortunately, all that extra-curricular work paid off and I passed, along with the other five from our school. I remember the day I found out – I actually cried! Not out of joy, but grief! I was distraught. To think that I would be going to an all-boys school when my best friends would be going to a boys AND girls school called St. John Fisher, which was just a ten-minute walk from where I lived instead of a three-mile uphill drudge every day!

Mum and Dad couldn't, or perhaps didn't want to understand why

I didn't want to go, especially my dad. As a natural athlete he'd excelled at the school, particularly at athletics, and we still have the medals to prove it. I'm sure he thought I would follow in his footsteps.

Soon enough, it was time to visit the only shop in town, Lingards, I think it was called, that sold the prison, sorry, *school* uniform. My parents couldn't easily afford it, but as it was my new school and my dad and brother didn't have their old uniforms any more to hand down to me (thank God), they bought everything I needed!

The outfit seemed very drab, with a tie that had red, white and green diagonal stripes across it and the FIDES school badge that mum hand-stitched on to the breast pocket. I thought I looked a right plonker, and my best friends agreed, delivering a never-ending amount of ribbing on the subject.

As I was quite a bit younger than my eldest brother, also named Ralph, and my dad, I never heard them speak much about their school days. I did know they ran all four teams of the Preston Catholic College ex-pupils football club, affectionately known as 'the Cath Coll Old Boys', who played in the Lancashire Amateur League. I often went down to Grafton with them, to help out and watch the games, before heading back to the warm changing rooms for a hot brew and biscuits.

That summer flew past in a blur, other than the day I met up with other future pupils for a trial for the first-year football team, coached by ex-professional Eddy Brown and soon enough 5 September 1977 had arrived. I set off for the long walk to meet with Bernard Moon as he lived en-route, and we made our way to Chapel Street for our first day at the 'big school', wary of any of the older pupils and kids from other schools, just in case!

Looking back, I don't remember too much about the first day, other than that I was put into the class of 1B (along with Bernard, I think), and that our class teacher was Mrs Proctor. I'm sure she would have read us all the rules and regulations that we were supposed to obey, but as usual I would find out the hard way for myself!

The school looked very worn and ancient to a young 11-year-old, but you could sense the years of history within its walls and winding corridors, right down to the old stone slabs in the playground where we were only permitted to play football with nothing more than a tennis ball. To one side of the playground was the 'Wendy House', a one-roomed building which displayed that month's 'Line', or literary paragraph as it should have been known! It was also where a couple of the head teachers seemed to spend their time observing our break time shenanigans. I came to visit the place many times over the next five years, to note-down that month's version of the penance that I would have to re-write time and time again as a result of some misdemeanour I had committed! Viewed from Winckley Square, the whole school was hidden behind a row of terraced four-storey offices on Chapel Street, with only the main entrance, which is still there today, visible to the street.

Our first-year classroom was separated from the corridor by an old varnished, wooden wall with opaque glass that rattled every time the doors was opened and closed, much to our amusement. The antique desks were aligned in rows, and I think we were organised in alphabetical order of surname. As mine begins with C, I was second row back. Too close to the front for my liking!

I'm sure that at the time none of us first-years were aware of the significance of our being the last ever intake at this historic school; for me, the fact didn't really sink in until I was probably in the third year, as by then there were far fewer pupils in the school, and the playground was a lot bigger – with fewer people to hide behind to avoid the teachers!

I was lucky, as I knew a couple of older pupils that were two years above us who gave me tips on which teachers to keep on the better side of, along with the short-cuts around the school – which seemed like a maze for the first few weeks – and of course, which of the older pupils to avoid, for my own good!

Most of the teachers we had were quite strict, but fair, and you could still have a laugh and a joke with them at the right time. We soon began to get the hang of the school day. I also began to enjoy the whole experience before too long, especially the sporting side of the curriculum. I had to endure the academic side, and try to get to grips with it, if I wanted to get on in daily life at school. We even had our own swimming pool, although it felt like we were swimming in the Baltic rather than the Med, and we didn't dally when getting dressed in the middle of winter in the changing room. I swear there were often icicles hanging from the ceiling!

We were encouraged to get involved in the numerous dinner time and after-school clubs. I joined the Dolphins Water Polo team, run by the Sports and Biology teacher Mr Steve Bradley, a portly fellow with a black belt in Judo and an innate ability to be able to hit you with the polo ball thrown backhand while looking the other way, if you were messing about!

Football was my real passion, and I played it whenever I had the chance. I was picked for the First XI football team as a winger and stayed in that position throughout my five years at the school, cementing it as my own. We had a great team with some really good players. We were managed by a really good guy called Martin Ainsworth who took us to the final of the Jack May Cup at Deepdale in the second year on a very wet and miserable evening, where we were victorious, winning 1-0, with me scoring the only goal of the game. We played on the full pitch, which was reported to be bigger than Wembley; it certainly felt that way towards the end of the game.

Although it was the pinnacle of my sporting life at that time, I'd nevertheless played in a pair of second-hand, moulded sole, Mitre boots, and a pair of odd socks, too! I remember drinking something fizzy from the trophy later in the changing room, where I read the name of Jack May on the cup and blurted out loud "Who the hell is Jack May, anyway?" Suddenly, I felt a hand grip my shoulder, and the man himself said "I am, sonny, and don't you forget it." Needless to say, I haven't!

A few of us went on a school trip to the Lake District that year, staying at Park Foot Camp Site by Lake Ullswater for a canoeing holiday, joined by some of the girls from Winckley Square. I'm sure I bought my first 'single' record while on that holiday, London Calling, by The Clash.

Unfortunately, my sporting prowess wasn't matched by my

academic abilities, and I slipped into the lower stream, where Metalwork, Engineering Science and Technical Drawing were our syllabus for the next few years. Still, I didn't think Latin, Chemistry and Biology would be my future anyway, and as it turned out I was right.

I was also picked for the Preston Town U12's football team, where a few of the players I would meet up with in later life had also been chosen. Even when playing football for the school we had to show up on a Saturday morning in our school uniform and tie; if we forgot the tie we were punished with 'lines', as it was drilled into us that we were representing the school and always had to behave.

Unfortunately, when representing the school, I wasn't always on my best behaviour. One particular occasion was when we were in the third year, I think, and we were playing a semi-final in Longridge against St. Cecilia's. Peter 'Singy' Singleton was our manager, and that afternoon he drove the school minibus with half the team in it to the opposition's school, where he then left us to go and get the rest of the team. I decided to have a cigarette in the changing room, and shortly after stubbing it out their manager came in, and I was forced to admit it was me that had been smoking. As punishment, I wasn't allowed to play the first half of the match. We trailed 2-0 at half time. I was allowed to play the second half but even though I scored we couldn't get a second and we lost. I had let the school, the team, and myself down. And didn't I pay for it, with six of the best the next day!

Corporal punishment consisted of 'ferulas', or 'cracks' as we more commonly knew it. I'll always remember the shame of standing outside Mr Jack McCann's office as all the teachers walked past, tutting or shaking their heads on their way to their Common room for coffee. The door to 'Jack's' office was enormous, and had a brass handle on the outside. When summonsed to enter, you had to close the door behind you, and explain why you were there, even though he knew the reason full well. Then he would produce the ferula, a thick leather strap of around twelve inches long with a handle made of whalebone on one end, which he administered with great skill onto the palms of your hands. When he had finished dishing out the punishment, we had to utter the words, "Thank you, sir", and then attempt to open the huge door, which, on the inside, had a brass doorknob! This was no easy feat with hands smarting as much as they did, and I'm sure it was just another form of punishment designed to deter us from returning for more of the same!

It really began to become more noticeable that there were less and less pupils in the school as the years raced by. In between classes and at break times it was far quieter than it had ever been before. There were even fewer teachers around, as some left for different schools and some retired.

Soon enough we were in the 5th year and (not) looking forward to the end of year exams, which seemed to be the only point in being at school, according to the teachers. I remember one of our classmates, 'Joey' Royle dying in a tragic road accident. We attended the funeral in a small church in Salmesbury, stunned by the shock that it could happen to one of us. I'm sure most of us thought we were invincible then, and imagining that we would all live to a ripe old age. I've visited Joey's grave on a couple of occasions when I've been in the area. It still shocks me that he died so young.

I also remember another pupil in our class, Franco Mastrobuoni, leaving just after Christmas in our final year as he had to take over the family business due his father's ailing health. The lucky so-and-so had managed to escape before the dreaded exams! Even the sports side of the curriculum seemed to be diminishing as the school, its facilities, and the numbers within it, steadily began to shrink.

Our games lessons consisted of a whole afternoon down at Grafton, off Factory Lane in Penwortham, most weeks. We had to make our own way down there, which generally meant going through Avenham Park. We used to have great fun getting there, and you can imagine what we got up to, even throwing some of our school text books off the disused railway bridge and watching them float down the River Ribble one day. Well, why not? We had no further need for them, and neither had the school as we were the last year there. Good job no-one found them though, as they could have traced our names in the front of the books!

The choice of games in winter was either hockey or football, weather permitting. If not, it was the dreaded cross-country run! In the summer it was either cricket or athletics. My choice in each case was the latter, and I never regretted it.

Someone who always featured amongst the top runners at cross-country was Shaun Daly. Shaun was a good friend during our school days, an intense lad with a love of punk music and someone who was always willing to have 'the craic'. I remember him arriving at the start of one term sporting red and green hair, much to the disgust of the head of year, Joe Bamber, who sent him back home to "sort it out". I also remember him wanting to skive off from games once, and forging Jack McCann's signature of approval on a letter from 'his mother'. There was another memorable incident when we left school for the summer holidays at the end of the fourth year. As we were walking back to my house with Ian Moore, we spied a beer wagon delivering to a local hostelry. With no-one around, we took the opportunity to liberate all we could carry and then spent the rest of the afternoon getting merrily sloshed! One slightly more dramatic event I'll never forget was when Shaun took on the hard man of the nearby rival school. The lad Shaun was fighting was a friend of mine from the junior school I had previously attended. When Shaun came away second best, I felt that I was to blame for organising the fight that he had lost. Luckily Shaun didn't seem to mind too much, although he did curse a lot when eating his dinner afterwards, as the salt and vinegar on the chips stung the cut in his swollen fat lip!

As the exams approached life turned to revision, revision, and more revision. And past exam paper after past exam paper. It was a good job the teachers knew what they were doing, as thankfully it paid off for me, as I received the five O levels I needed.

The only problem in my mind was that I didn't know what I needed these for; I was sure I would be a professional footballer and I didn't need exams for that! Following a three-month trial with Blackburn Rovers I decided to take a job offered to me at a local commercial heating company. My thought at the time was that I could get an apprenticeship and then return to be a professional footballer. Who knows, maybe one day I'll make it!

It was strange to leave the school and the friends we had all made, but we were moving on to our next step, and I'm sure the school breathed a sigh of relief as the last of us filed out through the doors. Looking back, I really enjoyed those days, and it's strange how a once shut door can open, when the person on the other side of it discovers that you went to Preston Catholic College!

As the exams approached, Mick Suthers, me and a couple of Mick's friends somehow managed to persuade our parents to allow us to go abroad on holiday together to the South of France, with the notorious holiday travel company, Club 18-30.

I'm not sure how we evaded their checks, as we were only just sixteen years old! But somehow, we got away with it, and that summer we boarded the train at Preston Station for London Euston, then on to Pimlico to meet with rest of the group who were travelling to our final destination in France in a 'luxury' coach for the next 18 hours! We had a great two weeks and met some rather interesting fellow travellers on that holiday, including some I'll never forget.

The return journey was delayed due to an horrific crash in France (thankfully not involving us), and we eventually arrived back in Preston at around 4am on the Monday morning of my first ever day at work as an apprentice pipefitter-welder! My dad met me at the station and we rushed home so I could have a quick shower and breakfast before he took me to my new company, C. Seward & Co. Limited, based in Ribbleton, Preston.

I had been awarded the job, along with another school friend, Ian Gorrell, and we were more than keen to get started and earn some money. The company was the fifth oldest in Britain, established in 1775 and owned by Tom and David Blackburn, two brothers from Longridge. Tom told me later that when they found out we had both attended the Catholic College, they dismissed the other applicants and gave us the jobs. The school's reputation spoke volumes for us!

I spent the next nine years learning my trade as a pipefitter-welder, working across Lancashire installing commercial heating and hot and cold-water systems in schools, churches, factories, hospitals, nursing homes and many more commercial buildings. The work was tough and demanding, but the camaraderie of my colleagues and the friends and contacts I made in those early years taught me a lot more than I ever knew before; many are still friends to this day.

My link to the old school remained throughout my early working years, as I played football in the Lancashire Amateur League for the team known as Preston Catholic College Old Boys, managed by my father and elder brother.

The club is still going to this day, although it has changed its name to Newman College, replicating the change in the school from a grammar school to a sixth form College. My elder brother and I still have an active part in running the club committee.

During my time at Seward's, I married my long-suffering fiancé, Michel, and we bought our first home in Lostock Hall, were we lived for 11 years having three children, Hope, Charis and Raife.

As the family grew, so did our needs, and in 1991 I joined a larger company called Crown House Engineering, based in Manchester, working around the country on much larger projects. Eventually I came off the tools to work my way up the ladder, becoming a Mechanical Contracts Engineer where again I began to learn a new trade, running my own projects under the tutelage of a Project Manager.

These were busy times both at work and at home, as the family grew and demanded more and more of my time. Both girls showed more than a keen interest in football and soon joined local teams, playing with the lads and then eventually PNE girls' team, much to the dismay of my wife! My son Raife however followed my wife's lead and showed no interest in sport at all, probably due to fact that weekends were spent being dragged around either watching sport of some description – I think we overdid it with him!

Having always been interested in one sport or another, I started to get involved in off-road mountain biking with a few friends in the local area, and somehow the receptionist at work heard about it. Without even asking, she enrolled me in a fund-raising cycling trip across Egypt! This was a fantastic experience, and one I would never forget! We even managed to raise a whopping £110,000 for charity, cycling along the Gulf of Suez, through the Sinai mountain range, and across to the Gulf of Aquaba. We visited the Pyramids, climbed Mount Sinai and were treated to a narrative by our full-time guide, who explained many of the stories of the Bible along the way, bringing to life what we had been taught in school many years earlier.

By 2001, we had outgrown our house in Lostock Hall, and we moved to a new place on a new estate on the outskirts of Hoghton. During our 18 years at this address, I have changed companies a few more times and moved further up the ladder in terms of my career, and I'm now Operations manager with a national company called Lorne Stewart.

Looking back over the last 37 years, I think the school set me on the right track, and I still meet with old school friends and colleagues regularly, sometimes in the least expected places!

Although long since closed, I think the school is still held in high regard by those that attended and some that didn't. It's remained a large part of my life, mainly due to the Old Boys Football team and my family connection to it, and the fact that some elder past pupils are still in contact due to having played for the club in the past.

As I still live in the Preston area I sometimes have cause to visit places close to the old school and I take an interest in finding out what is happening to the old buildings. I also enjoy telling stories to my children about when I was there, and what it was like 'back in the day'!

ALEC CROOK: FORMS 1C, 2A, 3A, 4A AND 5A

Background

If you are old enough, cast your mind back to summer 1976, otherwise known as 'the heatwave'. Temperatures reached a thousand degrees on the pavements (oh yes, they did!), and the water supply was cut off and rationed, with standpipes in the street – and this is pre-climate change mania. I am ten years old, working hard at primary school, and serving as an altar boy at St Augustine's Church. At the same time, I'm having the time of my life playing cricket with the Asian lads on the council estate where I live, and practising the piano. I'm fishing with mates in the River Ribble (this is when it had fish in it, of course), and I'm riding my bike for 1,000 miles every single day in this glorious summer of summers. I want with all my heart to be a doctor when I'm older and have my own microscope and science kit. The Hit Parade on the wireless (yes, that's what it's called) consists of The Wurzels singing *The Combine Harvester* and Brotherhood of Man singing *Save Your Kisses For Me.* Proper music. It's an era of no internet, no mobile phones, and no social media. In fact, looking back on it today, it's almost pre-historic.

Steve Jobs and Steve Wozniak had just created a little business called 'Apple Computer Company', with the intention of developing small, easy to use computers that could be used in the office or at home. Wow, if only they'd known what the impact of their work would be. It was the year in which 'Stretch Armstrong' was the toy to have, and the famous footballer Ronaldo was born. Agatha Christie and John Paul Getty died, and Jimmy Carter was elected president of the USA. Google these folks if you're uncertain of who they are. They're pretty famous for the time and era.

However, all this factual history fades into insignificance for me; more importantly, 1976 was the year in which my parents informed me that the teachers in my primary school, St Augustine's, had decided that I should be put forward to sit the entrance exam for the Catholic College. It would provide a fantastic start to my secondary education, and stand me in good stead for my aim to study medicine later in life. I was smart enough, apparently, and would benefit from a Grammar School education. You see, the simple fact is that the Cath Coll was an institution. A landmark of Preston. The envy of other schools. The best. Its reputation was known throughout the local area. There was no option, no discussion. I would be taking that exam. That was it, simple. Fortunately, a few of my schoolmates were also sitting it, which gave me a sense of belonging and helped with the process. I really, really wanted to make my parents proud and schoolteachers happy and pass the exam. I had sat some music exams playing the piano, so understood the pressures of 'examination' and everything that entailed.

We had homework the following year, to help prepare us for the test; this was pretty hard to fit in, alongside the other interests in a busy 10/11year-old lad's life! I would imagine that every student that year worked equally as hard, as we all did at St Augustine's Primary School.

After sitting the exam, there was a long wait for the result to drop through the letterbox at home. The hopes, dreams and pressure of being the first child in my family's history to attend a Grammar School were quite intense; I couldn't wait to learn whether I had passed, and whether my mates had succeeded, too.

The letter arrived. I will never forget my father's face as I watched his eyes roll over the words, hoping with all my might that I had been successful. He simply held his hand out and said, "Well done, son". A very proud moment for both him and me. My mum was overjoyed, and beamed with happiness. It was such a great high point in my young life. A super moment for my parents. I was a part of 'The Last Intake'. Fortunately, some of my mates passed, too.

Day One

No doubt others will fill you in regarding the school uniform, including the itching pants and emblem on the pocket! There was no 'first day at school' furore, posting photos on any network for the world to see. It was simply, the first day at school. We all arrived, probably filled with the same mixture of trepidation, excitement and hope as each other. Some kids had elder brothers already at the College, which perhaps made it a little easier, while some of us were completely on our own.

The Cath Coll itself was pretty old, having opened in 1865, and it had its own life blood running through it. The smell of the floor polish, the brass fittings, the creaks and groans of the floorboards, the old radiators (which were either hotter than the surface of the sun, or colder than ice), the high windows, the massive classrooms . . . it was all a 'proper' school. Old-fashioned, and full of character. I would imagine those not privileged to attend the Cath Coll would have thought it resembled some kind of Hogwarts (although we were there some 20 years before the first Harry Potter book was published). There was always a certain mystery surrounding this foreboding building. The great unknown. The caps and gowns worn by some teachers, the priests, the enormous reputation it held as a centre of excellence. You could almost taste the knowledge this building exuded. It all created a sense of gratitude at being able to attend the place, as it was really widely admired. A feeling of pride and pressure combined for the students.

Without wanting to bore you about every detail from the old wooden desks with ink wells in them onwards, the simple fact that we had to stand up every time a teacher entered the room, and everyone was called by their surname only, gives a sense of the place. And the fact that we all used Parker Pens with that refillable squeezy cartridge which got ink mostly on your hands. The simple questions you need answered are: Was this iconic institution a good place to spend five years of your life, in the company of just boys? Did the system 'work'? Would I have sent my kids there? Was the outcome a successful one? In today's 'speech' you might ask, 'Was the branding the right one? And was the product a market leader?' I'll come back to this. But needless to say, we were making history as being part of 'The Last Intake'.

Discipline

Yes. It was a disciplined place to be a pupil. There was corporal punishment. Actions had consequences. Don't get me wrong, the teachers were superb. Every one of them. We all had our favourites, often teaching whatever subject we personally excelled in, but at the same time, they enforced discipline according to the school rules. Some teachers were stricter than others, and some of them struck the fear of God into us all. I'm not sure whether this level of fear was merely a juvenile feeling that could be put down to our youth, or whether it was a good thing or not. It was certainly a genuine true fear at the time, though.

If you committed a minor misdemeanour, you'd be given the dreaded 'prefect lines' – writing the same phrase over and over again. This exercise was completed at home, not in school time. The number of lines could range from ten to over one hundred, depending upon the mood of the teacher and degree of punishment deemed necessary. Being called to the headmaster's office was never going to be for a quick word, or quiet piece of friendly advice! It was to receive corporal punishment, which would leave your hands stinging for a day or two.

I personally didn't mind these strict ways, as my own father was a firm but fair man. He had served with the Royal Marines in World War 2, took part in the D-Day Landings, and had a military manner which included military discipline. I enjoyed my upbringing within this environment and therefore it wasn't a problem. However, this kind of schooling wouldn't be allowed in this day and age, and perhaps the banning of corporal punishment in schools has attributed to an increase in violence and disrespect and crime today. All of which seem to go unpunished. Was it a bad thing after all? Who knows? In any case, 'The Last Intake' would be the final group of Old Boys to be facing such a regime in the Cath Coll.

Sports and Interests

The Cath Coll had an array of hobbies and sports you could become involved with. These ranged from Chess Club, to Rifle Club, Drama, Art, and of course we had our own gym and swimming pool. We had the opportunity to try most sports, including football, hockey, cricket, canoeing, badminton, basketball, and trampolining, and we had all the gymnasium equipment from climbing ropes and wooden horses, to free weights and table tennis. Excellent. There really was something for everyone. Competition both in the classroom and in sports was encouraged. Nowadays it seems to be frowned upon, and apparently there can be no 'losers' in life. How wrong is this philosophy? You would have found it difficult to survive in the Cath Coll if you didn't want to be first, or top, or the best.

On a personal level, my best achievements included cross country, badminton and water polo.

The Under-16's Lancashire Badminton Doubles Final involved two teams from the Cath Coll. I paired up with Mark Connolly (now Fleming) and we reached the County Final against our very own classmates Andrew Roberts and Phil Suddick. Unfortunately, we lost to the better pairing, but what an achievement for the Cath Coll to have these two teams in the final. Mark Connolly was also my best mate throughout the school years – so it was a great partnership. I also ran cross country and represented the Cath Coll in this discipline. I didn't achieve any great results with this, I'm sorry to say.

My biggest claim to fame was being the school captain of the winning water polo team and being presented with a 'Swimmer of the Year' silver cup after competing in a water polo final. I scored the winning goal. The local press was there, and my photo appeared in the

Lancashire Evening Post. Another moment of huge pride and self-achievement, which engraved itself on my mind and heart and was a large part of my experience of being included in 'The Last Intake'.

Friends

I truly believe that the school friends we form are lifelong friends. We all call each other 'Old Boys', and that's a testament to the Cath Coll. In life, friends come and go, but those friendships created during our teenage years, and the experiences we shared at the Cath Coll have, I believe, configured a certain bond and trust, which only 'Old Boys' would appreciate. Don't get me wrong, we are talking pre-Political Correctness days, and of course there was plenty of name-calling, jibes and bullying. It happened back then in that era. It was a boy's school. A lad's domain. A big gang of youthful exuberance which sometimes got out of hand. There were fights, which were secretly arranged so no teachers found out, and a winner emerged.

Of course, there were boys who you didn't get on with for one reason or another, maybe a different genre of music was the issue, or perhaps a fall out over politics. Maybe the disagreement was over 'acid rain' which was the topic of the day back then. Or even CND, which was another major talking point. We all were taught to have an opinion and speak our mind. Discussion, if reasonable and substantiated, was allowed, although the teachers did not appreciate a quarrelsome student!

Generally, however, we all got on pretty well with each other, as being at the Catholic College, we all had to attend mass on Tuesday each week and pray for forgiveness in the hope that God would still allow us into heaven. Even if we had perhaps made some other pupil's life a misery for the previous week or so!

My personal 'support network' (or 'mates' as we called each other back then), consisted of a small group of us who played the same sports and were in the same class. Indeed, we used to play snooker and table tennis at my house and badminton at another lad's house (he was lucky to have a badminton court, but he did live in an old school, so that explains it). This same group came to my 18th birthday party some years later, and we have mostly all maintained contact since our Cath Coll days through the medium of a school reunion and the power of Facebook. Namely Mark Connolly, Phil Suddick, Andy Roberts, Steve Barrow and Pete Naylor. As the photo shows, we've not changed one bit!

Were we posh? This misconception from others not involved in the Cath Coll was quite funny. We were anything but posh. The Old Boys came from working class backgrounds like myself. No posh kids here. No snobs, either. Some of our parents (well, mine, anyway) had decided to forfeit some luxuries for themselves to be able to send us to the Cath Coll and be a part of 'The Last Intake'. I cannot thank mine enough for their selflessness. I am sure that the majority of the other parents did exactly the same.

Mantra

If I was to provide you with one defining belief that the Cath Coll instilled in us, it would be that the teachers convinced us we could achieve whatever we put our minds to. It was almost a mantra of the school. Of course, good manners were always required. Being kind to others, forgiving those who did you wrong, striving to be a success at everything, and just 'doing your best' were important, too. The school ethos was something I took away and used in my future grown up life. Nothing was out of reach; nothing was beyond our capabilities. You could literally achieve anything you wanted. This was a very powerful message for a youngster to hear, and the preaching was a super building block to progress with one's career, business and general future. What a great mantra for 'The Last Intake' to take with us.

The '80s

So, the '80s are upon us, and it's a great time to be alive; music is brilliant, Cath Coll is brilliant, TV is brilliant, and the Rubik's Cube is invented. Pete Naylor, Old Boy and friend, can do this in about 12 seconds, with his eyes closed and one arm tied behind his back, whist reciting Shakespeare at the same time! Margaret Thatcher is the Prime Minister. The Iran-Iraq war has started, and every Old Boy in the Cath Coll fancies Madonna because she's 'Like a Virgin'. John Lennon is shot, and an old cowboy actor becomes the new President of America. Terrorists seize the UK Iran Embassy, which leads to the SAS storming the building, but most of our mums are more interested in tuning into a TV program called *Dallas*, to discover who shot JR Ewing.

We are all getting a little more homework and the pressure and mantra keeps building.

It's all about French and German and Latin and Maths, Physics and Chemistry with a little RE and History and Biology. Oh, and let's not forget English, English Literature, and Greek Mythology, too. That, my friend, is a whole lot of learning to be absorbed. I didn't do Geography or Art, or Metalwork or Woodwork. I wish I had. Apart from the odd pub quiz question, Greek mythology and the causes of the French Revolution have done nothing for me to date. You must remember that this is before the internet and iPhones and knowledge being at your fingertips. You couldn't Google anything. The nearest thing to a computer was a Casio Scientific Calculator which had more buttons than the Apollo 13 spaceship. You had to literally remember all this information, digest it, and repeat it in an examination situation. This was O levels we were studying for. Not CSE's or GCSE's. No 'course work' whatsoever.

It was about now that I realised my personal academic ambitions of becoming a doctor, were somewhat greater than my academic capabilities, so a change of plan was required to my own mind set. My thoughts led me towards running my own company rather than relying upon being a number on a payroll for some faceless corporation. My father had previously been in business and was a great inspiration to me. His ethos was that you never get rich working for someone else.

The ambitious, enthusiastic, driven, self-motivated part of me was about to be born. So much so that I even brought my camera into Cath Coll and took portrait photos of my classmates just before Xmas. I developed and printed them at home in my own darkroom, then mounted them in frames and charged a fee for my services. A perfect gift for the parents. I wonder how many of 'The Last Intake' still have those old black and white photos somewhere?

Final Years

As we approach the latter stages of the process and we reach the fifth form, preparing for exams, the teachers were as excellent as always. I haven't named individual teachers as I believe they were all as good as each other in their unique individual ways. I think they were inclined to ensure that every pupil had the best of their best, as we were the last intake. I think they wanted to do their utmost to make certain that each one of us reached our maximum potential. Indeed, it was perhaps a case of showing the authorities that by closing this first-class establishment they were making a grave error of judgement. The teachers were all scholars, fully committed to their chosen career and in educating us to the highest standard possible. They all made lessons interesting and encouraged everyone to get involved. Don't get me wrong, there was an absolute ton of writing to be done at every lesson, too. The classroom consisted of a blackboard, chalk and that was it. No computers, iPads, copy and paste or any of the everyday items we take for granted today, which make life easier for present day students.

The teachers said it, and we wrote in down, quickly. You could read it and try to understand it later, at home in the comfort of your own bedroom. That's if you could decipher your own handwriting. My hand used to ache after some lessons. My script looked like it was written in Arabic! That's the way it was. Simple.

One of the other good aspects about the Cath Coll was that it was right next door to Winckley Square Convent. Oh yes. A beacon of joy, shining amongst an all-male testosterone-filled environment. Babes, birds, girlies, chicks, senoritas, chicas, ladies . . . There were secret passages within the convent where you could have some innocent fun running through, hoping with all your might that the nuns would not find you out, and that at the end you may bump into a girl or two.

Maurice Black was a man who knew his way around these dark passages like the back of his hand. I don't know to this day how he secured this knowledge. I didn't know it at the time, but my first sweetheart was attending the convent next door! She was a pupil there, and not a nun, I hasten to add!

The Last Intake

I asked earlier 'Was the branding the right one', and 'Was the product a market leader'?

Did the Cath Coll deliver on its promises? Was it really a travesty to end an era of teaching, in this archaic building, and deny future boys the same levels of education as we received? Was it all down to politically changing parties, or were we always destined to go down in history as 'The Last Intake'? Well, personally, I believe that I could not have had a happier or more fulfilling education anywhere else. I would have sent my boys there if I had children. Oh yes.

The system was a success.

The brand worked.

It was a winning formula, for sure.

I would probably still call the teachers 'Sir' and stand up, if I was to meet up with them today. That's not through doctrine, or brainwashing, it's purely a result of the huge admiration and respect I have towards them, for giving me the best of themselves. Mother Teresa's poem *Anyway* contains the phrase 'Give the world the best you have'. It's one of my favourites, and a perfect way to describe the whole ethos surrounding the Cath Coll, its teachers and pupils, and final products. The Cath Coll produced generations of successful adults.

'The Last Intake' alone created opportunities for students to pursue highly successful careers within the Police Force, the Armed Forces, accountancy, and it produced some excellent scientists, science teachers and businessmen. It also helped some become top chief engineers in massive Blue-Chip organisations, and no doubt there's a lawyer or two amongst the Old Boys out there somewhere. A doctor or two also emerged from the system even if alas, I wasn't one of them.

We must also take a moment here to remember all the Old Boys who did not have the opportunity to write down their thoughts, views and memories of their time at school. I was saddened to learn that many of my fellow students passed away at young ages. No doubt they would have welcomed the chance to put into words their own experiences of those halcyon days. Bless them all. The same sentiment applies to the former teachers who are no longer with us. I am sure they would love to read this book and see the former pupils reminiscing about the Cath Coll. Bless them, too. My sincere thanks go to my much loved Mum and Dad as well, for believing in my abilities and always giving me so much encouragement and help.

Finally . . .

Jim Clune, the instigator of this project, (and whose own mother was my very first teacher, by the way – fond memories), has encouraged us Old Boys to participate in writing this book together, for posterity, if nothing else. He asked each of us to inform you, the reader, of our individual 'unique take' on life at the Cath Coll. Also, he asked us to provide you with a resume of our lives after Cath Coll a 'what happened next' scenario. The intent may have been to try and demonstrate the Cath Coll education delivered a successful outcome for us all. A final chapter to the story, with a happy ending. Proof, almost, that it was all worth it. Just like any good film! Well, by now, I think you have all gathered that I did not reach the grand echelons of life by becoming a doctor.

I elected to make my own way in life, through one business or another. I didn't relish the idea of working for a Corporate Institution for 45 years, getting a gold watch and a pension at the end of it. I began to value my limited time on earth in ways other than in success or money. I craved the freedom to do what I wanted, whenever I wanted. The only 'proper' job I held down, was for a short time working for a building society/bank. Other than that, I was involved in various enterprises instigated by myself and maybe a business partner or two, occasionally.

I left Preston for St Ives in Cornwall when I was 19 years old. I bought my first property aged 20. It was a small Guest House overlooking Porthmeor Beach, the main surfing beach in the area. I started another business in Penzance a year later – an investment and licensed credit brokerage. I bought my first Porsche when I was 21. I expanded the business to Newquay in Cornwall, and invested in more property, etc. I didn't marry or have children of my own during this time. But by the time I was 37 I had met my future wife to be, Tracy; I also wanted to travel some more. Fortunately, she also had a desire to lead a more Bohemian lifestyle. We emigrated to live in the Caribbean. I grew my hair long, got some tattoos, taught myself guitar, learned how to speak Spanish, and generally chilled out. By my 40th birthday, we were complete beach bums! I was on the Caribbean sands having a Long Slow Comfortable Screw and haven't looked back since! This 'Living the Dream' scenario was tinged with sadness however, as less than three months before my birthday, my father died. However, my mother had travelled out to see us and made my 40th an extra special one indeed. Thank you, mum.

From that point onwards, we've continued to travel, to cold and warm climes alike. We were ski bums in Austria for a couple of years, and have visited or lived in 29 different countries by now. When we're not at home in Devon with Tilly our dog, we spend the majority of our time travelling around the UK and Europe in our motorhome. We are the three amigos. We are discovering new places and enjoy hiking, biking and making new memories. So, I suppose now, we are motorhome bums! I don't recall seeing that as an option on the Careers Advice list at the Cath Coll!

I didn't work any harder or longer than any other pupil. I didn't do awkward shift work or go to war protecting our country. I didn't invent anything new or excel in any particular field. I didn't chase criminals and put my life on the line every day. Some of my fellow school chums did exactly that, and more credit to them. It was more a case that lady luck was kind to me during my time in business, and I always had a fair wind behind me. I do feel a little blessed for this. Right now, time is our friend and at the end of the day, that is all we have. It is also a very limited commodity. In many ways, if I had reached my initial childhood dream of becoming a medical professional, it may not have brought me as many life experiences as I have been so lucky to have had, or given me the time to 'drop out' at such a young age.

I hope you have enjoyed this book, and my own experiences written within it. Whatever the year you are reading it in, be aware that this was written in 2019 and I am currently 53 years old. We are talking and reminiscing about the years 1977-1982.

I shall leave you with the poem I mentioned earlier, by Mother Teresa. We can all learn from it, whatever our background or personal education, race, colour or creed. I believe this was part of the mantra of the Cath Coll and 'The Last Intake'.

Mother Teresa's *Anyway* Poem

People are often unreasonable, illogical and self-centred;
Forgive them anyway.
If you are kind, people may accuse you of selfish, ulterior motives;
Be kind anyway.
If you are successful, you will win some false friends and some true enemies;
Succeed anyway.
If you are honest and frank, people may cheat you;
Be honest and frank anyway.
What you spend years building, someone could destroy overnight;
Build anyway.
If you find serenity and happiness, they may be jealous;
Be happy anyway.
The good you do today, people will often forget tomorrow;
Do good anyway.
Give the world the best you have, and it may never be enough;
Give the world the best you've got anyway.
You see, in the final analysis, it is between you and your God;
It was never between you and them anyway.

Dedicated to my loving parents Herbert and Mary Patricia Crook.

ANDREW CROSS:
FORMS 1B, 2B, 3S, 4S AND 5S

Catholic College memories.

Looking back on my five years as part of the last year group at Preston Catholic College was an interesting exercise to undertake. They say you remember only the good things from the past, and this is largely true. Thinking back, I do remember many good, fun times. But digging a bit deeper, I unearthed other memories. Praying for the bus to come round the corner whilst shivering in the bus shelter in a mid-winter blizzard; being bored stiff in science classes as they held no interest to me whatsoever; and at times, thinking that school was the worst thing ever. However, sitting here now it was not bad at all; it could have been a lot worse, and I was lucky to have had that chance, whereas many did not.

I remember the first day, getting on the bus in Grimsargh, just outside Preston, in a new uniform two sizes too big so I "could grow into it". I had a briefcase, but that was soon ditched for a 'cooler' sports bag. On the same bus were Eugene Henderson and Andy Newsham, also from the same village. The Chipping lads, Steve Pye and the Rogerson brothers, were often up the back of the bus, and Simon Holden was also there from Longridge.

All I was ever interested in was Art. I could not wait for the double Art period with Mr O'Neill and later Mr Anderson. They helped me do what I do now.

Sport was another highlight of the week. Walking from the College through Avenham park, across the bridge down to the College sport grounds, come rain, hail or shine. I caught the bus back to Preston bus station, unless I had spent the money given to me by my parents on toffees. Football in the winter, cricket and athletics in the time just before the summer holidays. My performances on the cross-country runs varied, depending on my mood. Sometimes I tried and ended up in the top ten. Other times I hid a ciggie and a couple of matches down my sock and stopped for a 'breather' on the way with a couple of the other lads.

The swimming pool at the College was a memorable experience, and not in a good way. It was always freezing even in summer. Mr Singleton used to say, "Jump in, cringe, swim ten laps, jump out."

I was part of the College B team, at football. I always was amazed at how good the A team was and how bad we were. We mainly lost matches, and a draw was a cause for celebration. Mick Finn was the manager and must have been exasperated by the seeming lack of commitment from us all. I am sure we all tried our best; we just weren't that good. It was good fun and there was a great camaraderie amongst the lads. We did, however, win a seven-a-side competition in Chipping once against a team with the previously mentioned Chipping lads (I think they were all there). It was a bit of an upset, and my one and only football trophy.

My one regret was in the German class. Myself, Moz Black and a couple others (cannot remember who), gave the teacher, Father Praeger, a pretty hard time. We were generally disruptive in his class, to such an extent that we were summoned out on an excursion with him. He must have been advised to do it as a bonding exercise, and to be fair it sort of worked. It was a good day visiting Malham Cove and some steam trains. I still bombed at German, failing the exam miserably, but I think we eased up a bit in the classes. Also, having taught High School kids I now know what it is to be on the other side.

We once got the English teacher, Mr Thompson, a good one. A

blackboard duster was attached to a length of fishing wire and when he went to grab it, off it went. He took it in good humour, though.

On another occasion I was in the library prefect's room, where we were trying to see who could fit into a tiny cupboard. Being the smallest, I was nominated, and I just managed to squeeze in and get the door shut when in came a teacher wondering what all the cheering was about. However, being squished up just made me want to fart, which in turn brought on the giggles. I managed to just keep both in until the teacher left.

I have memories of a couple of school excursions. Early on, we went on a religious retreat to the Lake District for a couple of nights. My memories are fuzzy on this one, so hopefully some of the others have better stories to tell. All I can remember are long walks in the woods and long talks by someone in a hall.

However, the school skiing trip to Austria *was* memorable. It must have been in fifth year, as the legal drinking age in Austria was 16. What was the College thinking? Mr Singleton said, "We cannot stop you, but we can only advise you not to drink." Didn't work! The trip was a joint one with Lark Hill Convent, and some of the boys took the rare opportunity to interact with the all-girls school pupils. The skiing was fun and I only managed to end up on my backside a few times.

The last day of school involved going down to Avenham park and spraying shaving foam over each other and lots of plants and bushes. Then we all headed our separate ways.

I had some great friendships over the five years. Moz, Ashy, Harry and Mick Davis (did you ever have a nickname, Mick?).

It was certainly weird being the last year group to go through the school. Having no one below you and, in the fifth year, being the only people in the College. The teachers were also on their way out, and I am sure this affected them and the way we were taught.

After leaving the College in 1982, I went over to the Lark Hill site of Newman College to study A levels where a few of the old familiar faces were also studying. After that I went to the Blackpool and Fylde College of Advanced Education and completed a foundation course in

Art and Design. Soon after finishing the foundation course in late 1985, the whole family emigrated to Perth, Western Australia, where I have remained ever since.

I currently make things, and teach people how to make things, in the arts and entertainment industry. I am a lecturer in Prop construction at the West Australian Academy of Performing Arts, and co-director of Sabi Art & design, specialising in sculpture commissions and restorations. I have been married since 1994, and have two adult kids.

SIMON CUERDEN:
FORMS 1A, 2A, 3A, 4A AND 5A

As an adult, I passionately believe that school and education are incredibly important in shaping both an individual and what they can achieve in life. I recognise that there are many views, often linked to individuals' political leanings, as to whether selective grammar schools such as Preston Catholic College have a place in society. For me, the College, as it was known when I went there in 1977, was ultimately a gateway to a career as a white-collar professional. I am convinced that no other school in Preston that was accessible to me would have allowed me the opportunity to develop as the College did.

There is no doubt that my favourite period at the College was my first year. Joining a school that seemed so old (in fact it was only 100 years old when I attended), which was so well known in the Roman Catholic community of which I was part, was more fascinating than daunting. There was sport galore, with the school having fabulous playing fields at Grafton out in Penwortham – football (of course), hockey and cricket were all available, with fantastic playing surfaces. In that first year, I managed to make the football team, and from September 1977 Saturday mornings were suddenly all about playing for the school. The first-year team, third- year team and first team (sixth form boys) were grouped together – one week at home at Grafton, one week away travelling by coach. Those 'away trips' were just thrilling for a lad growing up in Frenchwood, whose previous travel experience consisted of walking to junior school in Avenham daily, being part of a family with no car. Off we went, every other Saturday from school in Winckley Square, to other grammar schools across the North West – Fylde Coast, East Lancashire, Manchester and Liverpool. We had a full roster of games.

Playing football for the school also helped in making friends. Six boys from my junior school went to the College in total. I had been friendly with all of them before – some more than others – but the catchment of the College meant that there were now boys from far and wide, particularly by 1977 standards. Boys came from within Preston and its surrounding areas of course, such as Walton-le-Dale, but they also travelled from Leyland, Chorley and Blackburn, as well as northwards from Grimsargh, Longridge, Chipping and Stonyhurst. These places genuinely seemed miles away back then. And with this mix of boys, a bit less than 100 in total, came new characters and new friends – some played football, some did not – and of course we all ended up with shorthand names. Mine were 'Si' or 'Cuey' (neither that imaginative, it should be said) and to this day, when I meet a College lad, sadly all too infrequently, I will always be called one or the other.

That first year was also when the school was at its most bustling. I was in the last ever intake into the grammar school environment before it began its journey to becoming a sixth form only College. There were boys everywhere, dashing through the playground and the various school buildings; the school was completely 'urbanised', being housed in various buildings and former houses which led on to and which were behind a façade on to Winckley Square. The uniform code was strict – grey trousers, grey or white shirt, school tie (always) and a black blazer, and definitely no trainers! You could get a hot pasty or a bacon butty at morning break in the dining room, there was a separate and modern gym on the school site, and we even had our own swimming pool (small, mind), which was the pride and joy of Mr Bradley, a PE teacher who had played water polo for Great Britain and who encouraged (with a fair degree of bark) boys to play water polo during lunchtime.

Then there were the teachers, and the education itself. I had enjoyed junior school and it would be fair to say that I enjoyed learning. In that first year we were split into three classes, A, B and C. We received fortnightly report cards detailing our progress, with a sentence or two on each subject from our teachers, and were introduced to the school exam grading system, with a grade zero being the highest grade and grade nine the lowest.

We had a mix of 'lay' teachers and teachers drawn from the Jesuits – the Jesuit and school motto was *Ad Maiorem De Gloriam* ('For the greater glory of God'). The 'lay' teachers had typically taught at the school for many years, with the occasional younger teacher joining them – Mr Ainsworth, for example, who also took us for football in that first year. The teachers all had a deep commitment to the College and the quality of the education that they taught. The Jesuit teachers were also committed, but perhaps were not as approachable, on the whole. My favourite Jesuit teacher was called Father Wareing. He had been born in Preston himself and attended the College as a boy before going on to become a Jesuit priest. He taught me English and Latin and had a wonderful intellectual air about him, with a particularly deep love for Classical languages. On a visit to Stonyhurst College in 2017 to look at that particular school for our daughter, one of the staff mentioned in conversation that the last Jesuit priest that had retired to the resident quarters at Stonyhurst had just passed away – that priest was Father Wareing, who had lived to the age of 86.

As the years went by and the school literally folded up behind us, the College strove to maintain its academic standards. Sadly, our sporting fixtures fell away, football in particular because we could not offer other schools an 'all school years' Saturday morning experience. However, football remained important and various College boys from our year – 'recruited' by myself and Peter Cooper – came to play for St Augustine's junior football team (St Augustine's being the parish that Peter and I grew up in). There was only one junior team in the parish, namely ours, but nonetheless it was one of the most successful teams in the area. College lads who played in addition to Peter and me were Bernard Moon, Jim Clune, Eugene Henderson and Phil Suddick. (As a footnote, I should recognise that I considered myself fortunate to be part of the team. I was a reasonable player but had the would-be footballer's Achilles heel; someone once told me that I had no need to fear losing my pace because I never had any in the first place!)

I've mentioned friendships, and I would say that my closest friend was Eugene. He was a larger-than-life character, great company, and a real wit. One truly memorable moment of humour came one Saturday morning when we were scheduled to play football down at Grafton. The weather was a bit frosty and for some reason our team was slow to meet up. One of the boys who had gathered with us was Jim Clune (see below), having been brought down by his father – Mr Clune, Senior, was a regular supporter and watcher of the team. Shortly before kick-off that morning, in walks Mr Clune to our dressing room, where he begins to count numbers. Off he starts: "Two, four, six, eight . . .", to which Eugene, quick as a flash, adds " . . . who do we appreciate?" It was priceless and brought the dressing room down, with Mr Clune bursting into laughter.

After my O levels, where I did ok, I stayed at the College for my A levels – it simply never entered my head to consider anywhere else. About half of the boys left for apprenticeships and farming (the school having a strong catchment from the farming communities around Longridge), and a small number went to other colleges, with the balance of what I would guess was nearly half staying on. Sixth form was where I, like others, began to mature. In other words, where I discovered alcohol (pints of bitter in my case) and girls, having had virtually no experience of girls beforehand, along with the vast majority of the other lads. In sixth form, the College combined with the girls from Winckley Square and Larkhill Convents, and with an influx of students (lads and girls) from other Catholic schools, particularly St Cuthbert Mayne school in Fulwood.

Socially, sixth form was a wonderful experience – with new friendships, girlfriends (at last!) and the infamous College 'do's', which consisted of us all heading to a specially booked Preston nightclub once a term, and where there were no drink restrictions whatsoever. I could not tell you who hired the various clubs and how it was even possible for 16- and 17-year olds to get in and get served, no questions asked, but I'd like to take the opportunity to thank them here!

At A level, I chose to do Pure Mathematics (I loved it – got an A), History (I loved half of it – got a C) and English Literature (I fell out of love with it – got an E). I also got a C in General Studies. Thankfully, the A and two Cs secured me a university place at Sheffield. In truth, I was desperately disappointed with my A level results, not because I did not deserve the C in History and the E in English Literature, but because I realised that I had coasted dramatically near the end and simply did not revise anywhere near enough. I had let myself down but, more importantly, I thought that I had let my parents down. In my first year at the College, the school was fee-paying for boys like me who lived in the Preston area. Paying those fees took money out of a tightly drawn family purse, with my father working on the outside maintenance 'gangs' at British Telecom and my mother a school dinner lady at the time.

At Sheffield University, I studied Pure Mathematics, Accounting and Financial Management and, determined not to repeat the complacency of my approach to A levels, I obtained a First-Class degree. After graduating, I joined an accountancy firm called Coopers & Lybrand, in Blackburn, returning to live in Preston and commuting from there. I qualified as a chartered accountant, went on to specialise in an area called forensic accounting, and ultimately became a partner in what was by then PricewaterhouseCoopers in 2002. I left to join Deloitte in 2006 as a partner, and remain there to this day. I have been based in Manchester and London since my time in Blackburn and now work full time in London, quite a distance from the family home in the west of Manchester, in the Altrincham area.

I am married to Lesley. I have a son called Oliver, now 23, who went to Hutton Grammar school and then Lancaster Grammar school to board for his A levels, and a daughter called Isabel, now 16, who boards at a public school, Stowe, in Buckingham – I have no doubt that my wife and I have the means for Isabel to go there because of what the College did for me and the journey that it sent me on.

When I reflect on the 36 years that have elapsed since I left the College, I am mindful that for the first 32 years of this period I had little or no contact with the lads with whom I went to school. The demise of the College as a school meant that there was no 'alumni' concept, and the nature of my work and personal life ultimately meant that I have not been based in Preston for over 20 years now. A huge thanks, then, need to go to Jim Clune, who organised a reunion for our year back in 2016 and came up with the idea of compiling this book.

My final reflection about the College is not about the institution itself, but the person who had the vision and drive for me to go to the school: my mother. To this day, she has an unshakeable belief that a good education can transform life and create opportunity, particularly when combined with hard work. She had huge faith in me when I began to prepare for the College entrance exams, always supportive and telling me with absolute certainty that I would pass on merit. As I noted above, finding the money to pay that first year's school fees was never going to be easy for my parents, but my mother never had any doubt that it would be an investment worth making. I will always be grateful to her and my father, who passed away in 2013, for the opportunity that they gave me. I will also always be grateful to the College and its teachers, not just for the education it provided me with, but also for the values it stood for and passed on to me.

RICHARD CURRAN: FORMS 1C, 2B, 3S, 4S AND 5S

It seems a long time ago that I first stood outside the Mount Street entrance to the College. I remember it well enough, though; an unmarked door set into a long red-brick wall that disappeared down the hill into an unseasonal mist. I felt uncomfortable in my slightly over-large uniform with the silver eagle on the breast pocket and green tie, and faintly ridiculous with my brand-new stiff leather briefcase. I entered, and eight years later emerged from the Chapel Street entrance feeling not much wiser than I had when I went in.

I'd always been interested in music; not in an academic or even an emotional way, but more because it was just something I could do. I'd started learning to play the violin some years earlier, and was progressing well through my grades by the time I came to the College. There was no music in the curriculum at that time, but after a brief and very public audition I was accepted for the school choir. There I came to love the early music and Latin masses we sang; I still do love them. I remember the choirmaster, Mr Duckworth, small of stature but big of voice, jumping up and down on his little podium during choir practice in the organ loft at St Wilfrid's, swearing like a trooper and scandalising the little old ladies cleaning the aisles.

He really was good, though. There were choir competitions, the

Eisteddfod, TV appearances and trips to Italy and the US. I'd never been abroad before, and there I was in New York! Sadly, for me, it wasn't to last. As the last intake we stumbled spottily towards puberty, our voices broke one by one, and when the alto section outnumbered the trebles by a comfortable margin we had to stop. I miss the singing to this day.

Around this time, just as I was starting my third year, my father died, and my mother descended into a mental illness that was to last the rest of her life. My academic and musical life seemed to stall, and I was drifting. I took an audition for the Royal Northern College of Music day school but I wasn't practising much at the time and quite rightly I didn't get in. I don't remember there being much in the way of pastoral care at the school, or even an acknowledgement of my grief, but I remember one of the Jesuit teachers was assigned to keep an eye out for my family.

Partly due to indifferent teaching and partly due to my own lassitude I had always found difficulty with musical theory. It seemed to have been based on mathematical principles that predated the Romans and in my mind at the time, defied logic. For this reason, I couldn't progress further with my grades. There was an equivalency though between the music O level and grade five theory, so when music was offered as an O level choice at the College I signed up. The classes were to be held at the convent school next door and given by one of the teachers there. I remember being strangely disappointed when we were presented at our first lesson with a nun in full battledress who would be our guide through the murky waters of proper musical study. I don't remember if it was at this or some slightly later stage but we had been invited to bring a recording of our favourite music to the class, presumably for a little sniffy analysis. Some of us turned up with LPs, singles, and cassettes. I can't remember my choice, probably something I would find unbearable now.

I've no memory of which of us it was, but the first submission to the music class was a jaunty little tune, penned by one Johnny Rotten, entitled *Friggin' In The Riggin*. Now in my opinion, that nun showed a lack of imagination. I'd like to think that we got as far as the bit where intrarectal circumcision was performed on the skipper by insertion of broken glass into the cabin boy's nether cavity, but I honestly can't remember. Needless to say, in a state of high dudgeon Sister Whatever-her-name-was positively ripped the offending article off the turntable and after a few mumbled imprecations stormed off. She could have played it differently. The punk movement was political for a start. The song itself is an old drinking song with origins that go back to the early nineteenth century. Also known as *The Good Ship Venus*, it tells the true story of a group of sailors who have commandeered their own ship at the behest of a female convict being held on board. The tune is an old one, the nursery rhyme it references is *In And Out The Windows*, although to me it owes as much to *Yankee Doodle Dandy*. It's profane, but not needlessly so, in my opinion. It's not clever, but who needs clever when you're giving the establishment the middle finger? However, like so many others who set themselves up as arbiters of morality and seek to make our choices for us, the Sister didn't see it through to the end, preferring to take her own moral high ground instead of mucking about in the gutter, even just to see what it was like. The course was discontinued.

After this, and my rejection from the RNCM, I decided to employ my own middle finger to the musical establishment. In retrospect this was a very good thing. In later years I've met many people who have been through the mill of classical music training. Some had not survived the experience as players, most of those that did are poorly paid and scratch a living from teaching and the occasional stint with the local Philharmonic. But very few seem able to simply perform for a living. On the occasions where I have rubbed up against them in recording studios, they always appear to be quite jaded individuals, hidebound by a dogmatic and highly proscriptive approach to music, with little freedom to express themselves beyond the dots and lines on the page in front of them.

Meanwhile, I matriculated with average O level results and went on to achieve somewhat less than average A level results at what had by then become Cardinal Newman College. Armed with these, a total absence of self-confidence and a lack of direction, I slid out of education at 18 and started looking for something to do. Some anarchists I'd met bumming around in squats in Preston were making music when they weren't too stoned to get up off their wrecked sofas, and I associated with them for a time. Even though I spent time with them I was always wary of their lifestyle, seeing how the drugs they took would debilitate them, and how any ambition or direction they had was subsumed by the desire to 'score'. The irony of the fact that much of the money they used to facilitate this life came from the very 'state' they affected to despise wasn't lost on me, either. Through them, though, I met people who were making records and I started working occasionally in local recording studios. Within a couple of years, I had joined my first proper band writing original music and getting some notice. After another couple of years of slogging up and down the M6 playing pubs and clubs, and the odd London gig, we got on the college circuit and started touring internationally.

This was a time of great change in popular music, when traditional instruments and styles came to be referenced increasingly, and it was no longer strange to see a fast, loud, and sweaty rock and roll band with a fiddle player. Although we didn't exactly ride this wave (having preceded it by a number of years), we did paddle in its wash, and for a time had great reviews and appreciative audiences.

I remember playing a concert hall in Turin during this time. The room was very old, and the ceiling barrel-vaulted, presenting enormous difficulties for our sound man, and generally shredding nerves. Now, being on the road for a couple of months has a distressing effect on your gear, your nerves, your clothes, and your personal hygiene. Suffice it to say that if I'd rocked up in the middle of a town in England at that point I might justifiably have been arrested for vagrancy. Indeed, I'd spent much of the previous day trying to find a pair of shoes for less than 10,000 lire to replace what was left of mine. Fat chance of that in Italy. So, it was with some misgiving that I saw some of the best dressed people I'd ever seen filing into the room to constitute our audience. Even by Italian standards in such things, these people were well turned-out. The hair, jewels, dresses, and tuxedos were all immaculate. It might seem at times like this that there are choices; that it might in some way be possible to adapt to circumstances, to play it differently, but there really is only one way to go. You just get up and do what you do. In our case this was to play wild and impassioned roots music very loudly, while looking like we wouldn't have seemed out of place dossing down on the bus station at midnight. We stepped up to the plate. At the end of our set, after the seventh encore, they called the riot police and we had to stop. I'll never forget one man in the front row. In my memory's eye he looked exactly like the cod opera singer on the 'Go Compare' adverts. Apoplectic, and purple with enthusiasm, he stood on his chair beating his fists on his knees screaming "BRAVI! BRAVI! BRAVI!" I've never attempted to pre-judge an audience since, and certainly never entertain the idea that there are choices.

I have never wanted to be famous, and fortunately for me I was never cursed with that tag. However, I have, on occasion, had fame brush up against me. Like the time I played Wembley Arena just before Johnny Cash, who even then took oxygen before he went on stage. A crowd of 15,000 watched us, and I was elated coming off stage and into the dressing room. Ten minutes later, while the techs were changing the stage, Johnny Cash's warm-up man (John McEuen I think, of the Nitty Gritty Dirt Band) came down, said he'd seen me play, and asked if I'd like to join him for a couple of numbers before the 'man in black' took the stage. By this point our lead vocal (an Irishman by birth) and I had made a respectable dent in a bottle of Bushmills whiskey, and I was forced to politely decline the invitation. Other less scrupulous performers may have gone ahead with it, but I'd already learned my lesson some years previously in Darmstadt at 'The Golden Krone'; an episode that even at a distance of years I find impossible to relate. Suffice it to say that on that occasion we were provided with an alcohol rider that a good number of young, healthy men were unable to sensibly dispose of.

I was lucky enough to have seen most of Europe in those early touring days, but Italy was the country I fell in love with. I fell in love on the shores of Lake Maggiore among the mountains, in Pavia where the setting sun lit the ancient red sandstone buildings, on the road bridge to Venice in the November mists, and with a group of anarchists in a derelict farmhouse near Pescara, watching the moon rise over a field of lavender. I was to go back many times and it never lost its charm.

There were grim times, too, and sometimes dangerous ones. I remember touring in Northern Ireland. This was the late '80s, and Belfast, still firmly in the grip of the troubles, was an unpleasant place to be. We played the bars in the dock area where every other pub was a burnt-out shell, the police stations looked like fortresses, and the British Army moved through the streets in formation. The sound of helicopters was a constant drone, and a lowering gloom pervaded everything. We often stayed with gig promoters on these tours and in Belfast we stayed with Molly who had put the dates together for our gigs there. Molly's place was also a safe house for the IRA, but we didn't know this at the time. Groups of men would arrive in the small hours to drink whiskey and listen to the old Irish music through a haze of fag smoke, occasionally talking with us, but mostly not. Somehow, we acquired a hanger-on, I remember talking to him in the toilets after one of the gigs.

"Are you in the band?" he asked. "Yes," I replied, "Does it show?" Dressed as I was, this was a stupid question. "The name's Wires" he said, ignoring this. "Hello, Wires," I said, "What do you do?" This was apparently another stupid question. With a smirk, he replied "I'm into politics, in an unofficial way." It was only later, after he'd described in detail the aftermath of one of his creations, that I put two and two together. By this time, it was too late. Wires had worked out that we crossed the border regularly and that our tour bus with its British plates and our English accents were unlikely to draw attention at checkpoints.

Wires travelled with us, occasionally ducking under a seat as we crossed the border. He would disappear for a few hours when we stopped to play, only to return at precisely the time we were due to leave. We eventually ditched him at a service station when he'd wandered off to take a leak and find some more vodka.

I found the inevitable returns to the UK depressing, not least because although I was touring and playing most of the time, I never made serious money. This was not in itself an issue for me but by this time I had a wife, a mortgage, and no day-job. A vaunted six-month road-house tour of the US had fallen through, and although I was doing occasional studio session work in London and Manchester it didn't feel like a proper job. So, when I was offered some casual work as number two sound on the Panto at the Guild Hall in Preston, I took it. Within two weeks I found myself chasing a six-foot-high chicken down a corridor with a radio mic because she was late for her entrance. I remember thinking that this might be an interesting side-line. And thus began a 15-year love/hate relationship with technical theatre, the principal attraction of which was that it was anything but a proper job.

I carried on with the music of course, and although I was playing places like Ronnie Scott's, The Marquee, The Montreaux Jazz Festival and numerous other places of similar standing, I found myself favouring the studio work I was doing. I had at this time what, for me, was a lucky break (not so much for the other guy). I had been doing a series of recordings for a couple of albums in a studio in London. The studio was called Heartbeat and was round the corner from PWL, the studios of Stock, Aitken and Waterman's hit factory (Kylie Minogue's ghost singer used to come in to score dope off the engineer, an enigmatic old hippy with a penchant for sticking daisies in his beard). The label I was signed to was also producing an album with the legendary and now sadly departed Bert Jansch. The fiddle player they had lined up for the sessions had unfortunately entered the end game of his alcoholism and was having one of his legs amputated at the time so they asked me to do the sessions. I didn't know who Bert Jansch was to be honest (and I know you're probably thinking *neither do I*), but for the cognoscenti of the roots music scene this was a very big deal and I've been dining out on it ever since. Bert was a recovering alcoholic, was virtually non-verbal, and had a face like a relief map of the Andes. I loved the music, though; its dark, introspective and brooding Caledonian undercurrents a suitable accompaniment to the hill walking I was doing around Torridon and Shieldaig at the time. I recorded the album and did a few gigs, and even though I can't say that Bert exchanged more than three words with me the whole time, it's still a very good thing to have on my CV.

This was also the time of my TV debut, working with the film composer Richard G Mitchell on the score for a BBC period drama starring the very lovely Tara Fitzgerald. Richard is a lovely man and we have remained friends ever since. In order to enhance my fee for the recording work he insisted I appear in a scene he had scored for a wedding that included a fiddler as a bit-part. The makeup artist declared I had very eighteenth-century hair and that all that was needed was a couple of stick-on sideburns, a stovepipe hat, a desperately uncomfortable but very authentic hessian shirt, and a heavy wool suit. I stood around in this outfit for several hours while they shot the scene, my part being right at the end when one of the principals (Toby Stephens, I think) stormed off and up a small hill past where I was playing. The delights of the catering van having been exhausted, I settled down to watch the lighting technicians attempt to make a freezing cold day in early March in North Yorkshire look like midsummer. My turn eventually came and even if I say it myself, I carried it off beautifully: sawing away like anything while the strains of the tune blared through a loudspeaker for sync and Toby stomped past. I think we did that take ten times, and in the end, like many great performances, the five seconds or so of footage ended up being cut to just being able to see my feet, then cut altogether, and what could have been a glittering career in acting was brought to an abrupt end. Oh well.

I did compose half of the theme tune for the piece, though, and still receive royalties for it every year, BBC period dramas apparently remaining popular in many countries. Richard won the Royal Television Society Award for the music, and sat back waiting for the phone to ring with offers of well-paid and rewarding work. I did the same. The phone didn't ring again for either of us for another two years.

Richard is a person that knows many people and my association with him has led to many other things. It was through our connection that I ended up working with award-winning media composers Ian Livingstone, Rupert Gregson-Williams, David Mitcham, Justine Barker and many others. It came as a surprise to me that many of these people were not particularly musically literate (indeed, often I have to make my own scores and even improvise my own lines), but had somehow transcended the strictures of theory and just wrote what they felt, or to be more precise, what they wanted you to feel when you listened to it. This was the key. For these people, technical brilliance (which I never really possessed) was of inferior value to the ability to emote in a way that supported the message of the music, to see inside it, to take what is there and make it more.

Meanwhile, I had started freelancing in theatre, touring a lot, doing re-lights and bits of production management. My love/hate relationship with the job had turned to one of pure loathing and I quailed at the prospect of yet another interminable production meeting, yet another week spent in a darkened hall, and yet another month or so on tour. I began to long for escape, but escape from freelancing is not so easy. When you're working from contract to contract and must keep the money coming in, getting off the train is tricky. However, after landing what proved to be a fairly unpleasant temporary post as production manager at the Bolton Octagon (at least it wasn't London), I finally came to the conclusion that my heart was very definitely no longer in it.

I left the Octagon and vowed never to return to theatre, whether for work or pleasure. Rather like chocolate cake, too much of something you like can make you sick, and I was sick of it. Returning to music as my sole source of income was not an easy decision to make. I had a good discography and lots of impressive names on the list of work I'd been involved with. I had regular composer/producer clients that were producing music for commercial purposes and sufficient experience to be able to walk into a studio anywhere and play without fear. However, as the following meme that has recently been circulating explains, things are never simple.

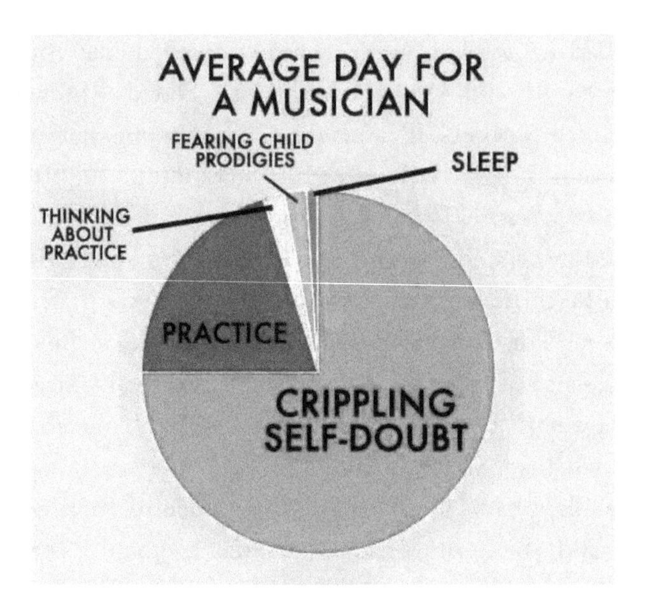

However, crippling self-doubt notwithstanding, I took the plunge.

One aspect of session work which I didn't much like had been the necessity to travel to Manchester, Liverpool and London to get the really good work. But with the increase in upload speeds that came with broadband internet connections, there had been a small but growing community of session players that worked remotely from their own homes developing. They would receive parts and audio from composers, record the parts themselves and then send the audio files back to the composer for syncing and mixing in their sessions. The advantages of doing this were manifold – the composer didn't have to hire a studio and engineer, parts could be recorded and returned within a few hours instead of waiting for weeks for available studio time, and nobody had to go to London any more. High quality recording equipment was becoming cheaper and more accessible, and with the technical knowledge I had acquired in my theatre days I was able to build my own recording studio capable of producing broadcast-standard stuff.

By this time, I had learned to play the cello and viola, and I'd managed to acquire a few good instruments. At the time of writing there are now many violinists across the world who do remote sessions. There are also a good number who play the viola, but there are considerably fewer cellists and thankfully there are only a handful that can play all three instruments.

So, this is what I do now, I have my own small but functional studio, and I work for people all over the world. I record for TV, computer game and film soundtracks, and I regularly do music for TV networks in the UK, USA and Europe. I've had some luck, like my recent connection with the composer who's working on the next Dreamworks animation, who happened to hear me on a music library track. I'm not rich, but I'm happy, and overall, it's been a lot of fun. I don't gig so much these days, except for fun, and I certainly don't tour, preferring the comforts of my own home, the occasional flop on a Greek beach with my partner Maxine, and doing the Times crossword on a Saturday morning in bed.

So, apart from giving me a slight edge in the Times cryptic crossword, I've little to thank The Catholic College for, but I've little to blame it for, either. Mired in its own history, and inextricably bound up with its Jesuit dogma, it was inevitable that as an institution it would be backward-looking and fundamentally perverse. One thing it did inspire in me though is an enduring and often vindicated distrust of religion and those who practise it, and for that I'm thankful.

TONY DIXON:
FORMS 1A, 2C, 3M, 4M AND 5M

My lasting memory of school? The only thing I wanted to do was leave! Quite right! There was no way on earth that I would have gone on to sixth form, that was for certain. The homework in the early years took me hours to complete, but luckily that eased later. I remember having to forge my Mum's signature on those report cards! The time spent travelling and lack of buses on the Clitheroe to Preston route was an absolute pain. On the plus side, I did learn some useful stuff, especially in Metalwork and Engineering Drawing, although what use Classical Studies could be to anyone is beyond me! The trips to Castlerigg, in Keswick, in the fourth and fifth years were great, too! After I left school, aged 16, I did an apprenticeship at GEC, mostly working as a welder/steel fabricator. For the last 17 years I have been self-employed. All that engineering drawing paid off, I suppose!

MARK HARRISON: FORMS 1C, 2B AND 3S

My mother Marian and father Anthony were working class; mum was a nurse, and dad a welder. They wanted me to have a good education, so they sent me to a private school for a year, St Pius X in Garstang Road, Preston. Their intention was that I would receive the education that would help me to pass the 11 Plus for the final intake ever at the prestigious Preston Catholic College. They decided to use their hard-earned money on my education, as even though at ten years old I was technically too young to go, this would be my one and only chance; such was the good name of PCC.

The differences between the posh prep school of St Pius X and the tough all-boys school of PCC were enormous! You can only imagine what a shock going to PCC was, especially at my age. I had to adjust very quickly. I think there were four pupils from St Pius X who went to PCC; myself, Matthew Iddon, Miles Hartland (whose nickname was Jam and who I believe has sadly died), and Damian Walmsley. I do not remember a lot about my first-year, education-wise, at PCC. I was in Miss Mangan's 1C class – she was very fair, but completely nuts on religion! I remember the size of Leonard Rogerson, son of a farmer from Chipping. Leonard was a large ginger-haired lad who had two other brothers who were even bigger.

I travelled to school on the Lightfoot Lane bus and later the

Plungington bus (this is where I first met Jimmy Clune, as we lived near each other and got the bus together). We finished the journey at the frighteningly big Preston bus station. I felt that I had to grow up quickly, walking from the bus station, through the underground to the Guildhall and then on a 15-minute journey to Winckley Square. I think PCC had the most miserable and depressing looking buildings I had ever seen – particularly the school yard and the 'underground' area where pupils would shelter or play games when it was raining. I remember there being fights in the underground area. Shaun Daly was the hardest lad in our year; I was sad to hear of his recent death. We all played football with tennis balls and I played 'pitch and toss' using two pence pieces with Russel Ashton against any available wall.

I remember the sports afternoons, when we'd head to 'Grafton', our playing fields. I did not enjoy the running and cross country! I'd always been used to being in the school football teams at primary school, but never got close to the PCC year team, there were too many good players, such as Jimmy Clune, Eugene Henderson, Phil Suddick and the 'creme de la crème', Pete Cooper. Pete was a great winger. I later played a lot against Franny Carr (who became a professional for Nottingham Forest), but I always thought Peter was better than him. I didn't like some of the teachers; Father Spencer, for example, who always said I was too small for football. I never took the Catholic religion seriously after PCC, and maybe I have him to thank for that.

PCC did not take cricket too seriously, but that was where I was slightly better than most, and I was chosen for the PCC year team. One of the funniest memories I have comes from our first game. I think we were playing away at Ashton school, and we had chosen to bowl first. Really only the guys from St Pius had played cricket before, so Matthew Iddon opened the bowling. I remember he walked back about 30 yards for his run up, while all our team in the field were looking at him wondering how fast a bowler he really was! The two batters for Ashton were looking at each other and looked worried; they were smiling nervously. Matthew was a little bit on the 'big side', and started to run in at a full pace. It was very quiet; all you could hear was

Matthew running in. He eventually turned his arm over, and bowled – he had a funny action so when he bowled, he was looking at the ground.

Everyone was looking for where the ball had gone, then all saw it, plugged in the wicket about two feet in front of where he had bowled it! There was complete silence for what seemed an eternity, then everyone started laughing and went on for what seemed like an eternity as well. Matthew, who was completely embarrassed by this stage, decided to bowl the rest of the over with a run up of about two yards. I don't think he ever bowled again!

The only other memory I have of the first year is of being a part of the choir. Mr Harry Duckworth was the choir master. We went to Yorkshire TV for *Songs of Praise* or something similar. I remember more of my second and third year. Me and my very close friends Shaun Daly, Moz Black, Ian Gorrell, Ronan Sargeant, Greg Wagner and a few others headed off to watch Punk groups such as SLF, Clash etc at Blackburn King Georges at this time. We were all rebelling. I started to dislike the PCC, and really had been too young to go. Because it was the last intake, we were always the youngest and we were treated as such. Education-wise I was not doing too well, and I left after the third year to go to St Cuthbert Mayne, where I started the third year again.

I was always terrified of the ferula (a small cricket bat made of bone, which was our version of the cane) and once got 'six' off Jack McCann, (the maths teacher), which was another reason why I left, I think. I remember in one of his classes, Moz Black and Shaun tied a fishing line to the blackboard duster. When Mr McCann entered the room to pick up the duster as he always did, Moz kept pulling the duster and Jack ended up chasing the duster along the blackboard. Quite original, really!

A sad event which I maybe never understood too well at the time, was the death of a boy who got run over. Michael Watterson was his name. Later I heard Anthony 'Joey' Royle had been run over and killed as well.

Like I say, I left the PCC and went to St Cuthbert Mayne, where I did OK. As I got older, I would go into the Black Bull pub, in Fulwood, and into town to meet up with a few PCC guys. I continued to take cricket very seriously (it must have been that Mathew Iddon ball that inspired me!), and I ended up playing for Lancashire Under 19s, club, ground and second 11's. I also played in the Northern League. During the off season I travelled to Pretoria, South Africa and was a semi-professional in Northern Transvaal province. Unfortunately, I did not quite make it in the professional game, so I decided to train to become an electrical engineer instead.

While out at 'Tokyo Joes' nightclub in Preston one night, I met Dave Keany, another PCC guy, who offered me a job as an automation engineer! PCC students were always good for contacts. It felt like because you had been to the school you had a bond, a link that was never forgotten. I used to meet Mick Suthers quite a lot in nightclubs, too. On one occasion Mick was with Jimmy White and Willie Thorne, the snooker players, who Mick had working for him. I think Mick sold second-hand cars. Good times.

After a few years working in Preston I got itchy feet and decided to travel the world. I became a freelancer and in 1991 started working in Thailand as electrical engineer on Steel Mills. I have been quite successful, working in many countries. My home is in Rayong, Thailand, now. I have two boys: James is 26 and a chemical engineer, and Phatee is 24 and a real estate agent. I have been married to my wife Somjai for 30 years. I live on a golf course named 'Eastern Star', and if I can work six weeks every year freelancing, I am happy.

The three years I spent at PCC made such a positive impact on my life. I believe the experiences and education I had are the reason I have done quite well. PCC made me grow up so quickly, maybe because I was a year younger than the rest of the intake. PCC was a very tough, all boys school of the smartest, and sometimes toughest guys. You also had to be mentally tough to survive.

We also offer a hearty welcome to the following boys who now constitute what is our last First Form.

Form 1A
Michael Ainscough
Paul Bryan Allison
Alexander C. Baker
Paul Baxendale
Mark William Beattie
John Bradley
James Anthony Clune
Philip Mark Connolly
Simon Derek Cuerden
Anthony Dixon
Edward Joseph Farrelly
Patrick Joseph Gardner
Andrew Keith Gornall
Miles Arthur Hartland
Simon Andrew Holden
Ian Peter Horrocks
David John Keany
Jonathan Clive Lace
Mark John Livesey
John Thomas McLaughlin
Francesco J. Mastrobuoni
Peter John Naylor
Stephen Richard Pye
Anthony John Rawlinson
David Bernard Rigby
Anthony John Royle
Neil James Slater
Michael William Suthers
Gregory Ronald Wagner

Form 1B
Roland Gary Anderton
Russell John Ashton
Stephen Arthur Baron
Simon James Begley
David Kenneth Blanchard
Michael Sean Brennand
Peter Anthony Cooper
Andrew Cross
Shaun Kurt Daly
Andrew Dixon
John Peter Dowbakin
Ian Joseph Gorrell
Michael B. Goulding
Edmund Michael Higgins
Anthony John Howarth
Philip Mark Huggon
Adrian Gawain Jones
Peter Leaver
Herbert Andrew Lovatt
Bernard Jackson Moon
Iain Edward Moore
Andrew Newsham
Paul Reynolds
Andrew Roberts
Peter Ryan
Thomas Smith
Damian John Walmsley
Michael L. Watterson
Mark Douglas White
Andrew McCarthy

Form 1C
Nicholas Paul Bajko
Stephen John Barrow
Michael Dominic Beahan
Maurice Black
Michael Brendan Browne
Simon Cahill
Alec John Crook
Richard John Curran
Michael Davis
Andrew Milton Finch
Paul Francis Garstang
Mark Harrison
James Eugene Henderson
Vincent Gerard Holme
Matthew Iddon
Keith Michael Jackson
Michael Thomas Kellett
Gary David McGrath
Robert A. McWilliam
Simon Morris
Timothy James Phillips
Peter Anthony Reece
Paul J. Richardson
Leonard Rogerson
Peter Andrew Rudd
Ronan Paul Sargeant
William James Simpson
Philip James Suddick
Michael C. Wilson

Also: Simon L. Mather (2C) James Archer (3S) Anthony Parker (4S)

The 'Last Intake'.

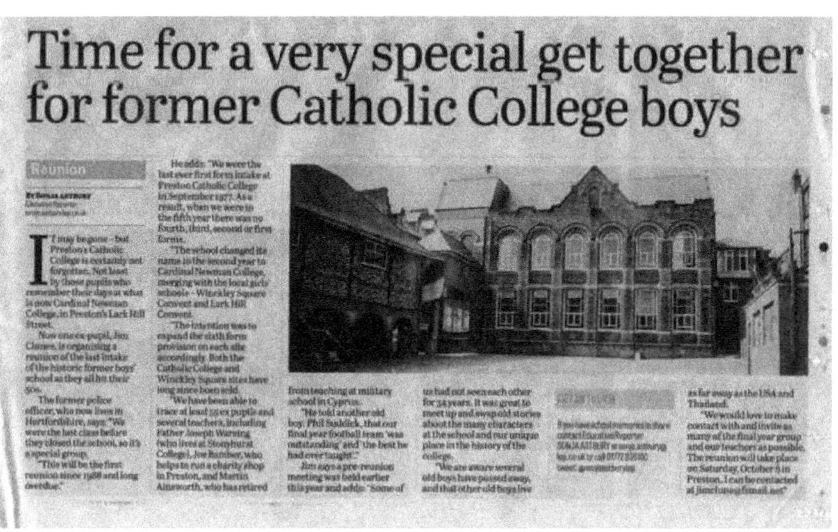

Time for a very special get together for former Catholic College boys

Reunion

It may be gone – but Preston's Catholic College is certainly not forgotten. Not least by those pupils who remember their days at what is now Cardinal Newman College, in Preston's Lark Hill Street.

Now one ex-pupil, Jim Clune, is organising a reunion of the last intake of the historic former boys' school as they all hit their 50s.

The former police officer, who now lives in Hertfordshire, says: "We were the last class before they closed the school, so it's a special group.

"This will be the first reunion since 1988 and long overdue."

He adds: "We were the last ever first form intake at Preston Catholic College in September 1977. As a result, when we were in the fifth year there was no fourth, third, second or first forms.

"The school changed its name in the second year to Cardinal Newman College, merging with the local girls schools – Winckley Square Convent and Lark Hill Convent.

"The intention was to expand the sixth form provision on each site accordingly. Both the Catholic College and Winckley Square sites have long since been sold.

"We have been able to trace at least 55 ex pupils and several teachers, including Father Joseph Waring (who lives at Stonyhurst College), Joe Bamber, who helps to run a charity shop in Preston, and Martin Ainsworth, who has retired from teaching at military school in Cyprus.

"He told another old boy, Phil Suddick, that our final year football team 'was outstanding' and 'the best he had ever taught'."

Jim says a pre-reunion meeting was held earlier this year and adds: "Some of us had not seen each other for 34 years. It was great to meet up and swap old stories about the many characters at the school and our unique place in the history of the college.

"We are aware several old boys have passed away, and that other old boys live as far away as the USA and Thailand.

"We would love to make contact with and invite as many of the final year group and our teachers as possible. The reunion will take place on Saturday, October 5 in Preston. I can be contacted at jimclune@fsmail.net"

Appeal to Old Boys to get in touch regarding the reunion.
Courtesy of the Lancashire Evening Post.

LANCASHIRE EVENING POST

SCHOOL MEMORIES

Re-union of the last intake from Preston Catholic College 1977-1982

Final intake at college make history at reunion marking 50th birthdays

Catholic college

A special group of former Preston schoolpals made history for the second time when they got together recently.

After an operation which took nearly a year to come to fruition, the last ever intake at Preston Catholic College met up for the first time since 1988 to mark their 50th birthdays.

Old boys travelled from London, the home counties, the west country and much closer to home, to Glovers, Glovers Court, Preston, 2016.

Jim Clunes, who was instrumental in organising the event and now lives in the South of England, said: "The evening was full of laughter, shared memories of our unique position within the history of the college and many a renewed acquaintance.

"There were messages from old boy's who couldn't attend, including Alec Crook from the Dominican Republic, Andy Roberts from the United States and Mark Harrison from Thailand.

"We were able to contact the college's most famous old boy, Mark Lawrenson, who kindly recorded a video message for us.

"We even received a good luck message from the Mayor of Preston. In total, 47 old boys and four teachers were in attendance."

Former Leyland Wellfield High School headteacher Martin Ainsworth who was the football manager in the first and second years, described the reunion as "a brilliant and moving evening".

Tributes were paid to seven of the former old boys who have died – Michael Watterson, Anthony Royle, Andy Dixon, Ronan Sargeant, Miles Hartland, Michael Browne and Dave Rigby.

The reunion was summed up by one of the old boys – Moz Black who said: "Just wanted to say thanks to everyone who helped to make it a fantastic night.

"What a myriad of stories, adventures, experiences, highs and lows we have had as a collective, it was really interesting and quite humbling to be part of it, thanks for sharing them."

From left, Shaun Daly, John Bradley, Bernard Moon and Damian Walmsley, Paul Reynolds, Simon Coarden and Matthew Iddon

Report and pictures from the Old Boys reunion in Preston, October 2016.
Courtesy of the Lancashire Evening Post.

The main entrance to Preston Catholic College, then and now.
Original courtesy of the school magazine.

Looking back at the school from Garden Street. The lower yard is in the foreground, with the wall of the gym on the left hand side. In the background is the upper school building. Picture taken in 1982.

The penultimate Catholic College Magazine, January 1978.

Catholic College year book/diary 1977-78.

THE COLLEGE CHOIR at the LORETO MUSIC FESTIVAL

Catholic College Choir, June 1978.
Courtesy of the school magazine.

The school gym after completion.
Courtesy of the school magazine.

UNDER-TWELVE FOOTBALL

The Season's Record:

Played 16 Won 12 Lost 4 Goals for 80 Against 43

RESULTS SINCE CHRISTMAS

v. Priory High School, Penwortham (L.F.A. Cup) . .	Won	4–1	Away
v. St. Theodore's, Burnley	Won	5–3	Away
v. St. Edmund Campion High School (Cup semi-final) .	Lost	1–3	Home
v. St. Kevin's, Kirkby	Lost	1–6	Home
v. Clitheroe Royal Grammar School	Won	8–1	Away

Bad weather was the strongest opposition the Under-12s met with during the second half of the season. Though keen and disciplined, the team had to learn patience. When we did manage to get on the somewhat moist field of play, our results were, not too surprisingly, inconsistent. Penwortham Priory High School became our third cup victims as we won, eventually, 4–1—Stephen Pye notching an excellent hat-trick.

There then followed an epic away game against St. Theodore's, Burnley. Wind-swept, bitterly cold rain and hail lashed off the Pennines down on to the diminutive frames of our team. Bravely and doggedly we went in at half-time 3–1 ahead. Sheer determination and 'guts' kept us ahead in the second half, when Peter Suddick, closely resembling an icicle, performed miracles in goal. It was a sterling performance, and, even on a day like that, one that warmed the cockles of the heart!

In the semi-final of the Preston Under-12 cup, we met Campion High School (the eventual winners) at Grafton. On a heavy pitch, strength was the deciding factor, and we were, in fact, overpowered by Campion's well-developed left-winger, and lost 3–1. The following Saturday, a dispirited side lost heavily 6–1 to St. Kevin's, Kirkby.

We then ended the season with a marvellous performance at Clitheroe where, in good conditions (!), we played excellent attacking football, swamping the opposition 8–1.

Over the season, each member of the squad has made significant contributions to the side, and, perhaps more importantly, improved individually as a player. Peter Suddick continues to improve as a 'keeper, and his bravery and agility have never been in doubt. Ian Gorrell's strength constantly cleared danger and prompted attacks. Simon Cuerden and Michael Ainscough are becoming a first-class pair of central defenders. Paul Alison, a great 'tryer' and tackler, has now left us. Stephen Pye exhibits outstanding potential as an 'all-round' player and, from midfield, was our leading scorer with 20 goals. Eugene Henderson captained the side admirably and was an unflagging dynamo in midfield. Neil Slater is a great worker and produces some amazing finishing. Peter Cooper excited on the ball and finished consistently well, scoring 18 goals. Jimmy Clune toiled unselfishly as a 'target man' and notched 9 goals. First Form penalty-winner, Andy Newsham, scored 11 goals and could become an even better player in midfield. Mick Suthers is beginning to use his strength and speed and is a very promising striker. Good contributions have also been made by Sean Daly and Michael Davis.

We have learned much and have still a great deal to learn. We will improve tactically as a side and will strive to achieve a better balance, in that, at the moment, we tend to be a 'right-handed' team. I have enjoyed this first year of management, and I am pleased we have a happy team that encourages rather than criticises. A huge 'Thank you' to everyone who has been concerned with the team. A particular word of thanks to Mr. Eddy Brown, who, quietly and steadily, has helped every player to improve and has provided invaluable advice. Like all 'originals', he will be irreplaceable.

M.S.A.

71

1977-78 first year football report, taken from the final Catholic College Magazine, June 1978.

MUD splattered but happy are the boys from Newman College who won the Under-13 Jack May final at Deepdale last night. Captain Eugene Henderson is chaired by his mates. Newman College (formerly Preston Catholic College) also won the Under-15 Ord Cup final.

Courtesy of the Lancashire Evening Post.

Winning the Jack May Cup at Preston North End's ground, Deepdale, in May, 1979.

LANCASHIRE EVENING POST
SCHOOL MEMORIES
Soccer stars from Preston Catholic College's last intake taken in Winckley Square in 1979 after they had won the Second Year 'Town Cup'. Below, the former Preston Catholic College in Winckley Square

First and second teams with the Jack May trophy, Winckley Square, 1979.
Courtesy of the Lancashire Evening Post.

Pupils on school trip to north Wales, circa 1978-79.

CATHOLIC COLLEGE, PRESTON. **REPORT** CHRISTMAS 1980/81

Name	Form	Number in Form	Place in Form	Absent Half-Days	Schools Re-open
JONES A.G.	VM	25	12	/	4 JAN. 1982

Subject	Grade	Place	Master's Report
Religious Doctrine	0	2	Very good progress [illegible]
English	3	5	A good result. Adrian always works seriously. [illegible]
Mathematics	4	13	Working well. He must keep up his efforts and remember to revise the memory work regularly. [illegible]
Latin			
Greek/German			
French/~~Spanish~~	8	8	Tries, but effort needed to improve written work and to learn vocabulary [illegible]
History			
Geography	5	9	More application needed if he wishes to gain O' level in June [illegible]
ENG. SCIENCE ~~Physics~~ (CSE)	2	=11	MECHANICS, HEAT 38% Tries but still finds the subject difficult. He must not give up. [illegible]
~~Chemistry~~			ELEC 73% – good result – generally works well. [illegible] 31% – good result [illegible]
Metalwork	4	8	Good steady worker – improving with recent effort, good theory exam. [illegible]
Eng. Drawing/Art			
Physical Education			Fair [illegible]

GRADE CODE: 0 = 80, 1 = 70, 2 = 65, 3 = 60, 4 = 55, 5 = 50, 6 = 45, 7 = 40, 8 = 30, 9 = 20

Form Master and Line Master: Hard work from now to June will give him a well-balanced certificate – and he is capable of gaining it. [illegible]

PP **Head Master:** Good work generally. [illegible]

TSC 77/8595

CATHOLIC COLLEGE, PRESTON. **REPORT** SUMMER 1980/81

Name	Form	Number in Form	Place in Form	Absent Half-Days	Schools Re-open
A.G. JONES	VM	26	12	32	7 SEPT. 1981

Subject	Grade	Place	Master's Report
Religious Doctrine	2	7=	Good progress. [illegible]
English	4	2	A good result, since this exam was of 'O' level standard. [illegible]
Mathematics	2	13	Good paper – a tremendous improvement. He must keep up his efforts throughout next year and revise regularly the memory work. [illegible]
Latin			
Greek/German			
French/~~Spanish~~	3	5/19	Tries hard always. There are still weak areas (i.e. oral) but at this stage the result is pleasing. [illegible]
History	7	11	His exams fall short of his achievement in term-time. He must beware of irrelevance. [illegible]
Geography	6	3	A good term and very competent exam. Well for this 'O' level type exam. [illegible]
ENG. SCIENCE ~~Physics~~	4	13	MECH. Only fair standard during year, [illegible] gave hope for the future. [illegible]
~~Chemistry~~			ELEC Only just satisfactory. POWER Showed interest. [illegible]
Metalwork	8	23	Has worked well and shown interest during term. Theory exam weak. [illegible]
~~Eng. Drawing~~/Art	2	1/9	A good year with some careful work and definite progress. Keep it up! [illegible]
Physical Education			Satisfactory [illegible]

GRADE CODE: 0 = 80, 1 = 70, 2 = 65, 3 = 60, 4 = 55, 5 = 50, 6 = 45, 7 = 40, 8 = 30, 9 = 20

Form Master and Line Master: He has really improved the standard of his work. He must have confidence in himself and just slog on. He is neat and tidy in appearance and his conduct is satisfactory. [illegible]

Head Master:

TSC 77/8595

Two of Adrian Jones' 'better' school reports!

CATHOLIC COLLEGE, PRESTON. **REPORT**

Christmas 1979

Name	Form	Number in Form	Place in Form	Absent (Half-Days)	Schools Re-open
James Clune	3M	27	9th	-	7th Jan '80

Subject	Grade	Place	Master's Report
Religious Doctrine	1	5=	James has produced some good work during the term and his exam result matches it. He is keen in asking questions. [illegible]
English	1	5	A very promising result. James has put a lot of effort into his work this term and maintained a consistently high standard of achievement. Keep up the good work! [illegible]
Mathematics	4	11	Fine progress this term. The grade would have been even better but for weakness in past exam. [illegible]
Art	6	25.	More serious effort required. [illegible]
Greek/German			
French/Spanish	1	5	Has worked steadily during the term and deserves this good result. JAC
History	4	4	Hard-working and showing fair promise [illegible]
Geography	0	1	A good term and excellent exam result. Well done. PS
Eng. Science	3	=12	Mechanics, heat etc. 41% Generally satisfactory. Exam showed lack of revision. [illegible]
Chemistry			Electricity 80% Good exam, keep it up.
Metalwork	3	7	Good standard all term – keep it up. [illegible] Practical Fair, more speed and accuracy req'd [illegible]
Eng. Drawing	9	25	Very weak indeed – I am still hopeful. [illegible]
Physical Education			Good PS

GRADE CODE: 0 = 80, 1 = 70, 2 = 65, 3 = 60, 4 = 55, 5 = 50, 6 = 45, 7 = 40, 8 = 30, 9 = 20

Form Master and Line Master: James has worked well in most subjects this term, although I expect a higher class position in summer. PS.

Head Master: [illegible]

Jim Clune's school report.

Paul Garstang, Mick Davis, Mick Suthers, unknown and Andrew Dixon (in the background), Austrian skiing trip circa 1981-82.
Courtesy of Andy Cross.

Tim Phillips and Mick Suthers on a skiing trip to Austria, circa 1981-82.

This picture was taken in front of the pavilion at Grafton playing fields in 1982. L-R: Neil Slater, John Dowbakin, Pete Leaver, Mr Pete Singleton (Geography and PE teacher), Pete Ryan, Simon Morris.

Lower yard at school; Science teacher Mr Louis Caton with Jim Clune (L) and Mick Brennand (R).

Teacher Mr 'TK' Henry in 5M.

Pictures taken at Avenham Park in 1982.

Top picture from back: Adrian Jones, L-R Howard Tomlinson, John Dowbakin and Dave Blanchard. Foreground L-R Jim Clune, Jonathan Lace and Mick Ainscough.

Bottom picture, L-R: Howard Tomlinson, John Dowbakin, Adrian Jones, Dave Blanchard, Jonathan Lace and Mick Ainscough. In the foreground is Tim Phillips.

At Grafton playing fields with Mr 'TK' Henry Engineering Science teacher. L-R: Jim Clune, John Bradley and Mick Brennand.

Grafton playing fields; Miles Hartland (L) and Eugene Henderson (R).

Grafton pavilion prior to demolition.

The headmaster, Fr Wren, leaving 5M's classroom after addressing the class on the final day of term, 28th May 1982.

Final day of term, Friday 28th May, 1982. In the foreground is Dave Blanchard. Lined up in front of the blackboard are, L-R: Mick Brennand, Jim Clune, Steve Pye, Mr 'JET' Talbot (Metalwork teacher), Pete Cooper and Andy Lovatt.

In 5M on the last day of term, 1982, L-R John Bradley, Simon Morris, Jonathan Lace, Jim Clune and Mark White.

Students in high spirits on the final day of term, L-R: Mick Suthers, Ronan 'Rex' Sargeant, Russell Ashton, Tony Dixon, Mark White, with Steve Pye above.

Lower Yard on the step by the Metalwork Department. From L-R: Mick Brennand, Adrian Jones, John Dowbakin, Mick Ainscough, Jonathan Lace, Miles Hartland, Howard Tomlinson and Mick Beahan.

John Bradley and Miles Hartland, 1982

The school tie of old boy Anton Rawlinson, which to this day is still tied in the same knot tied on 28th May 1982, the last day of school.

Form 5M, 28th May, 1982.

Eddie Farrelly, Jim Clune and Pete Leaver, 6th Form classroom, 1983.

Alec Crook's 18th birthday party. L-R: Phil Suddick, Alec Crook, Steve Barrow and Andy Roberts. In the foreground are Pete Naylor and Mark Connolly.

One of the old school ties and badges.
Courtesy of Ralph Cooper.

Winckley Square, present day.

Still displayed above the front entrance to the school is the Jesuit symbol and the letters IHS, the Paschal Lamb, the PP of Preston, and the date 1898. *Courtesy of Richard Blackburn.*

Preston Catholic College World War II memorial, now housed at Newman College.

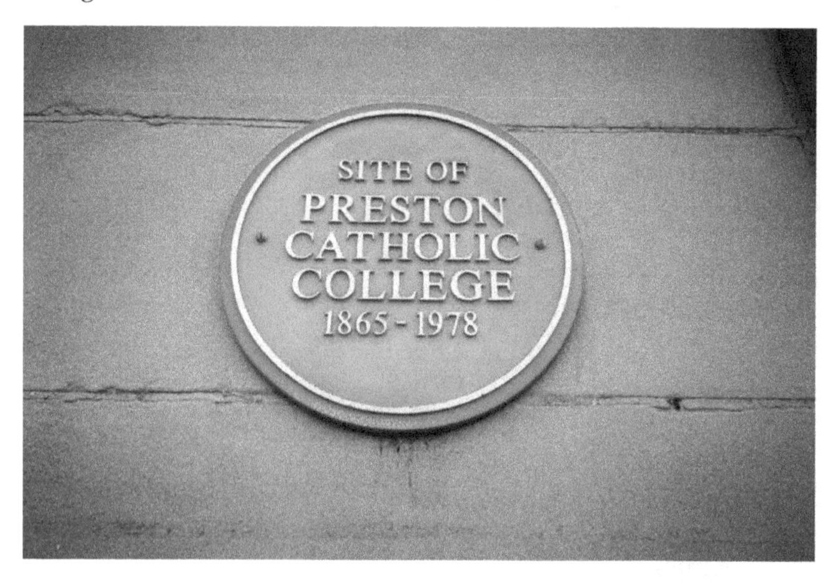

The blue plaque marking the site of the school on Winckley Square. *Courtesy of Richard Blackburn.*

With thanks to all contributors for providing these images.

EUGENE HENDERSON:
FORMS 1C, 2B, 3S, 4S AND 5S

To be honest, it came as something of a shock to me – and most of my family – when I passed that bizarre 11 Plus exam.

No one I knew had any training or a tutor; in those days it was all down to the lure of a new racing bike for the offspring of the more ambitious, or as we say these days 'aspirational', parents. Mine were neither.

One day in spring 1977, they stuck us in a room and left us to get to grips with questions like: 'There are 98 boys and 102 girls in a school. If there is one teacher for every 40 children, how long does an express train take to travel from Manchester to Aberdeen on a Sunday?'

I'd like to explain the answer to that conundrum, but for those who had to take the entrance exam (after failing the 11 Plus) it would probably be a waste of time!

How I passed is a mystery. It certainly annoyed my deranged Irish granny who, in a bizarre attempt to once again sabotage my future (she chose the name Eugene), stormed down to my primary school and told the headmistress: "He can't have passed, he's simple!"

Like most of my childhood this attitude had less to do with me, and more to do with 700 years of British colonial rule. Oh, and the small matter that her favoured grandson, my elder brother, had failed the self-same exam five years earlier.

Once the dust settled it was off to Hood's outfitters at Gamull Lane, where I was stuck in an oversized blazer, slacks (not grey, as I had no intention of joining the choir) black shoes, a smart white shirt, and a green, white and red tie. Apparently, I was now ready for academia. Or not.

With the budget blown on the outfit there was obviously nothing left for a decent haircut. But as the pictures from those early days show, I was not alone.

As the first Monday in September neared, little did I know that Lancashire's decision to go 'comprehensive' meant while the rest of the world was marching towards a bright new educational future, I was marching towards the film set of *Colditz*.

And to make matters worse we were going to be the last PoWs to be released by our captors. I hoped it might be over by Christmas. It lasted until May 1982.

What a dump I'd landed myself in! I'd seen more appealing crematoriums. Short of them land-mining the underground playground, it could not have been less welcoming.

Not only that, it turned out we had been streamed using no obvious criteria. So, there we were, stuck with each other behind the barbed wire in our very own Stalag. Mine was 1C – the following year it was imaginatively re-branded as 2B. I noticed little difference.

In those first years it became apparent my teachers ranged from the disinterested (the majority) to the deluded and the downright psychotic. Some of the masters had obviously been affected by the war, but why that was our fault I never quite fathomed.

When it came to female staff most of them seemed to be taking that 'ole time religion thing a little too seriously.

Only during break time and PE afternoons were we allowed to mix with the 'others' of our year. But there were always Wednesday afternoons (later it was Friday, which I preferred), when freedom beckoned along the Old Tram Bridge and down to Factory Lane. That's where the happiest memories of my schooldays are brought back.

What saved me from the desperate diet of dreary surroundings and even drearier lessons was sport, and football in particular. It was to be that way for the whole of my five years at Cath Coll.

I know many lads hated those afternoons, dreading being shoved into the vacant right-back spot or worse, in goal, and shouted out for their obvious failings, but this was my realm.

We were all similarly heartbroken when the pitches were unfit, though, as that meant the dreaded cross country. The secret of which was to never finish first and never finish last. And I never did.

After Mr Ainsworth (a liberal light amidst the bleakness) made me captain of the First XI I never really looked back. It gave me a natural outlet for my personality. As someone put it during our re-union, "You were a bit of a mouth, Eugene!"

Real bonds were forged with teammates, Saturday mornings spent travelling the North West to take on, and often beat, the best that Manchester, Liverpool and elsewhere had to offer.

That team remains very close to my heart more than 30 years later. Not everyone in it was a close mate, but they didn't have to be.

Many did become mates who played alongside me in other teams for the best part of a decade, and who often took me in when needed it. I still say Mrs Cuerden's double egg and chips is the best meal I've ever tasted. To those fantastic people, I will always be grateful.

Until I was 17, I never played for a team that didn't wear green. Luckily the colour went nicely with my yellow teeth!

Even now, if you asked me the best way out of either a midfield battle or Brexit, my answer would be to pop it down the opposition's left- back channel for Coops to run on to! Whatever happened I always knew someone had my back.

I only have positive memories of our second manager, Fr Spencer's team talks and his obvious delight at beating any Protestant school who happened to stand in our way. AMDG and all that.

Sadly, my only vivid memories of my time at school are of that camaraderie, both on the field and off it, as we spent our time navigating through the increasingly testosterone-filled environment.

Pre-arranged fights on the Miller Park bandstand, being barred for spitting from the upper floor in St George's shopping centre (that wasn't me), and jostling to get a look at the Lark Hill girls trampolining in the sports hall, all helped towards our collective coming of age.

Obviously, we weren't quite the finished article. I'm not sure being banned from the Bodega Wine Bar after a lunchtime visit to play the video arcade game 'Phoenix' while dressed in full uniform showed us to be completely streetwise youngsters.

Despite being 'a mouth' I was only on the receiving end of the Jesuits' chosen weapon of pain infliction – the dreaded ferula – once.

The bill was issued by our second-year chemistry teacher better known as 'Brenda'; a woman who although not an obvious 'Godsquadder' was also not an obvious teacher. My crime? Who knows? She had lost any semblance of control long before she dished out punishment to at least five of the class.

'Fat Jack' McCann – no body shaming intended – was the man handed the honour of ensuring Henderson would think twice before stepping out of line again. He gave me the usual "this hurts me . . . " routine before bringing a piece of whalebone encased in leather, he just happened to have hanging around in his office, down on across my palm.

It was a bit of a stinger to be honest, but the second was a killer. Jack's aim was off, and down came the ferula across the top of my fingers. Quick as a flash, and belying his nickname, he grabbed the same hand and gave me another.

"That's what happens when you move . . . ", he said. Looking at this rotund, red-faced man, nose covered in hairs, Himmler glasses, and sweat beads glistening on his forehead, I thought to myself, *that's what happens when you don't move enough, you fat b*stard.*

Perhaps three years staring at the back of Paul Garstang's head is the reason the rest is all a little hazy, but I don't think so.

Perhaps, instead, what we learned outside the classroom is the really important stuff. I'm sure today we would not have been left to our own devices as we were. I saw no pastoral care given to the pupils of

Preston Catholic College. When I had a family issue, no member of staff spoke to me, asked about my wellbeing, despite knowing what had happened, which I do not believe would happen these days. There were no action plans, interventions, or anything just to show someone was interested.

I think the education itself was functional for the majority of us. During my time at a grammar school, I was never given even the most cursory of introductions to Shakespeare, but usefully I did study classic Latin!

However, I did learn one quote from the Bard – it was one of the prefect lines dished out as a punishment:

'The quality of mercy is not strained.
It droppeth as the gentle rain from heaven

Upon the place beneath. It is twice blest:
It blesseth him that gives and him that takes.'

Looking back, it takes a pretty twisted mind to use the work of the greatest writer of the English language as a sanction. But with people like Pop Moulding in charge of discipline (I still have no idea what his real name was), nothing should come as a surprise. "Buns, bananas, brown bread!" is the only thing he said that I can remember. His material really needed working on.

Perhaps the oddest of all the staff was Mr Bradley – the man on whom I believe Phil Redmond based the character 'Bullet' Baxter in Grange Hill. Did anyone really believe the ball in the swimming pool games cupboard was the one used in the 1972 Olympic Water Polo final? He once called me over and gave me 500 lines for being a "nosey git". Nice man, and what a great weekend that was.

If only it had been 'Ten Timer' Turner – a maths teacher who did everything, including doling out lines, in base ten. It would only have been ten lines, or possibly 20, maybe 30. Well, you get the idea.

The schooling also lacked simple basics. There was no need for sex education; obviously it was intended we would keep ourselves pure!

And as for careers advice. . . Who needed guidance when you were automatically guaranteed a glittering future just by virtue of the fact you had studied at Preston Catholic College? Doors would open, and opportunities would knock for anyone from such a renowned alma mater, or so it was thought.

But that early post-war world was fast disappearing. The Tories had wreaked havoc in the North and there were more than three million unemployed.

I know this, because in 3S Mr Thompson wrote the figure on the blackboard, sat back and told us he didn't care if we passed our English as he had a job and wouldn't be down the Job Centre anytime soon, like the rest of us.

So, actually, a lot of doors were boarded up, and if opportunity was knocking, for many it was doing so with a sponge in its hand.

The majority in the A stream were destined to achieve academically. As for the others, some, like myself, stuck with studies because there was little else out there in the early 1980s, while others left and got a trade.

In truth I'm not sure how being at grammar school made a great difference to those apart from the exceptionally gifted, aside from the sporting life it opened up. Maybe, as one of my old classmates said to me at the reunion, we didn't realise the opportunity we'd been given. I think that's a fair point – what young man ever does at that age?

But I also think it's fair to say we were never a big priority, given what was going on around us. As we sat staring into the middle distance while Sandy McCann (and his unfortunate gaze) blathered on about the Haber Process, the world was changing, and our school belonged in the past.

It was transforming into a sixth form, many teachers were coming to the end of their careers and the real influence this well-respected establishment once had was long, long gone.

I landed eight O levels, but not one A. Other capable lads walked out the doors of 34 Winckley Square with not one exam pass, having long been left to their own devices to fail spectacularly.

For some it seems our schooldays remain the highlight of their lives. I think many of those saw a different side to the place, because they stayed on into the sixth form when beer was introduced to the curriculum.

For me, I believe in many ways, life only really started once I'd been released from the shackles of the old school and its antiquated system.

After A levels and attempts to avoid further education, I eventually moved to Manchester (mainly because I thought I'd meet The Smiths – and I did!) to study English and Politics at the Polytechnic. After three years I walked away with a gentleman's degree – or a 2:2 – a hangover, and an overdraft.

With an elder brother working in newspapers and not a clue what I wanted to do I decided to give journalism a go. Now, after 30 years, including spells on national newspapers including the *Sunday People* and *Daily Express*, as well as working in Hong Kong and Ireland, I'm getting ready to move on to another career and another country.

I've had an interesting life covering many major stories, and I've met and interviewed the great and not-so-good. I've also worked with some great people, and some you wouldn't cross the road for – and that isn't necessarily a dig at Piers Morgan!

Between work, children and living, there's not always much time to reflect on the past and possibly that's no bad thing. So, when you're asked to do so the experience can be very strange; trying to remember the boy you were four decades ago, and trying to dredge up how it felt to be a youngster growing up in a typical Northern town in the late 70s and early 80s, when only four colours seemed to exist (and two of those were brown and mustard!).

I stopped going to mass when I was 16, at about the same time I stopped studying French. It was the only O level I failed, and that could in part be down to me and Andy Newsham deciding to have lunch in Jackson's Chippy and turning up late for the exam. Sadly, the spotty teen I was then had no idea he might need it one day – the French, that is, not Catholicism – given that my wife Allison and I are doing up a dilapidated house in the country where we plan to live.

As for school, religion, and all that, I think about the old phoenix on the school badge and the Latin inscription 'Fides'! Looking back, I think we all needed more than Faith to survive . . . as George Michael later found out.

TONY HOWARTH: FORMS 1B, 2A, 3A, 4A AND 5A

While at Saint Mary's in Chorley I gained my place to study at Preston Catholic College in 1977, aged 11. My journey to the College involved cycling 15 minutes to the train station each morning, then getting the train for 45 minutes to and from College. Once I had discovered golf, this routine expanded to include a further bike ride to the golf course after school. I would cycle the three miles to the club and practise on the course or putting green until dark, no matter the weather. I didn't realise at the time how much benefit the cycling had given me; my legs grew stronger and that helped my game, but seeing as we hadn't even heard of a sports fitness coach back then, it was all accidental!

It is amazing how some things are meant to be. When I was a child, all I wanted to be was a football player. We kicked a ball around at school at every opportunity, and at home I spent hours kicking a ball against the wall or playing in the street. Then one day, at age 13, it all changed. The wonderful man better known to me as dad decided to visit the local municipal golf course, hire some clubs, and have a game of golf with his friends. A couple of weeks later, at the start of the summer holidays, one of them was unable to go and he asked me if I fancied giving it a try with them. I laughed and said no at first. "Is it because I would beat you?" he asked. That was all it took to get me to go! I laughed when the others hit the ball no further than 50 yards with their first shots, but stopped laughing when I finally completed the first hole in 14 shots myself (I still have *that* scorecard!). I was well and truly hooked, and I don't think a day passed that summer that I didn't play on the course, practise in the garden or putt in the house. Mum came home from work one rainy day to find me chipping balls over the sofa, trying to land them in the coal bucket. She calmed down once she realised they were plastic, not real!

Two teachers in particular had a big influence on my sport at the College: Mr Henry and Mr Ainsworth. Mr Ainsworth was always incredibly supportive throughout my time playing football, encouraging me to use my right foot for something other than just standing on, and asking me why I was obviously boycotting tackling! Mr Ainsworth and I had some great football chats on the way home from matches, and he was also very encouraging about me playing golf and my wish to take it up as a career. Mr Henry, meanwhile, was a big influence on my golf. He played the sport, and knew that I was passionate about becoming a professional. It was Mr Henry who managed to find a way of allowing me to sit in the staff room and watch the coverage of the Open Championship every year while everyone else was still in lessons! School then gave me time off to play in tournaments at a time when I needed to reduce my handicap to join the professional ranks. These extra tournaments ultimately made the difference, giving me the opportunity to turn professional a year early. Had I not played in them and performed well, my handicap would not have been low enough to join the professional ranks that year, and I would have had to wait another full 12 months for another opportunity.

Although I was lucky to have teachers who supported my golf ambitions at school, when it came to careers advice evenings, things were different. Many advisors tried to steer me away from a career in golf, telling me it was going to be far too difficult to make a lifetime career from a sport. I was advised instead to take a path towards accountancy. Luckily, I didn't take that advice. My family have always been hugely supportive of my choice, no more so than when my mum suggested to the careers advisor that maybe he should come and play 18 holes with me and decide if his advice still stood after that!

My first professional role was at Duxbury Park Golf Course in Chorley, the club where I played as a Junior. I turned pro at the age of 17, the third youngest golfer to do so in the country at that time, and something I'll always be proud of. It obviously took a lot of time and effort to turn professional, and I spent much of that period with Anthony Rawlinson (another of our College year and my best friend throughout school and beyond). Anthony would travel for miles to caddy for me in the early hours of Saturday and Sunday mornings while I was trying to gain my level to turn pro, and his help will always be remembered. He was always encouraging and would often chip in with a useful comment, such as "Why did you hit it over there when we are supposed to be going straight?" He took the game up himself soon after and unsurprisingly, the 'helpful' comments stopped!

Despite a couple of local event successes during my first few years as a pro, it became apparent that a playing career was never really on the cards. Alongside playing, I was coaching adults and juniors at Euxton Park Golf Range in Chorley (including giving lessons to Mr Huggan, my Latin teacher!). My passion and enthusiasm for teaching quickly became clear, and before long I was spending more and more time coaching others than playing and practising my own game. My coaching career has led me to meet some incredible people and has brought me as much if not more joy than playing for a living.

In the late 1990s I was fortunate enough to be asked to help create one of the first academic golf courses in the UK, at Myerscough College. In 1999 I was privileged to meet Prince Philip, and show him around our new golf facility at the College. As we were showing him round, we had students hitting balls in the nets and it was amusing to see his security detail leap to attention when the sound of one particularly well-hit ball sounded more like a gunshot than a golf shot.

It was at this time that my work with the Golf Foundation and the European Tour became more a part of my golfing life. I was asked to manage the coaching centres at European tour events and around the same time my work with local schools began to grow, developing coaching programmes and curriculum-based sessions to get more young people involved in the sport.

In the early 2000s I launched my own company 'Mini Marvels' as a hub for all my golf coaching and development work. I worked with several local authorities implementing golf across the curriculum in primary schools. As a result, I was appointed Golf Development Officer for Merseyside in 2003 and was awarded the Sinclair Award in 2004. (this is a national award presented to a PGA Professional who, as a direct result of his or her efforts, has made a significant impact in the development of grass roots junior golf; it was wonderful to have my passion for getting children involved in the game recognised). As part of my Golf Development Officer role, I worked closely with the ladies, seniors, and European Tour to put on events across the region. An event that always stands out for me at this time is hosting a coaching session alongside Jack Nicklaus, one of the sports greats, who turned out in person to be exactly the man I had hoped he would be.

As well as coaching beginners and club golfers, I've had the privilege to coach both Ladies' European Tour and Seniors Tour professionals; working alongside golf's elite players definitely counts as a career highlight and makes me glad (every day!) that I didn't go into accountancy.

In 2009 I started working in the UK with International Golf Development who implement first touch coaching and golf development programmes across the world, and in the following years I was able to expand my coaching to many countries across Europe, Africa and Asia. These trips were rewarding in many ways, with some emotional elements to a lot of them. By far the most rewarding of these was spent delivering golf into schools in the townships of Cape Town. It might sound like a cliché, but my experience in Cape Town was truly life-changing. I got to visit schools in the township of Khayelitsha, the second-largest black township in South Africa after Soweto. This visit opened my eyes to the happiness that can be achieved from having family and friendship even in an environment devoid of privileges. To see the youngsters loving playing football with a bag full of rolled up clothes as a make-shift ball reinforced my appreciation of the importance of happiness over possessions. I did feel quite sorry for the youngsters we visited, as I think they were expecting someone a little more exciting to come and coach them during this period. The last sports coach who had visited the township was none other than David Beckham – a hard act to follow by anyone's standards!

As my career has developed, I have been invited to speak at many events including the Inaugural Golf Careers Convention at the University of Northumbria, the UK Golf Show, The Turkish Golf Federation First Annual Coaching Conference and the Golf Europe Show in Germany. Since 2014 I have been the Academy Director at Scarthingwell Golf Course on the outskirts of York, and spend most days coaching players of all ages and abilities. The Academy has introduced many new people to golf and my passion for growing the game is as strong now as always. My work still involves travelling and delivering coaching seminars and clinics to golf professionals around the world, helping them improve their coaching styles and delivery.

Golf has provided me with a fabulous career, but mostly it has given me life experiences that have been priceless. My children, Zoe and Andy have played since the ages of four or five, and although they're now both in their twenties and working, we still enjoy playing together whenever possible.

Currently I am expanding my work with primary and secondary schools, with a new curriculum-based course ready for launch in Spring 2020. It's incredibly satisfying being able to put time, effort and knowledge back into schools as I will be forever grateful for the support given to me by everyone at Preston Catholic College, especially those who encouraged me to follow my dream and to forge a career in a sport that I love.

PHIL HUGGON: FORMS 1B, 2A, 3A, 4A AND 5A

Monday 5 September 1977 seems a long time ago, but memories of that first day at school are still sharp in my mind. With two brothers and various cousins at the College, not to mention my father teaching classics there, you'd expect mastering the dress code on day one to have been simple. Not so in my case – I was still wearing my grey battered shorts from Our Lady and St Edwards Primary School in Fulwood, Preston. Strangely enough, I was the only one in shorts that day, which I guess made me unique, although all the other lads and teachers (except my dad) probably thought *what a numpty*. To help make me stand out even more, I think I was the smallest boy in the whole year, and the youngest, so I really was 'special'. That evening, as we drove home in the car with my dad and two brothers (in their long trousers), I made it clear to my dad that on your first day at big school, you want to fit in, not stand out, so he'd better get me some trousers for day two, and he did.

I never looked back from that point on. We all knew that this was the last intake for the school, so I had skipped a year in primary, as had Eddie Higgins. We didn't appreciate how the school would empty, though, as with each year passing another year disappeared, until there was only our year left. I began life in Form 1B, middle row, behind

Higgins then Howarth then Huggon. Footie in the undercover playground area was probably the highlight in that first year, although I never won many headers (a height issue). I also remember being given my own money to manage, so it was chips and gravy every day for five years. One clear memory was singing the solo part in *Once in Royal David's City* at the school Carol Concert – I was up in the choir and as I sang the first notes, everyone looked back and up at me and I heard at least one voice exclaiming "Hey, it's Huggy!" The other poignant memory from year one was when Michael Watterson (who subsequently died from a cycling accident in year three) vomited all the way down the corridor, much to Mrs Proctor's displeasure. She asked if anyone would mind mopping it all up, and I promptly volunteered and got to work with my bucket, as I was used to mopping up sick from my mum at home – she was dying of pancreatic cancer so vomited every time she ate. The good news was that Mrs P thanked me in front of the whole class and let me off geography homework. My classmates looked at me as though they were slightly unsure as to my motives, but they were pure. Equally poignant was the sight of the whole school choir singing at Chipping church for the funeral of my mum who sadly died on March 13, 1978.

Year two is a bit of a blur, and I remember very little except for one incident where someone had the bright idea of seeing if we could cover the whole ceiling in pellets of chewed paper, expertly flicked with rulers. After three days, most of the class had joined in the task in a sign of solidarity, and we were close to achieving our mission. Sadly, someone tipped off Mr Billington who came in one day unannounced, with a face like thunder, and slammed his hand on the desk – it was quite scary at the time, and the whole class got detention, too. I can't remember if we had to unstick the collage we'd made on the ceiling (and if we did, I can't remember how we managed it), but it was quite creative.

Year three marked streaming, as we were all branded A, S or M. We never did understand why these letters were chosen instead of A, B, and C, but we all knew our place. A was for Academic swots; S was for the Special people and M more for the 'troubleMakers'. We were choosing subjects by this time, and science was something of a mystery to me, although chemistry teacher Miss Tyrell's long legs had their charms. I was marked out for languages and Latin was my thing, inspired perhaps by one teacher, Uncle Bernie as he was affectionately known (my dad), and Father Wareing, who later married off me and various members of our family. I remember my dad driving me home saying "I don't understand it" in relation to how well everyone had performed in a Latin test that day. Well, I did understand – I'd finished the test in record time and passed my paper round the whole class, so we all got close to full marks. I also recall the school motto, ADMG, or *Ad Maiorem Gloriam Dei*, which for the benefit of S or M (who I don't think did Latin!), means 'To the greater glory of god' – I even raised money for the ADMG fund by selling my auntie's sweets, with a small cut of the proceeds adding to my chips and gravy money of course.

Year four felt more real as O levels were looming, and more surreal as there were no underlings from years one, two or three around, so the place had started to feel emptier and you could hear the echoes in the playground. It was also the year when we began to share the canteen with the girls from Winckley Square convent next door. While it was interesting to watch the girls come round led by the nuns, can you believe we had to let them all eat first, then leave before we were even allowed in the canteen? I think this was also the year of the bandstand fight, where our own Shaun Daly challenged a guy from another school to fisticuffs at midday on Avenham Park Bandstand. There was quite an impressive turnout from PCC boys, as I recall, and even though Shaun got battered he came back a hero . . . That year we did two O levels, but it felt very early to be doing English Literature – maybe that's why I scraped a C!

And so, year five arrived – the last year ever year of Preston Catholic College for all 90 or so of us, and it felt the end of an era. The place had lost its soul; teachers were leaving in search of new jobs, and the school's previous academic prowess (so my dad later told me) was failing. The buildings were still lost in time, and the place always felt like a labyrinth of tunnels from the top forms through to the cavernous hall, with its secret passageway out to St Wilfried's church, and back down to the lower yard with the canteen, the gym and the ice-cold swimming pool. The clock ticked slowly to get us past O levels, and then we went our different ways. In sixth form, Science remained at the College, while arts went to Lark Hill College which was 80 per cent girls and 20 per cent boys – it was a no-brainer for me, with those odds: I went to Lark Hill in the pursuit of girls and never really came back to Preston Catholic College.

From school, I went on to study French and Latin at Oriel College, Oxford (the same College and subjects as my brothers, which made it ideal for borrowing essays). In my first year there, it was still all boys, only to become mixed in my second year. The upside of the change was that I then met my wife, Jackie, who also studied at Oriel; we had a great young life pre-kids, living in Paris, Lausanne, Lisbon and Brussels. As for work, studying dead languages helped my career no end as I worked with BP, then MARS and then Shell. The last ten years I have worked as a non-executive director with various organisations in health, education, and sport. Most important to me, though, has always been family, from my brothers and father at the College to my wife and three adorable kids, and we are happily living together in Hale, Manchester.

It's now 37 years since I left the College, but I still have vivid memories of the imposing Victorian brick buildings, the form register, and almost all the surnames, the presence of Jesuit priests and all the other teachers and friends who helped shape my character. And while I did eventually grow taller, I always was the youngest in the whole school, from the day I started until the day I left.

MATT IDDON:
FORMS 1C, 2B, 3S, 4S AND 5S

I still have the photograph of me that was taken on the evening before my first day at Preston Catholic College. I can remember standing there feeling slightly uncomfortable, decked out in my new uniform in our walled garden, squinting into the evening sun! I was holding a handed-down leather satchel in my right hand, nervously anticipating the journey ahead into my new school life. The uniform comprised a black blazer with an embossed Eagle-type figure badge on the breast pocket, with the Latin word 'Fides' underneath the bird's claws. Grey flannels, a white shirt and a green and black tie completed our garb.

The following morning, I began the oft-repeated ritual of bussing it to Preston Bus Station and the seemingly endless walk to school from there, through Guildhall Arcade, past the Harris museum, across the flagged market area with (what was reputed to be) an iron bear baiting ring sunken into the stone, and then along Fishergate to Winckley Square.

Walking through the main archway into the school, we were routed right down a covered alleyway and then left again through heavy old doors into the school, then onwards into the 'top' playground, which was in fact a large, flagged courtyard surrounded on all sides by three/four storey high classroom and offices. I always tried to get there as early as possible to play football with tennis balls, or throwing games which involved chucking the tennis balls onto the high roofs and then competing in a scrum to be the one to catch it on its descent. We gathered and played in a covered 'undercroft' when it was raining, and the odd game of lunch time football or cricket took place there too, it was roughly the size of a five a side football pitch.

The entrance to the first-year classrooms was close to the undercroft; the entrance door led out of the playground, past the Art classrooms, up two flights of dark bare-wooded stairs with thick mahogany hand rails, past the double doors to the Physics and Chemistry labs up to the classrooms 1A, B and C. I was in 1C, which overlooked Mount Street. The desks were very old-style singles with 'lift up' lids and old ink well cavities which everyone used to sharpen their pencils into. We got in trouble frequently for banging the lids in time to particular songs. I remember enjoying my first year and made some good friends. We learnt ancient history, about peoples like the Mesopotamians, and I can still recollect thinking *what the hell's the point of knowing about all this stuff?* The subtleties of a classical education were sadly always well lost on me throughout my time at PCC.

I can remember the class frequently took pleasure in putting drawing pins on the teacher's chair – sometimes it worked (resulting in much hilarity), but often it did not, whereupon pupils gathered round for a post-mortem type enquiry at the end of the lesson, when the teacher had left. I think I was a bit of a joker, or tried to be one – I got caught red-handed a few times doing silly things like dancing on top of my desk in between lessons while the class sung whatever songs.

Year one seemed to pass by OK; to be honest like much of my time at PCC, I drifted along, getting by. I managed to retain a 'middle of the road' position and was streamed at the end of the year into Class 2B which meant moving classroom out of the older Victorian buildings into a newer block across the other side of the playground on Winckley Square. It was a few floors up and I got a desk by the window from where I could survey the view of the top and bottom playgrounds and the short interconnecting concrete ramp which was a real bottleneck for the masses of pupils navigating between the two. I also had a prime view of the entrance door to the swimming pool, which paid dividends when the classes of girls from the convent school next door processed

Indian file to and from the pool for swimming lessons.

We had a swimming teacher called Mr Bradley who I think also taught Biology. Mr Bradley reminded me a bit of the wrestler Mick McMannus. He had a short temper and didn't tolerate mucking about. Once he gave our swimming class a punishment of 200 lines of 'I will not mess about with the organisation of a swimming lesson' with just two evenings to return them. My family were struck by the disproportionality of the penalty, and all chipped in to do forty lines each as much in the style of my scrawl as they thought would go undetected – which it did. I managed to get the various swimming badges that we had to pass which were duly sewn onto my trunks. It was 1978, and the Argentinian World Cup was in full flow – I don't think England had qualified but Scotland had, which one of the teachers, Father Spencer (a 'jock' himself) kept reminding us about. When Scotland were knocked out, we took much pleasure in repeatedly asking him how Scotland were "getting on" – he didn't see the funny side. Father Spencer smoked a pipe, and often he would arrive at the start of the class finishing his smoke off and laying the pipe on the desk to extinguish itself. One fantastic time he placed it into his jacket pocket instead, and after a couple of minutes a murmur developed across the class who began nudging each other excitedly, pointing at the smoke that starting emerging from his pocket. He saw neither us nor the smoke, as his back was turned to the class while he was writing on the board. We didn't alert him, and he only realised when he felt the heat of the fire as it started to burn through to his skin. To everyone's delight he started a bit of a highland jig around the classroom patting at his jacket pocket furiously.

We went to church once a week at nearby St Wilfred's, and I managed to get on the altar boy short list – this meant having reasonably free access to the altar wine, if one was careful enough. I got my first experience of corporal punishment later that year, when I thought it would be a good idea to enact a version of the ticker tape spectacle made famous by the crowds at the Argentina World Cup finals. From my vantage point high up in Class 2B, I waited for break time, then once I was on my own I ripped up dozens of sheets of white paper and cast the 'ticker tape' out of the window to the amazement of the school yard full of pupils below. What I hadn't accounted for of course was that the staff room lay on the floor directly below, and the snowstorm of paper appeared in full view of all the bemused staff having coffee. Caught red handed I was told to present myself for four 'ferulas' – a short, flexible thick strap made of whale bone with leather wrapped around it which was slapped hard on the palm of the hand. I received two on each hand, and although I forget who gave it to me, I remember that before each stroke the ferula was revved up by being swished up and down quickly to a point when it would hum. The punishment was meted out in a small office in the top playground. In the window of that office was where the 'line for the week' was displayed. If you received 'lines' as a punishment for something, you had to write out whatever the line was that was displayed in the window a number of times depending on the severity of the offence committed. The lines were sometimes a quote from Shakespeare, and I can remember one starting 'The quality of mercy is unstraineth, it droppeth like the gentle rain . . . ', which seems a bit ironic give that little mercy was ever shown in the use of punishment as a first line 'motivator'. In the fourth year I received a second set of ferulas, this time for burning my initials into a desktop during a Latin lesson using a strong lens to focus the sun's rays. I was so unfocused on the lesson content I failed to notice plumes of smoke billowing up from the desktop; I got four of the best for that.

The bell signifying lunch break saw an incredibly competitive race to the canteen to get as close to the front of the queue as possible; if you happened to be in the chemistry or physics lab for that lesson your odds were good as they were close by. Pizza, chips and gravy was top of the menu for me, and instigated a lifelong appreciation for gravy on chips – I have been doing missionary work around the UK, spreading the good news (and the gravy) ever since. Mr Andrews was our Chemistry teacher, a very earnest and strict man whose favourite shouted retort to the class members was "DON'T CONTRADICT ME, BOY!" He did have a bit of a dry sense of humour, though, and I enjoyed his lessons – if he felt the class needed waking up, he'd thrust open all the windows on a cold morning, telling us to breathe in some oxygen to liven up our minds.

I drifted through the third and fourth years. I remember having a good cross-section of mates, some of whom I shared a common sense of humour with; we'd recite lines from Monty Python and Spike Milligan together. Two of them, Michael Browne and Dave Rigby, have both sadly passed now, but they remained friends into sixth form and beyond. The school play one year was *The Importance of being Earnest* and the drama society had put up posters advertising the play – someone had amusingly gone around defacing all the titles to read 'The Impotence of Ernest'. The school had a big old drama hall with a proper stage, lighting, and even a green room with a heavily-sloping floor. As the school population gradually reduced in number, fewer plays took place, and the theatre was used by us to sit formal exams, including our O levels.

There was a good sense of camaraderie at the school, which was strengthened at times of challenge such as the cross-country run, which we helped each other endure. I was not a particularly strong runner, and I always tried, but failed, to be one of the pupils who'd be excused from games by being a course marshal for the day. I always looked for – but never found – shortcuts along the course, which ran through Avenham Park, across the old rail bridge and along a disused line which seemed to go on for an eternity before turning back along a parallel disused line through the park on the return route to school. It seemed like ten miles, but was probably much less than five.

Our school had a rivalry with John Fisher's school, which was also in the area. This sometimes manifested into one-on-one fights between school representatives or group fights, normally on the way home to the bus station after school. I remember our representative was Shaun Daly who fought our corner valiantly on a number of occasions behind the bandstand in Avenham park – Shaun was a keen angler and wore a badge on his blazer once or twice which read 'Next to fishing sex is number 1'. I also remember playing 'penny scrambles' in class between lessons, when someone would throw a penny under some poor unfortunate's desk, and the whole class would descend on them trying to retrieve the coin.

As we moved up years the number of pupils in the school reduced, because we were the last year's intake for the school. This meant that bits of the school were gradually sold off, and some areas in those buildings that remained fell into disuse. I can remember huge cloakroom areas in basements which once were used by hundreds of pupils becoming almost abandoned; it felt a bit sad to me. I remember the unexpected kindness of Father Wareing turning up at my father's funeral, and can vividly recall him marching us along the remnants of an old Roman road while reciting Latin verbs somewhere in the Pennines on a school trip. We went on another school trip in the third year, around the castles of North Wales. We stayed in a hotel near Betws-y Coed and had a great time.

Reading through my school reports, it's fair to conclude that I didn't try hard or make much effort, and I really wasn't motivated to learn. I somehow managed to do fine with my O levels, to the surprise and contradiction of many of my teachers, and far better than perhaps I deserved. The educational approach of drilling information into us suited me, I think, and I'm grateful to the school for giving me many interesting and happy memories. My enduring memories are of long, old wood-panelled darkened corridors, and small flights of stairs leading off upwards into mysterious small rooms which I never visited, nor it seemed did anyone else.

I proceeded on to Newman College sixth form, in the same buildings as the Catholic College, and with a lot of the same friends from lower school. I didn't fare too well in my A levels and joined the Merchant Navy to qualify as a Deck Officer. I collected many happy memories of hard work and great times with some terrific characters there. I left the Merchant Navy in my early twenties to join the Police and have just completed a thirty-year career in a profession I have been truly privileged to pursue. I've recently retired and am now enjoying giving some much-owed time back to my family.

ADRIAN GAWAIN JONES: FORMS 1B, 2C, 3M, 4M AND 5M

I had taken my 11 Plus exam, but hadn't really thought about the implications of passing it would be. I went to Brownedge St Mary's Junior School in Bamber Bridge, which was a smallish village-type establishment compared to many other junior schools. My mother had been a very successful teacher locally and had either worked with or knew most of the other teachers in the area. My current headmaster, Mr Pearson, had worked with my mum, and had also trained with her and clearly they were on good terms. I remember on several occasions he suggested she return to the profession, telling her he would gladly have her on his staff. When the results of the 11 Plus were released and I passed, he was over the moon, and congratulated me personally. Again, I was still none the wiser about what it meant, but my whole family seemed really pleased. That summer of 1977, though, my main thoughts were about the friends I would be leaving behind.

In August 1977 my father trooped me into Lingard's Gentlemen's Outfitters near Sweetens Bookshop at the top of Fishergate Hill. I discovered my dad had an account there; he used to be a Naval Officer, and this was where he obtained his uniforms. Lingards was an experience. I had never been anywhere like this before. Everything was wood-panelled, and the attendants were so smart. It was certainly very different from C&A, where mum usually shopped for me. I will always remember the deference the person behind the counter showed to dad, who was a known customer. After going into a cupboard to get a book (presumably with his account in), I was measured up for a blazer and several trousers and shirts, as well as two ties. Dad got a new suit at the same time, and I remember being stuck in that shop for what seemed like hours, but the reality was we were there for about 30 minutes. Every August for the next few years, similar such trips would be arranged, and purchases made.

Day one of school. Mum dropped me at Bamber Bridge railway station, where she also said hello to one of British Rail staff on the platform whose name was Andrew. It seemed that she had taught him at one stage, as he gave her a cheery "Hello, Mrs Jones". Two other new Catholic College boys were also waiting at the platform, Russell Ashton and Peter Ryan.

We got off at platform 2, Preston station, and made our way through to Winckley Square, passing Butler Street and heading down Fishergate, past the old ABC Cinema before finally arriving at the front gates. I went in through the front entrance to be told by a teacher that this would be the first and last time I would be permitted to use it, as it was reserved for sixth formers and teachers, and that I was to use to either use the front side entrance to the left of the main door or a side gate down Mount Street.

I remember us all being given a talking to in the main hall by a priest who I think was Fr Wren; he had what seemed a multitude of other teachers on stage with him. I also remember thinking how grand the building was with its wood-panelled front entrance, and how grand the teachers were in their capes, with at least one wearing a mortarboard just like they used to have on in old Will Hay movies. I also remember pictures of St Ignatius Loyola and other military-type people in renaissance-style gear and thinking *Wow!*

Being a town centre-based school and an old, long-established College as well, it was very different from the comprehensives that were popping up with their large playing fields and 60's/70's design. The Catholic College seemed ancient to me. Everything was pretty dark due to the décor, and the classrooms also showed their age. Obviously, we were the last intake, so they weren't going to redecorate them just for us. It had the feel of an old black and white movie school. The stairs were aged wood, while the walls were old and painted in a mid-neutral off-cream colour.

I ended up in Mrs Proctor's class, 1B, and I enjoyed my time there. I formed some very close friendships with David Blanchard, Peter Lever, Michael Watterson, Mark White and Howard Tomlinson in particular. Obviously, friendships change over the school years, but 1977 was the year of Star Wars, and Howard, Mark and Michael all were huge sci-fi fans, so that kind of pulled us together that year. Peter was a fellow train traveller like myself (I think he joined the train at either Pleasington or Mill Hill), and we often sat together with other kids travelling on the Preston to Colne line, including his elder brother, his sister (who went to the Convent), and others. As a side note: unfortunately, Michael died in an accident a couple of years later. I found it so difficult to take that I blocked the memory of the loss out until a long time later.

Like others will recall, one memory that stands out is of us having to write 'AMDG' at the top of the page of any work we did, meaning 'To the greater glory of God'. I think it was Fr Spencer who suggested 'Auntie Maggie's Dumplings are Good' as a way of remembering it. I also added a plus sign to it between the M and D, so it appeared as 'AM+DG' as I saw a sixth former do it and I thought it looked very grown up.

The teaching in that first year varied tremendously. Mrs O'Donnell, an elderly foreign lady (possibly Polish, when I think of her accent, but I could be very wrong), taught History, which was a subject I already loved; along with Fr Wareing, whom I will get to shortly, she instilled a greater passion for the subject in me. She lent me a book written by an archaeologist about his work in Mesopotamia, and I was hooked. Archaeology from that point on became a particular interest for me, especially Egyptian Archaeology; it was one of the reasons I travelled extensively in Egypt after leaving College, and why I took up the subject of my own accord in later life.

Miss Mangan took Maths. Good grief, she scared me! She knew mum (I saw them chatting very happily on several occasions, and mum casually mentioned that she lived very close to the College), but that wasn't a help. Miss Mangan was formidable and had a very powerful presence. I was OK at Maths, but her expectations were very high, and she threw the board duster at people if she thought they weren't paying attention. I remember a couple of classmates being on the wrong end of her anger, and being happy it wasn't me. That said, she was a good teacher and delivered the subject well.

Mrs Proctor, our form tutor, took us for Geography, English and Religious Education. She was a lovely lady and I remember her son was in the year ahead of ours. From memory I think he was called Giles, but I could be wrong. I really enjoyed her classes.

Fr Spencer took us for French, and he was also often seen at Grafton Playing fields refereeing football matches. French was never a favourite subject of mine. I had done it at Junior School and really found it tedious. I could do it, but I just wasn't interested. I remember him once seriously asking me why I didn't like it, to which I replied that French as a language and country just held no appeal to me. He nodded, and to be fair he just accepted it. I could have ended up with numerous punishments for that answer, in retrospect. I always found Fr Spencer to be fair, and he loved football with such a passion. One memory regarding him that sticks out was his asking for volunteers to sell programmes at an England international football match at Deepdale. I was coaxed into helping out. The game was on a Saturday and his enthusiasm was obvious. At the end we were all paid a couple of quid and awarded the OMB (Order of the Mars Bar) for our services to football, which unsurprisingly involved him passing Mars Bars out to all concerned.

One completely new subject for me in that first year was Classical Studies, which was taught by one of my all-time favourite teachers; Fr Wareing. He was an amazing teacher and a true gentleman as well. His enthusiasm oozed out of him as he delivered Greek and Roman

Mythology (mainly Greek) with tales of Homer, Troy, Odysseus, Jason and others thrown in for good measure. This cemented my love of the ancient world, and I lapped up his stories using the College library to discover more. I remember him referring to the class as "test tubes" at the end of the lesson on a regular basis, which always mystified me. I did ask him about this much later and found out he'd always been under the impression our next lesson was chemistry, hence the reference. It wasn't, which made it all the more funny.

The legendary Mr Duckworth took us for music. For part of the first term I had a decent voice and practiced a bit with the school choir, but alas, my voice broke and was unable to hold a note. To be fair, Mr Duckworth persevered with me for a couple of months before telling me what I already knew: I really wasn't up for a singing career. I tried again later in the year but literally fell flat. Music was a big thing for me, though. John McLoughlin, who also lived in Bamber Bridge, got me into Queen, Howard Tomlinson introduced me to Saxon and Rainbow, and I found The Eagles and Meatloaf myself. I stayed pretty much solely in the rock/metal groove until I came across Gary Numan, Blondie, Human League, Depeche Mode, Heaven 17, Prince and OMD in the early 80s. I may not have been musical, but I love it and am still really into my music today.

On the subject of music, one memory is of the huge ribbing that used to be given by some lads towards anyone who veered away from rock. Due to this I kept my varied tastes secret until sixth form, when it seemed to become a bit more acceptable.

Physical Education was the domain of Mr Singleton, another really good teacher, who also taught Geography. The gym we had was very new and located at the far end of the school. It was not a favourite of mine until sixth form when it became non-compulsory. As well as this there was Grafton Fields, already mentioned by others in this book, where football and other outdoor team sports took place. As it was located some distance away, we had a coach laid on to transport us there to begin with, but in later years we had to make the journey ourselves, through the park and along the old tramway.

The first year passed in a blur, and I am guessing my memories are being viewed with rose-tinted spectacles, but the memories I have are mostly good. Fond thoughts take me back to the library, which I enjoyed lots, using the train to get me to and from school, warm days sitting on the metal steps reading daft sci-fi and horror books and exploring areas of the school we normally didn't get to visit. These explorations took me to the attic area of the main block (which I later found out was referred to as The Attica), rooms that used to be classrooms in what was once a house facing Winckley Square (this was where the music room was) but were now mothballed, and science labs in yet another block in the lower school.

Other random memories that have come back include having to get exercise books stamped to obtain a new one from thc stationary room which was manned by staff at set times during the day. Also, the fact you could buy toast for 2p from the school canteen at break time. And of course there was a dodgy diner/cafe on the way to school called the Butler Street Diner; it had some cool arcade, pinball and fruit machines, so was often visited. We are talking Defender, Space Invaders, Scramble and Missile Command, here! The only place that beat it was a small taxi waiting room on Corporation Street, which eventually got the Star Wars Arcade Game in which you flew an X-Wing. Mind-blowing!

It's interesting now to think about how things changed as we moved up through the school. I was lucky enough to go on a school trip to Austria, which involved an extended pre-holiday shop in C&A to get some ski wear including 'Moon Boots', jumpers and the standard skiing gear. There was no room for us all in the main hotel on that trip, so a few of us ended up in an annex a short walk away and I ended up sharing with Simon Morris and Andrew McCarthy (plus someone else whom I can't remember, so apologies in advance). It was quite a buzz, but I ended up with some mad Asian Flu virus thing that affected me for quite a bit of the holiday and necessitated an additional week off when we returned along with a trip to the local hospital at the time, which came with a threat of "we may have to keep you in . . . " which fortunately they decided against.

I was rubbish at the Metalwork class, but really enjoyed it. The teacher, Mr Talbot, who travelled home on the train with us on the odd occasion, was always enthusiastic about what I had made, even when it was a complete mess. I was so proud of my candle holder at the time, but when I rediscovered it many years later it was cringeworthy. I loved the practical workshop, and one of my regrets is that I never got to try out the furnace and anvil that were sat in there. I think I only ever saw it stoked and ready for use on one occasion – probably for a higher year group. The smell of Swarfega and metal just wafted through the entire shop. I think the most successful thing I made was a plumb-bob using the lathe and power saw, but for that I was ably assisted by Mr Talbot; I always remember him wearing his brown overall jacket and having a file in his pocket that he would bring out when examining your latest piece of work, to remove sharp edges.

Technical Drawing was mostly taught by Mr Caton, who I recall being a calm man with an amazing sense of humour, who deliberately mixed up his words and waited for the students to correct him as a method of remembering what he was teaching you. One memory that sticks out fondly is his referring to "ellipses" as "eclipses". He also stepped in and taught Maths sometimes and he did the same there. It felt generally good to be in his class, and I can only remember one occasion on which he became visibly annoyed with a boy messing around.

The library was a great place to escape to for a break. It was rarely manned in the latter years and was huge, covering so many subjects. The room to the right as you entered was the fiction area, complete with large table, chairs and very warm radiator along with a window that overlooked the lower yard and swimming baths entrance. That was my favourite spot, especially on cold days. The room opposite was more open, with a magazine rack as well as windows looking onto Winckley Square. Thinking back, these were only 'rooms' because of the large floor to ceiling shelving; in reality, it was one large open room split up. It was there I first read Edgar Allan Poe, Mark Twain and

Arthur Conan Doyle. I rarely ventured towards the far end, which was more the domain of sixth formers.

Another favourite memory of mine is being taught Computer Studies. This was another subject that set me up for later in life, along with the purchase of a ZX81 which was followed not long after by a Sharp PC and Sinclair Spectrum. I really enjoyed learning programming languages as well as the background to it. I learnt more about this outside of school, and with Mr Holdsworth's help from the fifth year and into sixth form I worked on helping to maintain a computer network and the essentials of computer construction, maintenance and repair.

Thinking back, I enjoyed most of the subjects that were taught, and we had some great teachers there. Mr Henry, Mr Caton, Mr Billington, Mr Moulding, Fr Wareing, Mrs O'Donnell and Mr Singleton would all be up there for me, and I was fortunate to have a few of them as Form Tutors as well. I think "Pop" Moulding was my form tutor in the fifth year, and I saw a very different and caring side to him during a chat in his office next to the playground, after he had heard that my grandmother was seriously ill. I already liked him as a teacher (although God help you if you messed about after receiving a warning in his class), but he really was concerned about the boys in his care.

As we changed years, so did our form classrooms and the school itself. As we were the last intake, each year there became fewer of us lower school pupils, while the sixth form side developed and grew. Part of this change involved sections of the school being mothballed and abandoned, which provided a lot of new options for pupils to head to and chillout in during breaks and lunches. It became a strange experience as we seemed to dwindle away while the year groups above us left, along with their teachers. There seemed to be no real need for prefects, and the rules felt like they became more relaxed, possibly because the need for them was less, too.

A group of us used to gather in the park during lunchtimes in those final couple of years, just sitting, mainly, and chatting. We all parted at one of the benches there on the final day of College, agreeing to meet up at again in the future but never setting a date or time. In that group was Pete Lever, Howard Tomlinson, Miles ("Jam") Hartland, Jon Lace, David Blanchard, and some others. I don't get back to Preston often these days, but when I find myself in the area with some time on my hands I walk through that park, usually towards Broadgate, to visit the places we used to sit and talk, remembering those days and halting briefly by the grass banking we slid down, the bench in the Japanese garden, and the fountain. It's with sadness that some of those boys are now gone, but the memories are there.

As for school, The Catholic College, what I will always remember the most is the feeling of stepping back in time when I first went there, with the wood-panelled corridor, the strange smells of mustiness and polish, and the teaching staff wearing capes – I remember being laughed at by my friends at the local secondary modern when I told them this detail, as they thought I had made a joke or was making it up.

Since school (and in no particular order) I've been involved with archaeology (one of my huge loves) including trips to Egypt. I've managed a book, games and comic shop. I've overseen a Book Warehouse and a chain of bookshops including a distribution chain. I've been a baker in Cumbria and managed a coffee shop up there. I've worked as a frontline IT engineer, systems analyst and software developer. I've worked on a market stall in Preston, and another in Carlisle. I'm currently a manager in the Civil Service, based on the Wirral, and I also write and develop tabletop games in my spare time.

JOHN MCLAUGHLIN: FORMS 1A, 2A, 3A, 4A AND 5A

My life, partially digested

Those days at PCC/Newman College seem so remote, yet oddly recent at the same time. There have been threads that have flowed from that time till now, both in work and play, but diversions and experiences that I would have never predicted.

True for us all no doubt!

It is fair to say (and I'm sure classmates would confirm) that I was fairly good at science, and well beyond hopeless at anything sporty, pretty much always coming first and last in each, respectively . . . Nothing has really changed since then, aside from a couple of curious exceptions. I will expand later.

It was odd to enter a school which was winding down to become a sixth form College, meaning we would be the youngest year right through. The early days are a vague memory, but I recall our first form tutor Miss Almond (1A) being a warm and kind lady, counterbalanced by some slightly less benevolent types.

Being one of the youngest few pupils, and additionally rather on the small side physically, made for interesting dynamics. It probably explains why I was so hopeless at anything sporty, effectively I gave up around September 1977! Switching from football to hockey later was the only thing I vaguely enjoyed, much easier to hide in plain sight. Swimming in that foul little pool was probably the grimmest event of any week, but at least that teacher also appreciated I was hopeless at it and kindly left me alone. My angelic face had its uses.

Especially in the Choir! Of course, being the last intake meant the choir was doomed, the biological clock was ticking, and our sweet treble voices started to break. I think it folded around the third year, but may be wrong. I hugely enjoyed it; maestro Harry Duckworth was hysterical yet brilliant in equal measure. I loved the festivals, the coach trips, and the TV 'stardom'. Being so 'angelic' made me a good chorister for the cameras to home in on, so our performances on *Stars on Sunday*, *Granada Reports* and other shows I cannot remember, were quite frequent. The choir went to the USA in our first year; I couldn't go as my family could not afford it, and I was gutted to think I'd never ever go to America!

Not so. I've since lived and worked there awhile and have been over dozens of times, but your 11-year-old brain has a rather short-term set of expectations. I did get to go to Italy though, attending the Loreto International Music Festival in 1978. We went by bus, via Paris, Geneva, Pisa and Rome, attending Palm Sunday Mass in St Peter's Square before being instructed to "come back in a few hours". The idea that we 11-year-olds were allowed to pootle off up to the roof of the Basilica, or mess about on the open ledges of the Leaning Tower, fills me with cold sweats now wearing a parental hat! Safeguarding had not arrived at PCC in 1978. Fortunately, our parents never knew that!

To be quintessentially English, the choir were dressed in good old Morris Dance costumes. And why not! We trained in the cafeteria, and strode into the Piazza in Loreto chanting "Oggy Oggy Oggy!"

As you would.

Not.

We were then let loose to sing (beautifully) and wander around the town at night ad lib. This resulted in me busting my face on the Loreto fair dodgems and losing my front row place in the procession. I no longer appeared quite so angelic, with a bloodied face and fat lip! Fortunately, all was back to normal by the time we got home. I do recall how rough the ferry back was, with most folk vomiting merrily. I instead had a fry up. Maybe this influenced my future career choices. And I did get to record songs on an album with Queen at a later date.

My saddest time at school was when my best friend Michael Watterson was killed cycling home from Scouts. He lived just across the road from me at his mum and dad's shop in Walton-le-Dale, and we were doing loads together as we were both a bit geeky and sci-fi oriented. My mum told me the next morning when I phoned from Preston Bus station about something else. I was devastated. I still have his Latin dictionary, somehow, a treasured thing. His dad (John) had been super to me. He was a retired scientist, who ran a quirky grocer's shop, and one of the few people who understood my fascination with biology, especially dissecting dead things (Preston market's butchers were very obliging in that regard). John never got over the loss of Michael, and I deeply regret losing touch when they sold up and moved to the Isle of Man after I went to University.

Other memorable figures for me were Fr Wareing, getting us to march on the spot while reciting Latin vocabulary as if we were Roman soldiers, and Mr 'Jock' Malone, a wonderful (Scottish) English teacher who directed delightful plays and put up with my extraordinary inability to act, or to understand what poetry was for. Fr Wareing was a gentle and kind man, often taking the school minibus to drop us home after choir or drama events. I am sure he did it simply out of concern for our safety and well-being. I was sorry to hear of his recent passing.

Before too long voices broke, the years went by, and the sixth formers started to arrive as we approached our last year. Suddenly, not all pupils were boys!

Being told by a teacher early in sixth form we were a disappointing year with the worst ever O- level results achieved by the school was a little galling, the demob-happy style with which some of our teachers approached the last years can't have been unconnected.

Sixth form is a blur. I got to know some super people better, like Adrian Jones, but it all went so fast! I effectively taught myself A level physics and biology, as the teachers didn't seem to be able to get through the whole curriculum.

So, after achieving (rather successful!) science A level results, off I went to Manchester University to start medical school in 1984. Manchester was handy as my parents don't drive, and Manchester was going through an unusual period of not interviewing for medical school instead going on predicted grades and school statement on the then UCCA form, an approach unthinkable now (at the time of writing! Then Covid- 19 happened). So, thanks to whoever wrote my statement, probably my form tutor Mr Andrews (everyone's favourite chemistry teacher . . .) but I will never know.

The new policy was also significant as it was introduced by the then Dean, Professor Leslie Turnberg, a working-class genius from Salford who was Professor of Medicine at the University. This was important to me as my first job after graduating in 1990 was at Hope Hospital (now Salford Royal) with him in Gastroenterology, where I decided that this was the specialty I really wanted to train in. I will explain why later. Working for him was an amazing experience; he went onto become Sir Leslie as President of the Royal College of Physicians, and now sits as Lord Turnberg of Cheadle, an active healthcare-focused politician in his 80s. I get a mention in his autobiography, too, so it's only fair to return the compliment.

Winding back to 1984, medical school was huge fun, but tough – 'work hard, play hard'- was our motto. I prospered academically, taking a year out to do an extra degree in Physiology in 1987, and cheesing off more 'privileged' classmates by doing a bit better in exams. One decided I must be cheating as that was the only way I could possibly do better than him, given that his dad was a professor while mine was a caretaker. I think we have moved on in 2021.

I was fortunate to spend a summer working in a kitchen in Italy during my student days, after which my newfound Italian was, (and still is . . .) better than either French or Latin, despite four or five years of classroom learning. In 1989 I also spent an amazing summer working in a mining village hospital in the province of Bophuthatswana in South Africa, which was then under apartheid. The illness (TB especially) and poverty were shocking and never left me, nor did a weekend spent in Soweto. My hosts hid me from sight at one point when one of the infamous 'running funerals' passed by their house, as fatal violence was sadly common and unprovoked in those troubled and angry times.

I also got to deliver over 20 babies in Blackpool in 1989, and it's amazing to think they'll all be 32 this year. Another powerful memory I have is of being in the delivery suite on the dreadful day of Hillsborough, bringing new lives into the world while too many young lives left that day.

Shortly after this period I met my amazing and brilliantly talented wife Maureen, a music student. We've just celebrated 29 years of happy and rewarding marriage. We married at the then Jesuit-run Holy Name church on the University campus (which is well worth a visit), never expecting I'd still be working there 31 years on. This is weird, too, because you can see the very same adjacent medical school on some of our wedding photos, along with Paul Reynolds and Pete Reece, with whom I am still close friends, with regular pandemic Zooms of late. Maureen has moved on from teaching to become a highly active and effective local Labour politician in Warrington, where we live.

So zipping back to1990, I passed my finals, allowing me to become Dr John! After graduation, more nasty exams ('Membership') with only 30 per cent of candidates passing, but this was essential train in hospital medicine. My training involved time spent in Salford, Manchester, Oldham, Stockport, Tameside, Chester and Liverpool. Since 1993, I've been practicing in Gastroenterology and General Medicine, becoming a Consultant Physician in Salford in 2001, and working purely in Gastroenterology since 2012. Scarily, I find myself almost the most senior member of the team now.

Those early years were tough usually working 120-hour weeks (sic) (and so was I), while studying for exams. Having one, then two small children at home was also, erm, challenging. If you were on call on a Monday, you would work through till 5 p.m. on the Tuesday, then come back in on Wednesday. Weekends were special! Friday morning till Monday afternoon was the norm as far as they were concerned, then back to work on Tuesday of course.

We did get a 25 per cent pay supplement for overtime, so that was super! Although by this, I mean just 25 per cent of basic pay for anything we worked over 40 hours, not an *extra* 25 per cent. Apart from the hours, I loved it: sorting emergencies, cardiac arrests, inserting pacemakers, doing lumbar punctures, draining chests, 'biopsying' things, and loads more.

I have some sad memories too, of course, having often been required to speak to relatives about impending or recent loss, or breaking bad diagnostic news to patients. These are the most challenging parts of medicine.

Why Gastroenterology? At one level it came about simply due to having had inspiring senior colleagues and opportunities. But it is an amazing specialty. The digestive system has a huge range of disorders, making clinical practice interesting and challenging. We see patients with serious disorders such as gastrointestinal cancers, Crohn's disease, colitis, or liver disease. We also see patients with less serious but still very unpleasant conditions, like irritable bowel syndrome and reflux, and patients who need nutritional support due to disease. I have become a particular expert in the causes and treatment of diarrhoea, vomiting and constipation, and I have an interest in patients with gut problems that were caused by other illnesses such as diabetes, or following cancer treatments such as radiotherapy. Endoscopy (a camera test) is the main special skill in our occupation, and I have undertaken thousands of colonoscopies and gastroscopies. Preventing someone from bleeding to death by injecting a bleeding ulcer with adrenaline, or simply popping a rubber band around a bleeding blood vessel, is a privilege.

However, I stopped doing endoscopy a few years ago as my academic career was taking over, and it was no longer possible to do everything! I continue to do clinical work in Salford, and I'm the director of the GI Physiology Unit, where we undertake interesting tests to understand what is going on with gut function in patients sent to us from all over the North West.

The academic (science!) bit has continued in parallel to all of this experience. In fact, after achieving my BSc in 1987 I nearly left medical school to do a PhD and become a scientist, as I found the first clinical placements rather unenjoyable. That would have been a huge mistake and in hindsight it was simply because those placements were awful. Ironically, they were in Gastroenterology!!

Instead, after postgraduate exams in 1994 I was awarded a research post to come out of medical training and undertake a PhD in gastrointestinal physiology under the supervision of two outstanding mentors, Prof David Thompson in Manchester and Prof Graham Dockray in Liverpool.

I went on to develop strong research interests in gut physiology (function) and in how the gut and brain communicate in health and disease, with a big focus on gut hormones. This led to an opportunity funded by the Medical Research Council to spend a year at Harvard Medical School and Massachusetts General Hospital in Boston, before coming back to finish clinical training.

My current job is a 50:50 split of academic and clinical work. What I do not now about vomiting or diarrhoea is not worth knowing. Maybe that vomit-ridden ferry in 1978 had an impact.

Teaching and training are a major passion too, and I established a new 'Masters in Research' course at Manchester in 2008.

I was promoted to Professor in 2011. Research remains active in several areas of gastroenterology, and I've been involved in publishing an awful lot of stuff (some of which is actually awful, when I look back . . . I have supervised 18 research doctorates (PhD/MD), with 11 more currently working in my group. Most recently I obtained Medical Research Council funding to work in the field of childhood and pregnancy malnutrition, on projects in South Africa (Soweto again! An unexpected story arc) and Bangalore, India. A recent trip to Ghana representing Manchester will hopefully lead to more collaborations too.

More recently still, I became head of the University department in which I am based, and I have also chaired the National research committee in Gastroenterology for four years. Life is dominated by simply way too many meetings and forms to sign nowadays. Hey ho.

Another minor claim to fame was taking Nicky Campbell's pulse live on 5 Live breakfast while discussing the health benefits of coffee and the issues around caffeine withdrawal. Surreal.

What about the sport bit? I get invited to speak at Sports Medicine meetings about gut problems in athletes. My engagement with this field led to me becoming the author of the relevant chapter in the International Olympic Committee's Encyclopaedia of Sports Medicine, which is quite ironic/funny for this totally unathletic specimen. It is a sideline that has also seen me presenting at a Sports Nutrition meeting allied to the World Finals of Iron Man in Hawaii, which was quite an event. I do sadly prefer the Marvel version of Iron Man, having utterly failed to grow out of a tragic love of sci-fi.

I nearly forgot to explain how I got to sing with Queen on an album! OK, so it was a live album and there were 119,999 others singing along, too. But it turned out to be Freddie's last live gig before falling ill, so was a special place to be. Music remains a special thing in our family, but I won't bore you with that. While I can just about do three guitar chords, they can do amazing things on piano, clarinet, horn . . .

Those two small children I mentioned are now 24 and 26, both talented and delightful individuals. I hope they will have many adventures, interesting careers and more besides.

All in all, it's been a fairly mixed and busy old time, luckily with good health. I've not had a day off sick yet in 30 years, which alas means it has to be for something very serious now before I can make that call – hopefully not Coronavirus!

I have a wonderful family and amazing friends. Pete Reece and Paul Reynolds are regular curry eating partners; we all met back up in

Manchester in the late 80s and have kept in touch ever since. I do regret losing touch with so many super people over the years, and hope to renew those kinships as we all move into another chapter of our advancing lives.

Who knows what adventures are next? Certainly not me!

Prof John McLaughlin BSc (Hons) MB ChB (Hons) PhD FRCP

PETER JOHN NAYLOR: FORMS 1A, 2A, 3A, 4A AND 5A

I knew from the age of eight that I would be going to Cath Coll; my older brothers would both eventually sit and fail the 11 Plus Examination but I would have no such problems. Knowing what I do now, would I have been so eager to go? I choose not to live my life with any regrets, and as a young boy I certainly had no wisdom or experience to guide me. As I reflect on that time now, I have an appreciation of how different things could have been, and indeed how different I could have been. In truth, though, I cannot judge this in any better or worse sense, all I know it that things would have been different.

To put these reflections in context, I have spent over twenty years teaching Chemistry to 11-18-year-old students at some of the top Independent Schools in England. I have had the privilege to educate some of the best and brightest this country has to offer, doing all I could to guide, encourage and help my students develop confidence, resilience and independence, to believe in themselves and achieve their goals.

The modern-day nurturing and supportive education system bears no resemblance to the frankly dated, brutal and abusive experience of my years at Cath Coll. Some people would argue that tough love or strong discipline are important factors in child development, that they promote character and strength. Well, they are wrong. Such things are damaging both mentally and physically, they restrict proper emotional and mental development, and they compound problems in future relationships and life situations.

We did not so much join a school in 1977, more a long, drawn-out funeral procession. Rather than being invested in as a legacy to this Institution, we simply served as a constant reminder to the ageing and decaying fabric of the place that we were the very last of its kind. As the paint peeled and the mortar crumbled, as the Priests were retired off one by one and the yard grew emptier and quieter year by year, we witnessed the death of a College.

You certainly learnt to survive here, not in any taught sense, but out of necessity. Humour was my chosen weapon, although this proved quite annoying to the teaching staff and pretty useless in a fight! Nevertheless, it got me some notice and attention, so I stuck with it, even though it regularly got me 'six of the painful best'.

I have so many partial and incomplete memories of stories and events, some of which are even probably completely fictional by now. So, I choose to not name names or be very specific in case I am incorrect or offend the innocent. On this note I would like to apologise to anyone I hurt, bullied, or offended in any way during this period of time.

It was, as I recall, a very irreverent place, especially considering the religious purpose of the school. Banter barely does justice to the daily diet of abusive interaction that went on in all quarters, with actual physical fights being the norm rather than the exception. We constantly plotted ways and means of undermining the teaching staff and disrupting their lessons, not that many had ever been planned in any meaningful sense. I remember the Head telling us it would be blasphemous to go and watch *The Life of Brian*, so we all ditched games that afternoon to go and see it; what a great film!

Within the school there was a tribal divide between year groups, and even between forms within year groups, but outside on the mean streets of Preston we were as one. It had to be this way, as every other schoolboy in town would target a Cath Coll boy above any other; if we did not stand together, we had no chance. I recall one summer we had a big ruckus on Avenham Park, three or four schools were represented and plenty of police turned up for extra fun – happy days.

We used to have music lessons over at Winckley Square Convent Girls school, which was one of the few times we could go there legally; invariably on the other occasions we would be collared by a nun and dragged by twisted ear to the Head's study and deposited there for due punishment. I swear I saw him smiling once as Sister admonished him for not controlling his boys, departing with the line "keep your filthy boys away from my lovely girls". If only she knew what really went on in the basement corridors of her school. Music was always after water polo training, but we missed lunch on that day, so the teacher let us sit at the back and eat sandwiches on the proviso that we didn't disrupt the lesson. I feel I've left a big musical hole in my otherwise complete education as a result!

I will desist now, as I realise it's actually quite dull of me to avoid names and specific events, but I am not motivated to rewrite this piece. Suffice to say that at no other time in my life has each and every day presented me with such a challenge to survive, such an intensity of friendship, and such a misplaced notion that I actually mattered in life . . .

ANTHONY RAWLINSON: FORMS 1A, 2A, 3A, 4A AND 5A

Anthony. Even my name has changed slightly since I last stepped out of the main doors of what by then was known as Newman College somewhere around 34 Winkley Square, with 'Anton' appearing as I started at the University of Bradford for reasons I still can't quite fathom. So much has happened since June 1984, when I left sixth form, that I am sure that my recollection of events will be as vague and rose-tinted as anyone else's, whether they concern the chipped, dark wooden desks with inset ink pots that would not have looked out of place in a scene at Hogwarts, or the memories of running cross country in the mud and rain and really disliking it, ignorant of how much I would enjoy doing the same and more much later in life. I am therefore sure that some memories of people and events will occasionally clash with those of others. In such cases, I beg your indulgence to leave me in the romantic ignorance of my version of my childhood and in turn I will just as surely not lightly intrude on yours.

Getting in

I don't remember any particular drama around getting 'in' at Preston Catholic College. My brother Stephen had successfully passed the entrance exam two years earlier (not the 11 Plus, apparently that was something else), so in a manner which perhaps characterises other key points in my life since, I simply assumed that I would pass. My parents had encouraged me to follow in my brother's footsteps, and since we had always been academically similar through St Augustine's Primary School, I didn't foresee any problems. I do have a vague recollection of attending the exam and not being particularly anxious about the outcome – sorry if that sounds a bit pretentious!

I particularly remember a conversation with my dad later in life in which he told me that the reason he wanted us to go to "Cath Coll" (did anyone else ever call it that, apart from my mother?) was that he didn't want us to go through life doing the sort of hard, manual graft that he had to do. He worked at Leyland Motors Truck and Bus, and spent many an hour chipping sand off engine block castings, and he knew that the College offered the opportunity to get an academic head start in life, opening doors to university and better things beyond – so different to the 'university for all' approach of today. I'll always be grateful for both his insight and the sacrifices that he and mum made to give us such a valuable opportunity. I don't know whether it actually made a difference to what we eventually ended up doing, but their effort is beyond question. Neither do I know how much the fees were, but I do know that it was one of the reasons mum went to work part time as early as she did.

First Day

Sure enough, my casual confidence in the entrance exam result proved well-founded and I joined the likes of Bernie Moon, Coops, Si Cuerden and other members of the St Augustine's Junior School 'massive' who moved seamlessly if a little nervously to 'Big School' in September of 1977. We must have looked quite a sight in our oversized black jackets (they've got to last!) with the school emblem sewn onto the jacket pocket, our classic green, white and black striped ties, and briefcases, ready to face whatever the next five years could throw at us. I still have my old College tie. It remains fastened in the knot I tied it into on my last day in fifth form – it's not a perfect Windsor knot as my dad taught me, but it's lasted a few years, so maybe wasn't that bad. Although many of the cooler kids would wrap their ties endlessly round and round to leave only a few inches sticking down to avoid attracting the uniform 'plod', I personally thought it looked pretty naff and was happy to go for a more traditional length to somewhere around or just above the belt. Kept the 'naff' opinion to myself, though, obviously!

I had a new leather(ish!) briefcase in which to keep my newly plastic-backed schoolbooks (Peter Kay was dead right on that one), and an Adidas shoulder bag for my games kit. They would both get replaced like for like through my time at College and I did secretly quite like the idea of a briefcase rather than a shoulder bag for my school stuff, it just seemed to fit the look and feel of the school as a whole. The briefcase was large enough to fit my books, my pencil case with its endless supply of pens, pencils and drawing equipment, and later also my packed lunch.

My brother and I had two main ways to get to school. Sometimes we would catch the bus from Malvern Avenue for the princely sum of two and a half pence each way. We could either catch it to the top of Manchester Road and walk down the hill to Winckley Square, or else stay on all the way to the bus station, which would make the walk a little shorter. I remember having to jump off at the top of the hill to run back down to home because I'd forgotten my swimming stuff one day and was too scared of Mr Bradley to turn up without it. I managed to leg it home and still get to school before the bell, but it was worrying stuff!

More often than not, though, we would walk to school. We'd go up the steep cinder path from Malvern Avenue to the Ribble Motor Company office building, then probably along Manchester Road and past St Augustine's church and schools where Patrick Smith (who was my best friend in Junior School – he didn't go to PCC) and I had enjoyed our first, and at least for me, last puff of a cigarette, when we'd picked up a still smoking cast-off from lord-knows-who. In later years we'd often walk home down through Avenham Park, unless there were rumours of St John Fisher lads hanging around looking for trouble. I've never been one for a fight, discretion proving a far less painful route through life for me. I don't honestly remember much by way of violence between schools over the years we were there: I suspect the rumours were more myth than substance so will be interested to read anyone else's experience on that front.

My recollection of my first year is probably a good point at which to describe my impression of the overall layout of the school. It had clearly been much smaller at one point, containing some elements that were obviously part of the original school from 1900 or whenever, such as the 'olde worlde' staircases and in particular the bannisters that were studded with metal ornaments at regular intervals, presumably to stop people sliding down them. The original building at the top had old classrooms, and if I remember rightly the theatre was upstairs in that one, too. I can only imagine that the rest of the eclectic mixture of buildings around the main playground at the top, with a covered area on the side, and the lower yard with the swimming pool, canteen and gym, were gradually added over the years as the College grew. Looking at Mr Hindle's Centenary History of the Catholic College, Preston, this indeed seems to be the case. That book provides a very good historical overview of the College and its development over the years, incidentally. I wouldn't honestly say it's a riveting read, but it's been on my bookshelf for over 30 years and it's going nowhere. Over the course of the grand total of seven years I spent there I'm pretty sure I saw most corners of most of the buildings, including the insides of the both the head and deputy head's offices, more of which later!

First Year

My first day at school saw me put into class 1A. If I remember this correctly, we remained in the same letter classes – A, B and C – for the first two years, before being rearranged according to whether you did languages (French, German and Latin, class A), Geography and something else (B) or Woodwork/Metalwork (C). Although I had a few friends from Junior School in the year group, where you ended up sitting, and the class you were allocated, were allocated at random. I don't remember too much about the classroom layout of probably six desks wide by five deep, other than I think I was definitely near Miles Hartland and Anthony Royle. Miles was a happy enough soul and easy to get on with, but I do remember Anthony being a bit of a tough one with some, although not me. We sat near the door so were always the first to know when the teachers were upon us.

Do I remember rightly that the desks were all-in-one contraptions with the chairs attached to them? It seems odd now, but it definitely rings a bell for me. The wooden desk had a hinged top which slanted down towards you, opening from the top edge to allow you access to your books and stuff inside. Although there was an inkpot, we were much more progressive than that, with fountain pens which contained the ink within them, either with a plastic cartridge or a little sack inside, which you squeezed as you dipped the nib into your bottle of Quink ink to suck up a pen full. Blotting paper was one of our stationery essentials because the ink didn't dry fast enough, especially for us left-handers. Indeed, my handwriting leans to the left even today as a direct result of having to angle my hand so that my little finger didn't trail along my freshly written words and smudge them. It was while developing this style in first year that our Science teacher, a slim and small but fierce old woman called Miss Mangan, decided a better name for me would be 'Scrawlinson'. Fortunately for me, the name didn't stick, or if it did it was only until my other nickname CRJ came along to replace it later.

Miss Mangan was just one of a generally formidable array of teachers we had in our first year. I don't think it helped being referred to by your surname by the teachers, automatically putting a more formal slant on the teacher/pupil relationship than we had experienced in Junior School, but all the teachers had an authoritative air about them. I think Miss Almond was our form teacher and taught us a few subjects. Although French wasn't one of them, my favourite recollection of her was in perhaps second year, when our family looked after a French student named Remi, a family friend of our French teacher Miss Baron, later Mrs Wharton. He was a bit mischievous, to say the least, and when we went on a school trip to London, he was too busy larking about on the train back to notice Miss Almond sneaking up behind him to give him a good scolding in French. Now I don't know if the language was perfect, but the menace behind it certainly was, and he didn't say a word for the rest of the trip.

Two other teachers stand out from first year in particular. Mr Duckworth, our music teacher, was quite an acerbic wit. The College had a rather good choir, and the first thing he did was to get everyone in turn to sing a few lines of the national anthem. Now, I like to think that although my voice isn't brilliant, I can at least hold a tune and hit the right notes at the right time and the right order (think Pierce Brosnan in *Mamma Mia*), so I was quietly confident that within my limited range I would be worthy of a place in the choir. My turn came around, and I opened my mouth:

"Goood Saaave our Graacious . . . "

"Get back to the dogs' home, Rawlinson," came the immediate response. And with that, my singing career drew tunelessly to a close. I did in fact get offered a place in third year by another teacher whose name escapes, me but I think Mr Duckworth's words had already holed my singing confidence below the waterline and I wasn't to be persuaded to lower the average in the alto section.

The other teacher who had me avoiding his gaze unless spoken to would be Mr Bradley, our swimming teacher. I expect it was quite unusual for a school to have its own pool and in truth it was probably only 15m or so in length, but it was Mr Bradley's domain and there wasn't much messing about in his classes. I'd learnt to swim in Junior School at Saul Street Baths so wasn't too worried about the swimming side of things, and I did pick up my Bronze swimming award, but I remember him having us all try our hand at water polo, which was incredibly tiring. The first of my two other distinct swimming-related memories are of cheering on Alec Crook, who was making the butterfly look easy (can you still do it, Alec?). He was swimming on his own, and I think he must have broken some record or other because I remember the rest of us making the most incredible noise cheering him on in such a small place while Mr Bradley timed him. He turned around to the rest of the class at one point, with a thumb up and mouthing "he's got it." The other incident was no less dramatic; I also remember Mr Bradley having to pull Greg Wagner out to rescue him, diving in quite elegantly having thrown his clipboard and stuff to one side. When he climbed out, I remember him holding his watch up to his ear and saying to the gasping child whose life he had probably just saved, "You're paying for this if it's broken!"

The topic of school dinners is usually one that provokes strong memories, but in my case, I think I only had them for the first couple of years. You would race down to the canteen and form a long, snaking queue around the edge of the large building off the lower playground, picking up your cutlery which went straight into your shirt breast pocket (a habit I maintain today at times!) and then grabbing a tray before getting served the order of the day. The food was so unspectacular I honestly don't remember any details, which as much as anything probably explains why I moved to taking sandwiches with me in or around the third year. Four rounds of potted meat sandwiches ('Shippams' beef, chicken or crab paste most likely), a packet of crisps and a penguin biscuit kept me going after two or three slices of toast for breakfast and more for supper. The five of us in our house got through up to fourteen loaves of white sliced a week by all accounts. How I wasn't the size of a house by the time I left home I don't know.

Religion was clearly an important part of the school system and we all had RE as part of our curriculum all the way through to O' Level. I honestly don't think it was taught very well, though. Of all the subjects I took, I remember least about this one, which is ironic given the background of the school. I do have memories of walking up Chapel Street en masse to St Wilfred's church, sometimes with the whole school population in attendance. Such occasions would include the annual Christmas Carol Service, during which the choir would come into its own, in spite of my absence, to etch carols in my mind to a standard that is rarely matched live today. In particular, the descant of *Hark the Herald Angels Sing* sticks in my mind, and still sends a shiver down my spine in recollection of the superb version the choir did then. We also had our own version of Aled Jones in Phil Huggon, son of the mark-pinching Mr Huggon (more of him in a bit and no, I don't bear a grudge to this day), who was able to sing the solo pieces very well indeed. The church was also host to two distinctly sad occasions during our five years. We lost two pupils, Michael Watterson and my classroom near neighbour Anthony Royle, each to road traffic accidents. I know we have lost friends from our year in adulthood since then, but it was especially sobering to twice lose school friends in such an abrupt manner. I don't recall if their funerals were held at St Wilfred's – I suspect not – but there was certainly a remembrance service held for each of them.

I can't leave first year without a mention of Father Wareing. We had a number of Jesuit priests who taught us, but I regret that I only recall him and Fr Praeger, who couldn't have been more different – more of him later. Fr Wareing taught us Latin and one other class (English, I think), and he was one of the pupils' favourites. My two main recollections of him were his use of what he referred to as expletives in Latin – "mehercule" and "o me miserum" [note to editor – take these out if they're a bit racy]. We were to use these words with caution, as Peter Naylor found out to his cost when he thought he had good reason to shout "Mehercule". Unfortunately for Pete, this feeds nicely into my second memory of Fr Wareing, which was his preferred method of punishment to keep us in line.

Unusually for schools at that time as far as I know, we didn't have the cane at Preston Catholic College; instead, we had the ferula. This was apparently (I say this as I never saw it myself) a thick leather strap, which was administered to each hand by one of the deputy heads, Mr 'Fat Jack' McCann. Fr Wareing's tactic, which I've never seen or heard of anyone else doing, was to forego other methods of discipline such as lines or detention but go straight for the ferula, albeit in a roundabout way. He would write the names of miscreants on a piece of paper for any and all manner of offences and once he got to five or six names, he would ask someone to pick one of the pieces of paper out of his hand. The four or five losers were let off and the 'winner' . . . well, maybe that's not the right word. As nice a teacher as he was, and however much I otherwise enjoyed his classes, it was probably Fr Wareing's classes that I was most cautious and well-behaved in, just in case.

Of course, the other major novelty of big school was the introduction of homework. I don't remember having too much for most days, although I think it is true to say that we had something every night, but most Sunday evenings were spent scribbling a two- or three-page history or English essay into my plastic-backed books. I don't remember the homework getting in the way of a midweek game of footie with my dad and brother across the road in St John Fisher's playground, or *The Six Million Dollar Man* on TV.

At the end of each year, we would have an exam in each of the eight to ten subjects we had covered in the year. Until recently, my rose-tinted recollection had always given me pretty good grades all the way through, until my mum uncovered my results from one year which were, let's say, 'unspectacular'. Considering you 'only' needed 80 per cent to get an A and even 40 per cent was a pass with an E, they were definitely more ordinary than I had remembered. The percentages are pretty similar to today's pass grade in secondary school, but with A* ratings and the adoption of coursework that gets handed back with comments about how to improve it, I'm far from convinced it's easy to compare results between then and now. Let's just agree that it was harder in our day!

The Middle Years

I've grouped the second, third and fourth years into a single section, because with a few exceptions I'm generally a bit foggy about what happened in which year. Let's see how things unravel as I put pen to paper, or rather as I type this at my computer keyboard – an activity that would have seemed almost unfathomable in the time about which I'm writing. We didn't even have a telephone line in the house until after I left to go to university, using my grandparents' number until then, so the idea of owning my own computer would have been very strange.

One thing I'm pretty sure would have been covered in the second year is Biology. For some reason best known to the powers that were, 2A were either taught the subject by our Geography teacher Mr 'Piggy' Poole or our erstwhile swimming teacher Mr Bradley. The lessons inevitably involved sex education. Now, for a bunch of schoolboys whose collective experience of sex would have been summarised by the magazines that did the rounds at the back of the school bus on the way to the sports fields at Grafton, this was always going to be an interesting area. You might remember Monty Python's *Meaning of Life* sketch on the same subject at an all-boys school, in which the school children were bored by John Cleese's efforts to teach by inviting his wife along for a practical. However, our experience couldn't have been further from this, with a red-faced teacher mumbling his way through the lesson while there was a mixture of embarrassment and cringing on our part. I do, however, recall the memorable phrase "Stick it in and wiggle it about a bit"! It would only be later in life that I'm sure we all learned that even to wiggle it a lot would have been much better advice!!

The same classroom, (so I guess this was also our second year), was where our Latin classes were delivered, in which Mr Huggon, father of Phil, found lasting fame in our house by cheating me out of a 100 per cent exam – at least according to my mother who tells this story far more often than I do. Now, Mr Huggon had compiled our exam in two parts, the first being marked out of 36, and the second out of 64, and when it came to the results, he read out each number to each pupil, to which they replied with the total. When he got to me, he read out the first mark – "Thirty-six"! The class let out a collective gasp. The second mark came – "Sixty . . . three"! An even bigger "Oohh!' was heard. I'd achieved 99 per cent – the highest mark I ever got in an exam. However, at parents' evening that year, Mr Huggon confessed to my parents that he had made a mistake in the exam, and that the total number of marks available was 101. He had said he was getting increasingly worried as he went through my paper that he might have to award me 101 per cent, but apparently I got the last letter of the last word of the paper wrong, giving him the excuse he needed to cheekily knock off two marks.

That same classroom was the one in which Peter Reece got me a three-page essay punishment for laughing in class when he wrote 'Speling Test' at the top of the page he passed to me as we swapped to mark each other's tests. However, this was easily trumped by Phil Suddick, who was in a competition with another pupil to see who could collect the most three-page essays in a year – the standard punishment from 'Piggy Poole'. In the last class of the year, the two boys were becoming increasingly disruptive, until the exasperated Mr Poole called "Right – Suddick!" "Yes!" exclaimed Phil, raising his arm aloft in triumph. "Detention!" the voice continued, much to the amusement of the rest of the class.

The second year was probably also where I got more into the sporting side of things. The mainstream sports were football in the winter and cricket or hockey in the summer. We would be bussed down to the sports fields at Grafton, where there were a couple of pitches near the pavilion for the summer sports, while the football pitches were more spread out. I was reasonably sporty, enjoying both football, where I was on the fringes of the school team (think squad rather than first 11 here), and cricket, where I opened the batting with a Chris Tavare like stoicism that made me look good in comparison to most of my team mates, who would tend to swing the bat more but with varying degrees of failure.

Football is clearly one of the staples of any young boy's upbringing. Or at least it was, until the advent of the games console, which I have no doubt I would have succumbed to as much as has been the case with more recent generations. However, in our day we had the usual routine to contend with of standing in a line while the captains chose their teams based on a combination of friendship and ability. I started off as a left winger, following on from my career in the 7th Preston cub scout team where Fr Spencer would expect to see white paint on my boots from running so close to the touchline, but I did end up moving into goal because I was briefly one of the tallest in the class until I stopped growing in third year. I think I did OK, although for some reason I remember being chipped by Russell Ashton once and then standing motionless (as us goalkeepers occasionally do when taken by surprise) when Jim Clune toe ended one into the top corner from the edge of the box. I must have had the occasional good match because I also remember being hit on the back of the head by a chunk of mud, thrown by Shaun Daly after a match, presumably delivered because I'd saved so many of his shots during the game. I turned to him to say something along the lines of "You scored two, how many more do you want?"

Thinking of Fr Spencer, it was he who volunteered a group of us to sell programmes at Deepdale when England played there. I think it was a youth match of some sort, rather than the senior team. It was a freezing afternoon, but Fr Spencer kindly gave us each a Mars bar as a reward, and awarded us the letters OMB, IPS after our names (Order of Mars Bars, International Programme Seller). It's bizarre what sticks in your mind sometimes, isn't it!

The school turned to either hockey or cricket in the Summer. I managed to take advantage of others' recklessness with the bat as a result of my own patience, catching the eye of Mr Ainsworth, who appeared to confuse my inability to hit the ball hard with the steadying influence of someone dabbing ones and twos in the style of a typical opening bat. I think I opened the batting for the school team more often than not, although this was later perhaps more as a result of the 35no I scored in our first season than anything approaching that level afterwards. I remember the nadir came off the back of the schoolyard game and its 'tap and run' rule, which was intended to speed up the match and make it more interesting during playtime. As the name of the rule suggests, if you hit the ball with your bat you had to run even if it went straight to a fielder. The trouble came when this reaction became automatic, and spilled over into the game proper. One games afternoon I was opening the batting for my team and facing the first ball. As you might have guessed by now, I struck the ball very sweetly out of the middle of the bat, and set off like a rocket for the other end. The problem was, I'd struck it straight to a fielder at mid-on, who threw down the stumps at the bowler's end long before I arrived. Run out, first ball! Still, I did have the school team match later on that day to look forward to. Opening the batting, this time at the non-striker's end, I watched the receiver hit the first ball and we both instinctively set off. And . . . I was run out again, making it out twice in the same afternoon having only faced one ball. My cricketing career did continue into my working life, where I opened the batting for Blade Cooling for a few years, and I'm happy to say that fateful afternoon was comfortably the worst of my cricket life, even beating the occasion when as an adult I was hit twice in the face in the same innings while batting!

I'm not entirely sure how or when hockey came along, but I only played a couple of times. It was generally played in the same manner as most football matches; that is, with the ball being closely followed by the vast majority of both teams while the goalkeepers and those who were only there on sufferance left everyone else to it. Since we had at least ten years less experience of playing hockey compared with football, there was no doubt a lot of swinging and missing going on, as the hard cork ball bobbled around the relatively rough grass pitches. Every so often there would be a vaguely good contact and the mini scrum would move up the pitch. There was however, one distinct occasion when this didn't happen. Picture the scene, if you will . . .

Two teams are scrapping it out, ours defending the goal to cover the unlikely event that the opposition actually hits the ball in the right direction. But instead of them getting a shot on goal, one of our boys manages a good defensive slog, taking the ball trundling up and over the halfway line. As one, we turn and leg it after the ball.

Now, I was at the front of the charging pack, spurred on no doubt by the fact that all that stood between me and a clean shot at goal was a solitary, disinterested defender. This was no ordinary defender, though. This was Miles Hartland, my friend since first year. He had never been particularly sporty, but for some reason his parents had bought him his own hockey stick – a go faster stripes version of the wooden hooks with string handles that the school supplied. As I bore down on him, he took an almighty swipe at the ball, and caught it absolutely spot on, sending the high velocity lump of solid cork straight into my chin. I don't know to this day how I kept my teeth, let alone my good looks, but suffice to say that was the end of my hockey career.

Of course, you didn't always end up playing the sport you wanted to do on games afternoon. If the weather was bad enough in winter, or bad at all in summer, then the dreaded words 'cross' and 'country' would be uttered by Mr Ainsworth. Off we'd trudge, left out of the sports field and gradually forming a longer and longer snake as the quicker ones pulled away from the slow-coaches. We'd head to the railway bridge at Miller Park and back, along the muddy, tree-lined track that was Tram Road. I would inevitably be one of the stragglers (I was more of a sprinter, back in the day), arriving back cold, wet and bedraggled; even the showers that we would otherwise try to dodge would be welcome, for once. It clearly stirred something very deep down, though. I'm now a regular runner and occasional triathlete – I guess we all start somewhere.

While we're on sports, let's turn to a more highbrow version – chess! The College had a couple of chess teams which I think were divided by age, so I'm guessing they were under 13s and under 16s. We (the College) had a pretty good record, and both my brother's year and mine performed well. One year, the College had all four finalists in the Preston school district chess finals in the under 13s and under 16s. My brother Steve played against Andrew Jackson from his year in one match, while my opponent was Peter Naylor. Andrew and Pete were always just that bit better than me and Steve, and sure enough they won the competitions, but not before we'd had our photos taken under the watchful eye of Mr Starkie by the Lancashire Evening Post. Pete and I always played boards one and two in our best of eight match competitions against other schools, and my recollection is we didn't lose too many between us. Indeed, I think Pete played for Lancashire a few times, too, a feat I managed just the once, when I managed to draw my match.

I reckon third year was when additional languages were introduced, at which point those who had a more practical bent went off to do their thing while the rest of us got stuck into German and Latin at the expense of Geography and Biology. I never really enjoyed Geography at school so it was no great loss at the time, but I think with hindsight I did miss an opportunity to learn something that would be of greater interest later in life.

It's possible to nail down a couple of events in the fourth year. The first occurred in May 1981 – the attempted assassination of Pope John Paul II. This sticks in my mind because we learned of it in the school minibus while at a cricket match. It's a slightly bizarre memory to recall, but I do clearly remember it. It also seems slightly far-fetched for personal reasons, as I had broken my wrist playing football only a month earlier . And I know *that* date is accurate because at the time was devastated to think I was going to miss the first ever space shuttle launch; luckily, I didn't, because it was delayed. The injury happened while I was playing in goal during games at Grafton; someone had a shot from close range that bent my hand back awkwardly and really hurt my wrist, so I finished the match playing in defence. I walked home on my own with my jacket around my shoulders as it was too painful to get it on, and my parents took me straight to the Preston Royal Infirmary where I found I had fractured the radial bone in my right wrist. I suppose it must have healed quite quickly for me to have got into the cricket team by the May.

I suspect it was also in the fourth year. The second significant development I can remember taking place in the fourth year was the arrival of a new breed in school – girls! I don't know how different school life would have been if we had been a mixed school from the outset (very different, I'm guessing), but it brought a new dimension to the place when our Winckley Square Convent neighbours started to pop over to use our canteen and gym. Lark Hill and Winckley Square Convent Girls Schools were combining resources with Preston Catholic College to form a single sixth form Newman College, which made sense as the size of our lower school dwindled. As far as I can remember, we didn't tend to mix other than for lunchtimes and occasional sports in the gym. I remember playing mixed basketball, if only because I was called for a foul on one of the girls for 'reaching inside'! I didn't live that one down quickly. On the other hand, I did garner lots of attention and sympathy when I turned up with my lower arm in plaster, after the wrist-fracturing incident above. I got quite a few get well soon messages from the girls – and a QTπ ('cutie pie – geddit?!) as well.

You might be forgiven for assuming that the school's standards wouldn't so much slip as at least move with the times as younger generations came through, particularly one with such a fine tradition and history. You'd be wrong to think this, however; it didn't really seem to be the case. Even the last intake were subject to 'old-fashioned' punishments, such as prefect lines. I managed to get 30 of them (they were more like small paragraphs than lines, so 30 was quite a bit) from the deputy head teacher, Mr Bamber. I don't know why I got them, but when I met him last year at the funeral of my uncle, with whom he and his wife were good friends, he was gracious enough to apologise for giving them to me anyway! This is typical of my recollection of JB. He didn't act a hard case because he didn't need to. He had two deputies, Mr McCann and Mr Billington, for that. Mr McCann – also known as 'Fat Jack' – was a tallish, stocky, and stern-looking man, with crew cut hair and a prison-like suit that created an air of menace to match his actions. I only saw the inside of his office once, on the only time I crossed him was when a friend and I (perhaps Pete Reece) were in the wrong place at the wrong time. Fat Jack asked us a question, and I remember we both denied knowledge of the answer. Thankfully for us, he bought it, and we legged into the playground knowing we had dodged a bullet that time. Actually, that's not quite right. I think I also ran to his office when Pete Naylor cracked me on the top of my head with a cricket bat that he was swinging round in the classroom at the end of break. Not only was I dazed, but I put my hand up to my head to feel blood all over my fingers. I immediately ran downstairs to get assistance, honestly not thinking about the trouble I was about to get Pete into until the obvious question about how it happened came. Sorry, Pete!

I remember Mr Billington being more of a menacing presence. In spite of sporting something like a tweed sports jacket and 70s moustache, he seemed to have that air about him. We had a couple of days off school when there was a very heavy snowfall one winter, but a few of us had made it in and were enjoying a snowball fight on Winckley Square outside school when Mr Billington emerged from the building. Was this our chance? He came slowly through the crowd of armed teenagers. As he walked past, one pupil maybe just started to lift his hand. Without even turning around, let alone flinching, he said "You just dare, boy", and walked slowly on his way in complete silence, unmolested of course. I always had a grudging admiration for him after that.

Of the rest of the teachers, only the Chemistry teacher, Mr Andrews, was consistently overly strict with us, clearly keen to hang on to the past, as he demonstrated in sixth form. I don't know why this would have been the case, since I was doing Maths, Further Maths and Physics, but he taught me for one of my first classes that year. In sixth form while we were still calling the teachers Mr or Miss so-and-so, they had mostly relaxed their stance, and were resorting to calling us by our first names rather than our surnames. However, in this class with Mr Andrews, he announced that although he was aware of the policy the other teachers were following, "We're not going to do that in this class, are we, *Kellett*?", spitting out the K of Michael's surname and sending it reverberating around the room, to leave us in no doubt that modernisation could wait outside the door when he was in session.

Mr Andrews couldn't have been more different from the other Chemistry teacher we had for the last couple of years before sixth form. Mrs Fox was a lovely lady who was inclined to let the more boisterous class members get away with far more than almost any other teacher. She drew the line at being called 'Brenda babes' by Peter Reece, though – sorry, Pete, but that phrase has stuck in my mind for too many years for it not to be right! Certainly, Tony Howarth and I used to play classroom golf with impunity; we'd flick little rolled up balls of paper, trying to get them into the round hole sunk into the lid covering the sinks at each pair of stools in the chemistry classroom.

The only other teacher with whom we could generally get away with being tearaways was Mr 'Jock' Malone, a quaint wee Scottish gentleman who did his best to control the class while trying to teach us English. However, he was so nice that even I was emboldened to nick his chalk and board rubber alternately (with Pete again – the more I think about it, he got me into quite a bit of trouble over the years!), while Mr Malone resorted to asking the class which "light-fingered Louis" had pinched his equipment again. I remember him teaching us the correct way to label an envelope so that the address didn't disappear into the bottom right corner every Christmas (unlike when my wife puts the names right in the middle. Grrr!)

The other rather notable teacher I remember was Fr Praeger, a slender, wiry individual who sometime wore a cape – very old school indeed! He didn't put up with any nonsense, but unfortunately brought out the worst in one or two of our class. He's the only teacher I ever heard of who stormed out of a class mid-lesson, presumably after some antics by an unidentified miscreant, saying "Good luck with your exams, gentlemen" as he marched out of the door. Otherwise, Mr Higgins (father of Edmund in our class), Mr Norcross, Mrs Wharton (Nee Baron), Mr Turner and the other teachers we had over the years, all contributed to getting me to where I am today with minimal trauma and drama.

I mustn't forget 'Pop' Moulding! He was another characterful teacher; a small and stocky man, most obviously characterised by the pointed hat he wore, which I recall looked straight out of the film *Zulu*. He got on well with us kids, often referring to us by our nicknames. In my case, this was CRJ, which stood for 'Crawly-Rawly Junior', a carry-over from my brother who had carried the sobriquet CR before me. I don't remember many other nicknames that weren't simply shortened versions of actual names – 'Wammer' and 'Coops' spring to mind, here. In fact, the only exception I can think of was Gary Anderton; Gary was a slight and bespectacled blond-haired lad at the time, who looked unfortunately a little too much like the character from the associated TV ad not to be referred to as MBK – Milky Bar Kid. I don't remember it being particularly intended as offensive; looking back I think it was a pretty cool nickname, and probably better than mine! I must admit it never bothered me though, I just blamed my brother for it.

Final year

By the time we'd reached our fifth and final year, we were in the unusual position of still being the youngest in school. I was now in 5A, one of a few of us who by chance stayed in class A all the way through school. While the conversion to a sixth form College had continued, our skirted guests from next door, along with those boys beginning the sixth form to occupy the space left by the dying Catholic College. The playground had grown more spacious for our particular version of catch, which involved throwing a tennis ball up onto the roof of one of the school blocks and fighting with a crowd of others to catch it before it bounced so that you got the privilege of throwing it up there next. It actually proved to be good training for a cricket qualification a bunch of us did with skills which included throwing and catching. Having played that playground game, it was trivial to catch a mere eight out of ten balls thrown to you. It may also have played a part in my adult cricketing life, as in addition to opening the batting for the Blade Cooling office team I also ended up keeping wicket.

I kept the blue diary that each of us was given as one of my memories of final year; it's buried somewhere in my loft. I know it contains the dates and details of each of our O levels, along with those of a few of my friends' birthdays, and of the nights Tony Howarth and I took part in a mini darts competition with Ian Horrocks, including which buses we needed to take to get there! This information was added in addition to the usual class listings and a standard prayer, if I remember rightly. A few term dates completed the diary itself.

The final year was certainly quite a bit tougher than the others in terms of homework, but it seemed to at least pay off well enough to get me into Newman College sixth form. I don't know what the total of six As and four Bs would equate to these days but I'm pretty sure my 'U' in English Literature would still be a U by any marking standard! Ironically, I genuinely thought it was one of my best exams, and the common assumption of Mr Bamber and my parents was that my handwriting might simply have been judged so illegible that the examiner didn't think it was worth bothering to mark the paper – maybe Miss Mangan had a point all those years ago! Or maybe it reflected my genuine inability to relate to Homer and Shakespeare, which was demonstrated when a friend and I watched the school's production of *Macbeth* (I'm certain of this, as there were witches at the start). We'd been very grateful when the lights came up to applause, joining in with great enthusiasm and perhaps with different motivation to most, before happily legging it home in the dark. It wasn't until the following day that we found out we had left in the interval!

I feel slightly cheated that I don't really remember what should have been one of the most auspicious moments in my life – my last day at school. I have a vague recollection of contentment, rather than happiness, perhaps because I knew I would be back in a couple of months to carry on the adventure with many of my fifth year friends staying on too.

Memories

When I look back at my time at Preston Catholic College, it throws up several interesting contrasts with schools of today. It occupied the slightly rare ground between state and private school, as far as I could tell. To be honest, if my parents could afford to send two of us there then it couldn't have been that expensive, at least not in comparison with the schools which might be considered equivalents in Derby, where I now live. I have no doubt that we were sent there because of the superior academic results it presumably delivered relative to the local state schools, although I don't know what official standards were in place that could help parents make such judgements, other than gossip that "Everyone knows . . . " When we got together as a group for our 50th birthdays celebration I didn't get the impression that we had done too badly as a group, so maybe there was something in it.

I don't think the idea of single sex schools is as popular today as it was in Preston when we were growing up, where there were at least three from which to choose. I expect the fact that these three merged to a single sixth form College tells its own tale there. Since I never attended a mixed sex school, I am no more in a position to judge the merits of it (or otherwise) than someone who's never attended a single sex school could judge my own experience. I can say with confidence that sixth form was more enjoyable than PCC but it's impossible to make a proper comparison of this, too, because in addition to the female presence in those final years we were also studying subjects of our choosing (having chosen to come back at all), and the teaching was much more relaxed (unless you were in with Mr Andrews!). The fact that Fiona Doyle in my sixth form class was an electric-blue-haired, mini-skirted and stockinged version of the girl who had left an 'I Love You' pendant in my school drawer at the start of our last year of Junior School 'was undeniably a bonus'. (We never discussed it, but I could tell from the look in her eyes the first time we realised who each other was that she remembered!) I reckon I've still got that pendant somewhere . . .

You would never get away with the school's corporal punishment regime nowadays, would you? Not just the ferula but Fr Wareing's mind games. Although we had a few unruly types, I don't honestly remember much in the way of bullying at all. There were one or two hard cases, yes (step forward Shaun Daly for one!), but I never had any trouble with them personally. I'm not saying for a moment that my behaviour was such because of the threat of the ferula, nor am I saying it 'never did me any harm', because I never suffered it, but while I sympathise up to a point with punishment as a form of deterrent, I'm not sure many children are mature of thought enough to be able to view it in that light. Indeed, I suspect many adults would struggle with the concept, so I'm quite comfortable with its demise over time. I honestly believe that the challenge of teaching has never been more difficult, for reasons I won't go into here, but I'm personally satisfied that bringing back corporal punishment would do very little to help staff in that respect.

So, where to go from here? I've probably expanded my original text by about 50 per cent (or 51 per cent, if Mr Huggon is reading this!), as I've gone back and added more things as they've occurred to me. It would be lovely to see others' memories corroborate my version of events, but that might be asking too much. Maybe all I can hope for is that I've provided a few memory joggers, as I hope the others have done for me. I have really enjoyed writing these memories down, and I think they're indicative enough of a happy and productive time at Preston Catholic College. It only remains for me to thank my friends for the memories, especially Jim Clune for prodding us into writing them down, and Peter Cooper for being instrumental in getting me to the 50th Celebration last year – my mum recognised him straight away when he knocked at the door, so he clearly hasn't changed much. Most of all, however, my thanks go out to the staff and my own teachers for providing me with an education that enabled me to earn a job with Rolls-Royce; this itself has taken me all over the world, and allowed me to take my family on the sort of holidays we could only have dreamed of when I was growing up. Dad, your advice was spot on!

PAUL RICHARDSON: FORMS 1C, 2B, 3S, 4S AND 5S

I was the second member of the Richardson family to attend Preston Catholic College. My elder brother Mark was already there, so perhaps it wasn't such a big deal to walk through the arched entrance on Winckley Street for me as it was for others. This, together with the fact that I came from St Augustine's Primary School in Avenham, meant the journey to school was similar and therefore not too onerous, unlike those of many lads who travelled a long way by bus or train from various parts of the county.

School was fairly routine. I neither loved nor hated it, although looking back now I probably have more good memories than bad. I made some good friends, some of whom I still see on a regular basis. I wasn't particularly interested in the usual school sports of football, athletics or cricket, so don't have any long-lasting memories or funny stories; all I really recall is the long walk to Grafton playing fields every Wednesday afternoon to stand aimlessly on a football pitch in the rain, and the cross-country run over the old tram bridge if football was cancelled. I enjoyed the water-based sports of swimming and water polo (more about that later). I didn't make the school choir, either, so never made the trips to international singing events that those who were more musically gifted were offered.

My main memories are of school-organised holidays, and the

teachers. I distinctly remember a trip to Betws-y-Coed, in north Wales, which I think took place in our second year. We stayed in an old residential manor, that sounds grand, although it was more like a youth hostel than a five-star hotel. Anyway, it was about a two- or three-hour coach journey, so we had a half way stop for a leg stretch in Conwy – you know, the walled market town famed for its castle and history. Not that anybody was remotely interested in this, of course. What was more appealing was the joke shop that myself and Matthew Iddon spotted – how could we resist?

After much childish laughter and debate we settled on our purchases. I went for the 'fart powder' and Matt got some 'luminous eyes'. I decided to let the fart powder loose during that evening's meal, with my chosen victim being Pete Reece, who was sat opposite me. When he turned around to talk to somebody on another table, I took the opportunity to tip the entire contents of the packet into his soup. What I hadn't bargained for was it settling on the surface! I had nearly finished stirring it in when he turned round and caught me! Pete was normally quite a mild-mannered lad, but today he was furious. He gave me two choices – I could either swap dishes with him and eat the lot, or he would grass me up. I took the soup, along with the added ingredient. Despite what you may think about the quality of the products you buy from a tacky joke shop, this purchase was the real deal. I would now like to formally apologise for the resulting stink to my suffering room-mates, who were, from memory, Michael Davis, Andrew Finch and Matthew Iddon! The powder was so good it carried on working the next day! To this day, every time I put pepper in my soup I think of Betws-y-Coed.

If the first night of that trip was eventful, the second turned into a riot. What else do you do on a lad's school holiday at 12 or 13 years old? Well, one thing you do is run round the residence playing 'knock a door run' on each other, especially if you've been to the joke shop and have extra fun to throw into the mix. We decided to play a prank on one of the lads (this time I think the intended victim was Paul Reynolds, otherwise known as Riff – another mild-mannered lad). Matt Iddon got ready with his luminous eyes and we set a trap. I ran across the landing and knocked on his door, hoping that he was going to come out to investigate and receive the shock of his life. Unfortunately, we were the ones who got the shock. I had knocked on the wrong door, and out came Mr (Sandy) McCann, who was less than impressed. He chased me back into the room, where Matt, unaware that Mr McCann was in hot pursuit, sprung out with his glowing eyes! As you can imagine, Mr McCann was in a combination shock and anger, but after he calmed down he must have seen the funny side of it, as apart from receiving a mild telling off, we got away with it. I think he gave us as much of a scare as we gave him, actually – he was quite scary anyway, with his two top front teeth missing . . . reminded me of Dracula!

I also recall going on a ski trip to Austria in the final year of school. We headed to St Johann im Pongau, stopping at Gasthof Goldener Hirsch. Why I can remember the name of a hotel we stopped at 40 years ago but not what I had for tea last night, I'll never know! Our group consisted of about 25 lads from Cath Coll and Winckley Square, and possibly a few girls from Lark Hill Convent as well. I was one of the lucky ones, as there were a limited number of places available, and names were drawn out of a hat. It was to be an action-packed holiday. Although most of us would only have been 15 or 16 at the time, a couple of six formers were also with us, and they'd decided to buy some Schnapps at Munich Airport. That was just the start of it! The Schnapps (which was ridiculously strong and only supposed to be drunk in small portions), was shared around a small group of us with abandon on the coach from Munich to the resort. I'll never know how I held it together and didn't throw up. I literally staggered off the bus and went straight up to my room, along with my room mates Mick Suthers and Maurice Black. We never made it back down for the evening meal. Despite the excitement of my first ever ski holiday, the first day out on the slopes was a disaster. A few of us were still hung over, so we did well to stand up, let alone ski (which wasn't pretty), and I think Maurice injured his leg, which must have been due to the alcohol, as he was a competent skier.

We were given an hour's free time after our evening meal on the second night of our stay, , after which we all had to be back in the rooms (our allocated rooms, that is – no mingling or socialising with Winckley Square or Lark Hill girls allowed!). So, what else were we expected to do in our spare hour, other than head to the local off license where, despite concerns about age and nationality, we found the purchase of alcohol to be extremely straightforward. After careful consideration, I decided to buy the cheapest two-litre bottle of red wine I could find. It certainly wasn't an award-winner! We got back to the Goldener Hirsch just in time to be unceremoniously escorted to our rooms. After about an hour, once we thought all was quiet and the teachers would be tucked up in bed, we decided to have a wander out to find our mates. Armed with cheap red wine, we met up with others – Andrew Cross and Andrew Finch spring to mind. After around half an hour, loaded up with said cheap wine, we must have got quite raucous, as we heard Mr (Pete) Singleton prowling, and growling, along the corridors outside the rooms. Knowing the consequences would be bad if we got caught, I dived on the floor (with the bottle of red wine in hand) while the lads pushed a bed over me as cover. Unfortunately, this did not work, as Mr Singleton came in, saw my feet sticking out from under the bed, and dragged me out by my hair! To my horror, worse was to follow . . . I had to watch him tip the rest of the wine down the sink. There was plenty of skiing, a little more alcohol, and many more laughs on that holiday, which remains one of the best I've ever had! It must have made a lasting impression as I love skiing and have been on many winter holidays since. I even have the odd schnapps, for old times' sake.

Teachers

Teachers shape your memories of school and probably contribute to life after school in terms of further education or careers, both in terms of what and how they taught you. There were good teachers and some that weren't so good, some I liked and some I didn't take to, and some that made a lasting impression, if not necessarily all for the right reasons. For instance, I remember Mr Bradley, the swimming teacher, whose favourite hobby seemed to be using our heads as target practice during water polo lessons, and who would push lads up against the cold wall while they were waiting to go into the even colder pool. I'm sure he used to like a couple of pints at lunchtime.

There was also Mr McCann, the Maths teacher affectionately known as known as 'Fat Jack', who could draw a perfect circle on the blackboard using a handkerchief. One day, in our Maths class on the top floor overlooking Winckley Square, we were trying to answer some testing questions when we noticed that Fat Jack had dosed off while sat at his desk. Out of nowhere came a huge clap of thunder. Mr McCann bolted upright, looking stunned – we didn't half laugh! It's funny what you remember.

A final couple of honourable mentions should go to Mr Henry, the Physics teacher who was particularly good at throwing the board duster when anybody talked in class (I got a couple of bruises to prove it), and Mr Thompson, the English teacher and form master, who possessed a memorable wig. Others will also know what I mean when I say 'fennel seeds' . . . !

Life after Catholic College

To be honest, and as some will remember, I was never the greatest academic while at school; I couldn't wait to escape and get stuck into proper work, actually. (Having said this, I might have thought that I was escaping academic work when I left, but it got worse when I went to college during my apprenticeship!)

At the age of 16, I started an apprenticeship with a local electrical contractor, based just a stone's throw away on Mount Street behind Catholic College – it seemed I would always be attached to the school, somehow! Mr Bamber, another teacher from school, was absolutely delighted when I applied; so much so that he told me, "Richardson, I will write you a reference and personally hand deliver it to them." I thought that was very kind, then realised he was only offering because he didn't want me to go into sixth form or ever catch sight of me again! My career progressed smoothly enough, and over time I gradually expanded my interests into contracting, building refurbishment and mechanical services. Up until September 2020 I was employed as a Building Services Contract Manager.

Having been with one company for 38 years, I realised I was ready for a change, and decided to become self-employed to take control of my own destiny. I've started my own company, working primarily in electrical contracting but also carrying out advisory work for building and mechanical services.

Hobbies

My main hobby is spending time in the Lake District with my lovely wife Gemma and our family. We spend most weekends walking and relaxing around Windermere, usually staying on our classic cabin cruiser, which is moored at the Swan Marina, Newby Bridge – my perfect place. I also enjoy water sports such as wake boarding, water skiing and fishing – I did tell you football, cricket and athletics weren't my cup of tea! That said, not every sport I learned at Catholic College was wasted, as I do try to get away every year for a winter snow holiday. I love snowboarding, and of course 'Apres-ski', although now I'm older and more mature I only drink one bottle of red wine a night! I still toast Mr Singleton every time I have a glass of red wine, and think of St Johann. Unfortunately, we missed out last year due to the Covid restrictions, but we'll be back!

Family

Family is important to me, so whenever there's an opportunity to spend family together time together we take it, whether it's a day out, a BBQ, or a holiday. I have two sons, James and Ashley, and a beautiful grand-daughter Lilly – I can't believe I'm a Grandad! Fortunately my mum and dad are still around, so it's great when we all get together four generations plus dogs!

NEIL SLATER: FORMS 1A, 2B, 3S, 4S AND 5S

I remember my first day at Cath Coll well; I was proud to have got in, as I was following in my Dad's footsteps who had attended the school some 23 years earlier. It was now September 1977, and on that first day everyone gathered in the top playground, huddled around with the lads they knew from their previous schools, and kitted out in oversized blazers with the school badge depicting an Eagle with the word Fides (Faith, in Latin) written underneath, clutching briefcases and, if I remember rightly, bibles as well! A tennis ball started to get thrown around, and as it gathered pace it unfortunately cracked one of the lads right in the eye. So not a great start for him!

I was assigned to Class 1A, and my teacher was Miss Almond. Miss Mangan looked after the other class, and both teachers had been there for many years. As Miss Almond ran through the register on the first morning, I remember her asking "Are you James Slater's son?" to which I replied "Yes, Miss." "I remember teaching your father," she said. I confirmed this with my Dad that night – he remembered Miss Almond, too.

I'll always remember having to put the letters 'AMDG' in the top left-had corner of the margins of our books, meaning 'To the greater glory of God'. We were taught by quite a few Jesuit priests; I particularly remember Father Wareing, or 'Wez', as everyone called him. He was highly intelligent but also a great laugh, and had everyone in stitches.

As well as enduring academic lessons, sport (particularly football) was a big thing at the Catholic College. Miss Almond was proud of this fact, and hadn't wasted any time in telling the class that Fred Dewhurst – England international and Captain of the Preston North End 'Invincibles' Team who won the first league and Cup double in 1889 – had been a teacher at the school after his playing days were over.

I remember the school holding trials for the football team at their impressive Grafton Sports fields in the late August, before we started the following month. There was a massive turnout, and the trials went on for at least a couple of days. I was a keen footballer and a big Preston North End Supporter, with all our family being season ticket holders in those days, so I was hoping to get into the team. You got moved around the different games as the trials progressed, and I began to see that there was a good team being formed on one of the other pitches. I was small but quick in those days, so I played my heart out to try to get into that group. The trials were being run by Father Spencer, Mr Ainsworth and Mr (Eddie) Brown, who had been a professional player for PNE (who were a top team in the top division at the time), Orient, and Birmingham City, and had even played in the FA Cup final in 1956. The three men came over to watch our match. I remember putting in some good tackles and playing the ball around well (if I dare to say so myself). Eddie Brown pointed at me, and told me to go to over the pitch where the 'good' team were playing. I had done it! I knew that was going to be the first team, and from that point on I was in the First XI Football. We were a good side, and I really enjoyed the Saturday mornings, both home and away. My mum and dad always came to watch me, which was great, and Jimmy Clune's Dad was a big supporter –I remember his shouts of "Come on, James" as Jimmy went for goal! Our greatest achievement was winning the cup at Preston's Deepdale ground in 1979; it was a close game, and we beat Cuthbert Mayne 1-0 with Pete Cooper scoring. I remember sliding in to kick one off our goal line at one point. It was a great night, and we even got our photograph on the back of the Lancashire Evening Post newspaper.

We had to write our names and the year in the front of our schoolbooks when they were issued to us each year, and I remember once opening mine to find the name 'Mark Lawrenson, 1970/71' staring back at me. Everyone came and had a look. The player had just left Preston for Brighton at the time, but would go on to become a big star with the powerful Liverpool team of the early 80s, and a Match of the Day presenter after that. Indeed, at our School reunion in 2016, Mark sent a video message through to us all.

The other sports related story I remember concerns athletics – we were all taking part in trials for the 100m, under the watchful eye of Mr Bradley on Friday afternoon. You didn't mess with Mr Bradley; I think he was in the 1968 GB Judo Squad, or something similar. I ran first, and he handed me the stopwatch when I'd finished as he had to talk with another teacher. "Slater," he said, "you mark down the times – I'll be a minute or so." One of the lads came over and asked whose the watch was. "It's Bradley's," I replied, innocently. Mr Bradley was in ear shot. When he had finished talking, he came over and asked, "Slater – whose watch did you say that was?"

"Mr Bradley's," I replied.

"No you didn't, lad. You said 'Bradley's'. See me on Monday morning for six of the best."

I was well-behaved at school, so as you might expect, I was gutted. Imagine that happening now! Anyway, on Monday morning I went to the gym to see Mr Bradley. The other gym teacher, Mr Singleton, was there. I asked where Mr Bradley was, to be told "Sorry, he's not well today."

"Okay I'll come back tomorrow," I replied. I went back the following day, but he still wasn't in. I didn't go the next day, and luckily Mr Bradley completely forgot by the time he returned, so I went through school without having the dreaded 'cracks' as they were known!

The school choir was another interesting facet of the school. It was well known, and toured the world to Germany and US. Mr Duckworth was the music teacher, and everybody had to audition. You either got an A, B or C, or he just blew a raspberry. As you can imagine, a lot of the lads didn't want to take part so they sang terribly on purpose in order that Mr Duckworth would blow a raspberry at them. My voice wasn't great, and I got a C. Not good enough to get in, thankfully.

As we were the last year group to enter the school, the number of pupils grew smaller and smaller as each year progressed, until in the final year we were the only pupils left. We had some fun in the classes. I'm sure I remember Maurice Black bringing a mouse or hamster into school on one occasion, and scaring one of the teachers. I also recall a game in which we used to throw a penny and whoever's desk it landed under nearly got turned over in what was called the 'penny scramble'. I used to sit with Mick Suthers a lot in the laboratories, and we used to chat quite a bit; I remember our Physics teacher Ms Tyrell having to keep saying "Slater, Suthers, please stop chatting."

Unfortunately, there were some sad times, particularly when Mick Watterson was killed. I had gone to infant and junior school with Mick, and he sadly got knocked off his bike on London Road Bridge coming back from Scouts one Friday night in 1978. I still remember finding out on the Saturday morning from my friend and fellow Cath Coll pupil Simon Cahill, who lived two doors down from me. Also, Anthony 'Joe' Royle was sadly killed in an accident. Life can be cruel.

We finished school in May 1982, and I managed to get seven O levels. I then went on to to Newman College as had become known by then, where I studied for my A levels. I passed three A levels and got a place at what was then Newcastle Polytechnic (later Northumbria University) to study Librarianship and Information Studies (don't laugh). I had a great time in Newcastle. After graduating in June 1987, I came back to Preston to apply for some jobs while doing temporary work. I got an interview with British Gas to work in their Research and Technology Information Centre down in Fulham, London. So in February 1988, off I went down to the 'Smoke'. I then discovered that ex-Cath Coll boys Paul 'Riff' Reynolds, Jimmy Clune and Phil Suddick were living in London, too. Jimmy and Phil were both in the Police. I met them quite a few times for drinks and general merriment in the capital. After nearly six years in London, my job relocated to Loughborough in Leicestershire, and soon after that I moved over to the company's Communications and Marketing department. After many mergers and takeovers, I now work for a company called DNV in Marketing. I am still in Loughborough and enjoying life. I got married to Sue, who I met through work, in 2001, and have two daughters, Alice and Edith, who are now teenagers and keep us both very busy.

I was proud to say that I went to Preston Catholic College. It was a pity that the school closed as it did, but I guess times move on. I have some great memories of those days, and I hope to see the lads again soon, as our recent school reunion in 2016 was a fantastic night.

PHIL SUDDICK:
FORMS 1C, 2A, 3A, 4A AND 5A

In the words of Oscar Wilde, '*To live is the rarest thing in the world. Most people exist, that is all.*'

I like to think I have chosen to live. I have the most wonderful wife, two amazing sons, and a fantastically close and supportive family. I have also had the privilege and opportunity to experience two amazing and exciting careers. For all these things and more, I am extremely grateful.

But what part did 'schooling' at Preston Catholic College have to play in all of this? Honestly, I don't know, but maybe at the end of this short exercise I will have a better understanding, as the flashbacks start to appear, and I am able to draw more firm conclusions with a clean and clearer insight.

At the ripe old age of 53, memories are tempered by many things. The truth is probably tempered within these, as over time such a cacophony of events, both good and bad, can be misremembered or even (God forbid) over-embellished. This occurs not for any particular reason, but it happens, nonetheless. Thirty years' experience as a police officer, working in the capital city, creates many hundreds of amazing, scary and life-changing events. Sadly, however, the vast majority of these are forgotten with the passage of time. And like these days at work, one school day becomes another, and events come and go. At the time, school days, like workdays now, became the norm, whatever the nature of the events that unfolded happen to have been.

Remembering historical events, and generating thought processes, sometimes results in an unintentional creation in the mind's eye of the person remembering the event, a complete and overwhelming belief that what they remember is the truth. The inescapable fact, however, is that it isn't the truth; these thoughts and memories are blurred at the edges, and perhaps not as fine-tuned or polished as they should be.

I have no bad memories from school, in fact I have very few memories of school at all. I was not bullied, and corporal punishment was applied to me only as and when necessary. They were the rules of the day. However boring it sounds, it was just normal. I fell in line and stayed (mostly) within thc boundaries set by the staff, and time went by. Perhaps I had an underlying 'fear' of getting into trouble, so consequently I tried not to.

In general, the 'day to day' life of a grammar school seemed normal then, and seems normal to me now, even in our modern age of reflection and super-scrutiny. Criticism is readily dished out by a myriad of twenty-first century 'concerned' persons, who themselves have no understanding of what it was really like. I had no real benchmark at the time, and still have none today, from which to make an adequate comparison of whether it was good or bad time. It was just school.

People readily criticise the grammar school system, and its process of selective discrimination. I am rightly or wrongly apolitical; I have never voted, not even for Brexit. I know the 11 Plus was good for me and many other children from similar but not privileged backgrounds. We were given a chance to extend and develop our individual skills and abilities, and I am grateful for that.

We were told we were the last of the 11 Plus generation, the final part of an historical phenomenon. In reality, I only remember the school getting quieter and quieter. With every year that passed, we lost the chance to be the older year and to exert our influence throughout the school by leading younger pupils and educating them in its ways.

We were always the youngest in the year, and missed out on the opportunity to be in charge.

Please bear this in mind as I write my short collection of thoughts. I have no axe to grind nor criticism to make. These recollections are in no particular order, but hopefully they will make a modicum of sense, allow people to reminisce, and perhaps raise a couple of smiles along the way.

I remember being told I had passed the 11 Plus and would be going to a school where I was to be taught by Jesuit Priests in cassocks. The prospect was daunting, to say the least, especially as my sister was already at the Convent next door being taught by a sisterhood of Nuns.

The journey to school every day seemed to take a long time. There was none of this 'school run' thing we have now. There were no mobile telephones, no 'helicopter parents' and no health and safety high-visibility jackets. It was a 20-minute cross-field walk, often in the dark in the winter months, carrying a torch, leaving wellington boots at a family friend's house near the bus stop. This was followed by a similar length bus journey (244 Rochdale) from Hoghton to Preston bus station, and a walk down Fishergate to school. As I got older (and quicker), and if my timings were good, I could find time to go to the Black Cat café near the train station or sometimes the mini cab office nearby to play on the arcade games 'Cosmic Alien' or 'Defender' before school. No mobile apps or even Nintendo in my day.

The return journey was a run though Fishergate to get the first bus home, often stopping to spend a few pence on some hot potatoes in a white paper bag from a man at a brazier stall by the bus station entrance. This amazing forerunner to the now trendy 'street food' was covered in copious amounts of salt. Not a good idea in the twenty-first century 'Jamie Oliver' world, but a great one in the twentieth-century real world of dead tasty grub.

I also used to stop at a sweet shop, whose name escapes me, where I would buy coloured sherbet which I would eat the next day in class, sucking up and ingesting the wonderfully sweet molecules though a 'Bic' plastic pen casing in a vain attempt to disguise my nefarious activities.

The school building itself was a collection of odd buildings that appeared bound together by the glue of history with no real semblance of order or architectural plan. It was certainly no 'Grand Design' in my view. The bricks were dark reddish, and were in no way welcoming.

St Wilfrid's Church opposite the school was used for religious events. There was no outward appearance of grandeur or over symbolic religious rhetoric. But when I entered and smelt the heady fragrance of incense, and heard the Gregorian chanting of the school choir, the hairs rose on the back my neck. I am tone deaf, but the school choir was a renowned institution and I remember having to have an audition. Simon Cowell pressed his red buzzer. I didn't have the X-factor, apparently.

'Ad maiorem Dei gloriam' translated means 'For the greater glory of God'. This expression was abbreviated by staff to 'AMDG'. At the start of each lesson the teachers would instruct us to write these letters, and the date. The stock phrase was immediately written in the margin of the page. I still remember it to this day.

"Pens poised, gentlemen . . ." This is a quote from Father Wareing – Latin teacher extraordinaire. And the giver of 'bops', too – hard clips to the back of the head for misdemeanours – which were probably always justified. Corporal punishment came in the form of a ferula – a piece of bone covered in leather, which was administered with a number of strikes to the hands. These were colloquially called getting 'cracks'. I got them on a couple of occasions, and trust me, your hands swelled up and really hurt after they'd been delivered.

For some reason I used to cover my textbooks in boring white anaglypta wallpaper. It was all we had; all we could afford. It got covered in graffiti and ripped to shreds.

The wooden desks assigned to us were linked to a seat by a solid bar that ran across the back of the chair. These desks were marked with scratches and graffiti carvings and were covered in blue ink, especially around the hole where the inkwell would have been. The bar behind me wore into my back as a result of the constant tirade of "sit up straight" and "stop slouching" I received throughout the day. As I grew in height, I felt the marks of the back bar rubbing on my spine, scarring me with notches of age. I think I remember being forced to kneel at front of the class in some lessons, having to keep a book balanced on our heads to keep our backs straight.

I remember one of the 'new' school clubs being offered to me. It was called 'computer studies'. I was told by one of the old Jesuit teachers that it was a fad and would "never catch on". You can't get it right all the time, I guess.

Sport was one of my favourite memories from my time at the school. I played a lot of football, cricket and badminton. To the boys and teachers, a heartfelt thank you for the camaraderie and coaching. Mr Ainsworth and Mr Singleton in particular were gentlemen and role models.

I remember playing football in lots of godforsaken places. Somewhere near Kirkby, Liverpool, springs immediately to mind. I had to the clear the glass off the pitch from round the goal area before we started. It didn't make much difference, as I still ended up with numerous cuts to my knees and elbows. Another that springs to mind is a match in Burnley. My hands were so cold I had to wear my dad's driving gloves. Unfortunately, they were the ones with leather inserts, which become very slippery in the relentless rain.

We played and won a cup final held at Deepdale one year. It rained, and the pitch was very muddy. As a result, we were in the Lancashire Evening Post – fame and fortune beckoned. Perhaps we all had the X-factor that year.

There was a boy two years up from me called Simon Farnworth who was selected to play for England schoolboys. He was on television. He was famous in my eyes. He was an early role model, as we were both goalkeepers.

I remember freezing certain parts of my anatomy off while playing water polo under the supervision of Mr Bradley in the school's minuscule swimming pool. In addition to having to wear ridiculous numbered cloth caps you had to survive what was really just a game of

British Bulldog under water.

Cross-country was a steep learning curve, in as much as you learned to find new, creative and innovative ways to avoid doing it completely, or how to cheat during the run by only completing part of it and not getting caught or 'grassed-up'.

Break time for me consisted of playing football in the covered area with a tennis ball. In addition, we sometimes played a game where one person, hit a ball high onto the sloped roof of the school with a cricket bat. A large group of schoolboys at the other end of the school yard would fight to catch the ball one-handed as it came off the roof at pace. The successful catcher would then become the new batsman. This was great fun for me, as I was taller than most and could therefore leap higher to catch the ball. I am not sure this game had a name, it just happened. Also, I vaguely remember football cards, which we used to flick up against the wall in competition to win the cards of an opponent.

So, what happened to me after Preston Catholic College? I went to the new sixth form, Newman College, and took A levels, leaving to join the police in London in early 1985. In my formative years I walked the beat and progressed to driving pursuit cars. I then diversified by managing a specialised crime unit involved in covert drug-buying operations. I then spent many years working in a highly secret role investigating organised corruption in the police, government agencies and departments. My favourite role, though, was in another unique role in the force, where I was individually tasked with hunting down some of the world's most wanted fugitives. I spent eight years tracking global terrorists, murderers, serial killers and other serious and organised criminals who had evaded justice.

I retired from the police in 2015 and took up a role with the Tennis Integrity Unit, utilising my unique skillset to investigate global corruption in professional tennis. And there you have it, a short essay on my school memories and work life to date.

I have spent many, many years linking things and solving other people's problems, but I am finding it hard to relate my school time to work and private life. Did school make me the person I am today? Common sense says it must have helped form and forge me into the person I am to some extent at least.

Did the school instil in me the values I hold today? Yes, I think so. Despite not realising it at the time, I guess the teachers must have nurtured and complemented the work started by my parents.

I have only one regret concerning my school life. It is one I cannot blame on anyone but myself. I wish I had kept in contact with the boys I grew up with at school. I should have made more of an effort to maintain these friendships. Life overtakes friendships, but it shouldn't. For many years at school we were close friends, and work and family shouldn't have got in the way of those relationships. I apologise to those with whom I lost contact.

MICHAEL SUTHERS:
FORMS 1B, 2B, 3S, 4S AND 5S

The famous stone archway of Preston Catholic College on Winckley Square was initially pointed out to me in 1976 by my mum, Pauline. We were on our annual family Christmas shopping trip. There were cars parked all around the square, as this was an era of no parking meters, and fewer traffic wardens or double yellow lines! On this and many other occasions I was told "that's probably the best school in Preston", always by someone pointing to the famous stone entrance that still stands today. At ten years old I didn't take much notice; I just wanted to fill my boots in Mears toy shop on Fishergate, Zodiac at St. Johns Shopping Centre and Willie Cunningham's sports shop for some new football boots. Senior school was the last thing on my mind.

But early in 1977 I was sitting the private entrance exam, on a Saturday morning, with probably another 150 lads. With only probably thirty or so places available, the stakes were high. After attending St Oswald's Primary School on Chapel Lane in Longton, from where I'd picked up many happy memories, my automatic route would have been to go to All Hallows Catholic Secondary School in Penwortham. Mum had different ideas, while dad and the siblings didn't really get over involved on decisions relating to education. This was strictly mother's department!

A month or so later, the postman delivered a large brown envelope;

even I deduced what the contents might be – the results were in! Mum opened it. "You've passed! You've passed!" She shouted around the dining room, dancing better than Michael Jackson, overjoyed with excitement.

This was my senior school destination, then, the start of my journey at the College. Mum was ecstatic and immediately called Dad at our family business to break the news. I still wasn't convinced, but Mum and Dad eventually sold the school to me on the basis of its sporting facilities and traditions. They both said the College had the best football, athletic and cricket teams, and that they even played water polo in their on-site swimming pool. More on that swimming pool later! I hoped she was right about the football, because I knew we'd be battling against my mates from Penwortham at some stage and losing was not an option (luckily we didn't!). I was very apprehensive going to the College, though, not least as I was the only student from my junior school attending. But it turned out well.

I soon found myself being measured up for the College uniform, in Halliwell's Menswear on Lune Street, with Mum and Dad in attendance. To be fair, I felt very proud wearing that uniform for the first time; the importance, history and fame (if that's the right word) regarding the College was beginning to sink in. I was going, it was official! On the school crest read 'Fides', meaning 'faith' in Latin. It also differentiates to belief, trust, credit, loyalty and confidence, which are all attributes I believe the College instilled in many of its pupils over the years.

I can't remember my first day at the College, but I was placed in the middle stream of three classes, which suited me perfectly. The lads in the top stream were extremely bright boys, and many will have undoubtedly gone on to become doctors, dentists, solicitors and surveyors. Any accountants out there that can get my accountancy fees down, give me a call!

You could enter the school by three routes – the main entrance off Winckley Square, on Garden Street opposite Winckley Square Convent School, or via the small entrance on Mount Street. Briefcase in hand, I chose the main entrance, heading down the outside sheltered alleyway, into the corridor, past the notice board, and into the sloping flagged school yard. Approximately 450 lads, the school population at its peak, appeared from nowhere! Suddenly I was surrounded by the sights and sounds of shouting, footballs being booted against the brick walls, tennis balls being thrown everywhere, occasional swearing and a scuffle here and there. This was my welcome to a big boy's world. And it was my first lesson: I'd have to grow up quick and fast, as this environment was not going to take any prisoners. It didn't. The teachers were strict but fair, right was right, wrong was wrong, and over time you learnt things were told no more than once, or twice if you were really lucky.

The experienced teachers Joe Bamber, Jack McCann, Steve Bradley, Mr Moulding (Pop) and Pete Singleton, all knew how the school ticked, and kept things under control. They couldn't show weakness to four hundred-plus, sometimes very rowdy lads.

Mum worked at the TSB Bank in Preston (now the 'Twelve Tellers' public house), and dropped me off for the first couple of months in a Mk1 Escort, later upgrading it to a Mk11; most impressively for the time, it was a second car! Dad worked long hours in the family garage business, with mum's part-time wages purely paying for two lots of school fees, one set for myself at the College, and the other to my elder brother Chris, who attended George Fox in Lancaster. Our younger sister Gill attended All Hallows, so didn't cost much to run, God bless. Paying those school fees was hard work for many a family in that era. The year was 1977, Red Rum had just won a third Grand National, and Kenny Dalglish signed for Liverpool; It seems just a blink of an eye away! Frightening how time passes us all by so quickly.

We probably came from what would be considered a 'middle class' type of family, finance-wise, in the mid-Seventies. However, as youngsters we were all encouraged to get part-time jobs outside school hours to earn some extra pocket money. Delivering 485 South Ribble Weekly newspapers around Longton, Hutton and Walmer Bridge as a thirteen-year-old was hard work. The pay was one and a half pence per newspaper back then, earning me £7.27 in wages. I got a promotion eventually, serving petrol at the family business for Dad, earning better pay and working better hours!

Back at school, Miss Almond became my form teacher, a very strict lady who was very much part of the old -style College teaching regime. I think she taught us History and Maths in the first year. Some of the classrooms in the old part of the school were very old-fashioned, with pull-down benches attached to the desks. These older-style desks had inkwells set into them for fountain pens, which were preferred in the early school days.

All the lads were arranged in alphabetical order according to surname around the class, and were addressed purely by surname when being spoken to by a teacher. This felt a little strange and formal, but that's how it was. Neil Slater sat behind me and Greg Wagner in front; we had a laugh throughout school, if only in the classroom.

Like the majority of boys, I also attended the pre-school football trials at Grafton in August 1977. Mr Ainsworth and Eddie Brown organised the trials and cast their expert eyes over us, assessing which players might have the potential to be part of the first-year football team. It was a completely disastrous start for me. I didn't perform well and played well below par; I think nerves kicked in. I was probably the best player at junior school, but suddenly I was surrounded by an incredibly talented bunch of lads.

A month later, the football First XI team was pinned on the notice board. I wasn't even one of the two substitutes. This was my biggest disappointment in life so far; I was devastated. I knew my ability and I was determined to make that team, by hook or by crook.

I just had to keep scoring a few goals down at Grafton on a Wednesday afternoon and trying my best to impress Martin Ainsworth. Three weeks passed, then one day Mr Ainsworth said, "Suthers, go and join Suddick, Clune, Cooper, Pye and Henderson in that six a side team." I knew now I was knocking on Martin's door. Walking back to the pavilion on that cold, rainy Wednesday afternoon, Mr Ainsworth said to me, "Suthers, you'll more than likely start

Saturday morning's game." I still didn't believe him until my name was on that team sheet , , , *come on Martin, pen me in!*

At break time that Friday, I rushed down to the notice board to view the line-up for Saturday's game. There I saw it: Cooper, Clune and Suthers, the front three. I was overjoyed with excitement. All three of us remained the College's attack for the next five years.

Our school football team was a strong side, winning the schools cup at Deepdale in 1979, with Pete Cooper scoring the only goal in a 1-0 victory against St Cuthbert Mayne. Fr Spencer sent me to trials for Preston Schoolboys in the third year, and I represented them in several games, from the third to the fifth year. Gary Kelly and Franz Carr also played, both of whom went on to play professionally in the Premier League. I'm sure if Martin Ainsworth had remained at the school, that team would have won at least one more school's cup, if not two. The lads enjoyed playing under him, and he could be very detailed in tactics and organisation.

Many moments stand out from schoolboy football. Laughs, giggles, goals, saves, fights – you name it, it happened. I was on a two-man attack one time with Pete Cooper. He should have squared the ball to me, but passes from Coops were sometimes rationed – just ask Jimmy Clune! On this occasion, Coops rounds the keeper after beating about three of their players, stops the ball on their goal line, kneels on all fours, and heads it in – talk about arrogance! Peter Singleton, the PE teacher shouts, "No need for that Cooper, less of that." Coops was a showman, though, and had it not been for a few cigarettes and an early interest in girls distracting him, he probably should have made it into the professional game. I played with Pete to the age of about 25 in the Lancashire Amateur League – all those years I had to put up with him!

At lunchtimes we played football in the underground, which was a type of open building made of brick with goals painted at each end. Elsewhere in the school yard many formidable characters plied their trade. Maurice Black and Franco Mastrobuoni used to run the card schools, where dinner money was won and lost, with many a lad going hungry all day. Anybody who got involved knew the score so there was no sympathy, and some days the place looked like a scene from *Casino Royale*. Neither Maurice nor Franco would have passed for Daniel Craig, but then again, who would!

Down at the Grafton pitches, if anybody mentioned they needed some new football boots or a new football strip, Franco would always ask them "What size and colour do you want?" He was always wheeling and dealing. His dad was a jeweller, and he always had a watch, a ring or a bracelet for sale. He'd have definitely passed auditions for the *Junior Apprentice* with Sir Alan Sugar, if that had been on our TVs in the Seventies! What a personality he was; larger than life, brightening up the day.

All the teachers seemed very committed to the school. Miss Baron taught us French, and Fr Wareing taught English in our early days. If 'Wes', as he was known, lost his temper in a lesson, you kept firmly out of his way. He went ballistic, with board dusters being thrown our way and everybody taking cover. But he was a great guy. Elsewhere, Jack McCann was a brilliant Maths teacher, who could silence a class from a 50-metre approach; you could just sense he was en route. On entering the classroom, he would throw his opened briefcase on the desk from five metres out, then for the next forty-five minutes in his company you could hear a pin drop. Jack's office door was always left open near the staff room, and lads would stand outside at lunchtime waiting for the strap, or 'cracks', as they were nicknamed. Cracks never cured you, but they did slow you down for a month or two! When you did have find yourself in the unfortunate position of standing outside Jack's office, his stare over his spectacles towards you was sometimes as punishing as the cracks themselves. I received a few myself over the five years, along with Coops, Steve Pye, Franco, Maurice Black, Greg Wagner, Shaun Daly, Leonard Rogerson and young Mark Harrison (Harry). I call Harry 'young', because he looked about 12 when he left in the third year. He wasn't in my class, but if there were any pranks or adventures to be found, Harry was never far away.

Derek Thompson taught English. He'd come into teaching late, and he just couldn't control our class. But again, he was a top-class guy, and he also got most of the lads an English O level.

Miss Tyrell joined the College when we were in the second year. She was a very stylish, well dressed and extremely attractive young lady, not your normal Catholic College teacher by any measure. Undoubtedly most of the lads fancied her, hence why the physics class as an option got over-subscribed! Unlucky for some of the lads who couldn't get in to her classes!

Steve Bradley taught Biology, but he was better known for running the school's athletics with Peter Singleton, along with the cross country. However, his real notoriety came from being in charge of water polo and swimming in that infamous minus five degrees swimming pool. David Attenborough could have discovered penguins in that pool on some days, it was that freezing. Even the benches we sat on at the pool side shivered and shook before us as we entered. You didn't mess with Mr Bradley. He was a proper 'lad's lad', and soon had us all in that pool working hard up and down. Steve would sometimes turn up in full tracksuit, and sometimes in his famous pin stripe suit. If Steve said it was Monday, Monday it was!

I was a very good swimmer and at lunchtimes and after school I played relentlessly for the water polo sides. I had many a race and battle with Alec Crook to get the best times for crawl, back stroke and breaststroke. It hurts me to say that Alec just had the edge, but the competition was intense. If you gave 100 per cent in that pool, Steve Bradley would push you and ultimately get 110 per cent. He set high standards; you had no choice but to deliver. On one occasion, Greg Wagner got into difficulty in the centre of the pool. Despite being fully suited up, Steve Bradley dived in, shoes and all, and rescued Greg, dragging him to the side of the pool. In the changing rooms afterwards, Steve came over to me, putting me in one of his not-so-friendly head locks. Talking straight into my ear lobe, he said, "Suthers, why the hell did you not go in for Wagner? I've not taught you life saving for nothing." He was back in his tracksuit by now, after hanging his dripping suit on a peg and lecturing the class for about five minutes about the £4 dry cleaning bill he now faced. Perhaps surprisingly, Steve

Bradley was my favourite teacher by a mile. I think it was just the way he pushed you to your absolute limits that appealed. Plus, I loved all the sports he taught. Steve Bradley was 'friend or foe' in the eyes of many pupils, and didn't take much messing around. He didn't need Jack McCann to sort things out.

I must also mention Paul Allison, who was a good mate of mine in the first year but left the College later that year, in 1978. Paul was also a great little footballer and would have definitely made us a stronger team, if he had remained at the College. I mustn't forget Ian Gorrell either. He was also a great and loyal mate.

All the lads lived for our Saturday morning games. We travelled to Blackburn, Burnley and even Liverpool, playing in Lancashire Cup School competitions. During the match, if it wasn't Jimmy Clune saying "on me head" it was his Dad on the sidelines, whom you could hear from a country mile away! We had some good runs in the Lancashire Cup, with captain Eugene Henderson rallying us on. Outside school all the lads were passionate about Sunday junior football in the Central Lancashire League. I played with Steve Pye and Andy Gornall from school for Newman Wanderers, winning both the under 16 league and cup double in the fifth year. I also finished as the league's top scorer that year, which gave me great pride – I must have had a load of tap ins! Coops, Eugene, Jimmy, Simon Cuerden, Phil Suddick and Bernard Moon played for St Augustine's, who were also a very good side. We all had friendly banter at school, trying to give our side an advantage for a forthcoming Sunday game.

Mercers coaches would take us to away games from Winckley Square for school matches, and everybody had to represent the College in full uniform. As soon as the coach pulled away though, school ties were put inside blazer pockets and various card schools would break out, depending on the amount you were prepared to lose. Nothing changed on a Saturday morning! Coops and Steve Pye, still like an 'Ant and Dec' duo, would be joking around. By our third year everybody was mixing in mini groups more at lunchtimes and breaks, or we could all be found playing football together in the yard. However, lunchtimes sometimes got monotonous within those four walls, and more adventurous activities were required. Leaving the school premises at lunchtime was not allowed until you became a fifth year, but that rule was regularly broken.

The safest and preferred route of exit from the school was to climb the bike shed and drop straight over the wall into Mount Street. Our little army platoons could range from three boys, to half a dozen. We always had to wait a little longer for Franco, who was slightly overweight and needed two attempts to scale the sloping bike shed roof. You wanted to be out of sight quickly once you dropped down on the other site, and we usually ventured to Avenham Park, or a café on Butler Street called the 'Black Cat to play 'Space Invaders'. They were great days, looking back. Getting back into school was always harder than leaving, as we'd be trying to avoid teachers who were also coming back from lunch. In the mornings I would exit the bus outside Tommy Balls shoe shop, opposite the train station; that café was always packed with College lads at 8.30am early mornings.

After leaving school with six O levels and two further A levels in Economics and Business Studies, I completed a Business Studies course in Manchester. At the age of twenty-one I joined the family business, and still run it today in partnership with my elder brother. We have also done some smaller property renovations over the years, and generally have been reasonably successful in buying, selling and keeping property projects along the way. Happiness, health, friends and family are worth more than anything in life though, that's for sure. A big thank you to all the staff and students of Preston Catholic College. God bless you all, and what a time we had!

MICK WILSON:
FORMS 1C, 2A, 3S, 4S AND 5S

As a teacher of 32 years, I can say with conviction that schools are VERY different today than they were back in 1977. I remember my very first day in September of that year; being dropped off by my Mum at the very grand school entrance at the top of Winckley Square, having never visited before. Despite there being no pupils or teachers to greet me, I eventually found my way (exactly how I have no idea) to the central area of the flagged playground. From there we were sorted into forms and taken away to what I remember was an antiquated classroom with lots of wood panelling, to be seated at desks which had lids for storage underneath them and inkwells from days gone by when children used ink-pens. A very stern looking elderly lady called Miss Mangan was our form tutor. There was no 'banter', no humour, and no sense of kindness or affection, and that will always be my abiding memory. Metaphorically speaking, it was a very cold, dark, and soulless place. No posters, no pictures, no colour. A little bit like Hogwarts, it was a place steeped in history and tradition; held in high regard in the community and staffed by teachers who, like characters from a Dickensian novel, rarely smiled, and gave an impression of being emotionless. Many of the staff were Jesuit Priests and lived at the Presbytery attached to St Wilfred's Church, opposite the school. Fr Wareing was the pupil's favourite. His tales of the 'scrutineer' were legendary. Every term ended with mass and hymns at St Wilfrid's, it was a nice way to finish for the holidays!

'Lines' were the preferred punishment for misdemeanours. If you received lines your name was published on a noticeboard on the 'Wendy House', an office half way down the main school yard. Each 'line' was at least two lines long (it would be a prayer or a quote from a book), so 25 lines (which was the norm) was actually more like 75 lines, or two sides of A4 paper. Failure to complete and return the lines was unthinkable, as doing so would result first in the lines being doubled, and after that you'd be sentenced to 'ferulas', or 'cracks' as we called them. Punishments in school were quite barbaric by today's standards. Father Maghull liked to make pupils kneel on a stone flag, holding a dictionary in each hand with arms outstretched. As your arms tired and they moved below the horizontal you would be punished further. I remember 'fear' being an emotion I experienced a lot at school.

Breaktimes and lunchtimes were challenging. With limited areas available in which to 'play', due to the school's structure, design, and location, we became experts at 'tennis ball football', pitch and toss and 'escape the fifth years' who would drag you into the toilets and 'nipple' you. As we got older and more confident, we would manage the odd excursion into Avenham Park, or into the town centre to a café to play on the arcade machines, to escape the boredom. Behaviour in the classroom became more adventurous as we grew older, too. After working out who was who, it was fairly easy to play up with the 'nicer' teachers. I remember one of the few female teachers we had, a Mrs Sharratt, once stated that she quite liked the look of a man in glasses. Some of us came to school the next day with glasses from home with the lenses taken out! In another, a history lesson I seem to remember, we set up an elaborate design of drawing pins and fishing wire so that we could snatch the board rubber off the runner underneath the chalkboard as the teacher reached for it.

I was one of the Catholic College Choir Boys. The school had an amazing music teacher, Mr Duckworth, who was a fantastic pianist, organist and choir master. He took us all over the world to compete in competitions and Eisteddfods. We travelled to Wales, France, Switzerland, Italy and America, visiting Paris, Milan, Rome and New York along the way. We appeared on programmes such as *Granada Reports*, *Songs of Praise* and *Psalms on Sunday*. Of course, we got some stick from the other boys, and there was many a reference to us being 'queer' or 'gay' because we could sing! How times have changed. Strangely enough we didn't really mind – it was almost expected. Mr Duckworth was a renowned local musician, who used to play the organ at Fulwood Methodist Church. He was passionate and committed but eventually we had to disband as we ran out of sopranos and altos!

PE lessons were my favourite. At the time, I was not a team or games player, so I didn't make the football teams, but I was a keen swimmer, and Steve Bradley introduced me to water-polo. We were lucky enough to have a swimming pool at school, and water-polo became my favourite lesson. Mr Bradley was a difficult man to please, and if you made a mistake you knew about it. He would pick up a ball and throw it at your head as hard as he could. Ducking was advisable! We had two other PE teachers, Eddy Brown, an ex-PNE player who I never knew to smile, and Peter Singleton. Although I didn't know it at the time, it was Mr Singleton who sowed a seed that was to lead me to my chosen career. Games lessons and cross-country were conducted at Grafton, near 'Vernon Carus' Cricket Club, Lower Penwortham, and we always walked down through Avenham Park on a Wednesday afternoon (something unthinkable today – the safeguarding implications!). Football, hockey and cross-country were the chosen activities in the winter, and we switched to cricket and athletics in the summer. There was no coaching or teaching, just playing and performing – again, the exact opposite of PE lessons today. Cross-country was a run to the Old Tram Bridge at Avenham Park, where one pupil (usually Simon Morris, as he seemed to be permanently excused from PE for some reason) would tick off your name before you'd head back to the changing rooms where Mr Singleton, Mr Bradley and Mr Brown would be waiting with their feet up on a chair . . .

Peter Singleton was one of the few teachers who smiled or took the time to forge relationships with pupils. I seem to remember him being a great trampolinist and canoeist. He nurtured and encouraged us, and under his tutelage I gained confidence and a love of PE and sport, playing everything with enthusiasm and thirst. By the time I moved onto sixth form at what became Newman College, I was a keen runner, fitness enthusiast and badminton player. As I gained confidence, I went on to play team sports that I hadn't really tried before, like football and rugby. I eventually went on to play most sports at a competitive level, and went on to study PE and Sport at University, before launching a career as a PE teacher. Even today at the age of 54, I am a keen bodybuilder, and coincidentally teach PE to the children of some of my school peers, something they would not have believed I would have been capable of when I was at school. Peter unfortunately died prematurely of cancer, but I owe him much. If nothing else, he taught me that a teacher can be immensely influential in a child's development for both good and bad reasons. He taught me the power of a smile and the importance of empowering a young mind to have confidence and self-belief, that making mistakes is ok and is to be expected, and that failure is part of the journey. Shame on you, Mr Bradley!

Other teachers I remember fondly are Mr Sanderson (Biology), Mr Turner (Maths), Mr Thompson (English), Mr Huggon (Latin), Miss Almond (History), Miss Tyrell (Physics), Mr Poole (Geography), Mr Norcross (French) and Mrs Warton (French).

They say school days are the best of your life, but I am not sure I would agree that was the case with my own. I certainly look back with fond memories of all the fun we had, but that came in spite of the lack of nurture and encouragement we should have been given. I did of course make some amazing friendships which still exist today, forty-plus years later. Where school failed us is that when we made a mistake we were punished or ridiculed. Most teachers would not take the time to help, guide or support – it was not the way then. You simply swam, floated or sank. Despite these obvious flaws in the system, I regularly pass by the buildings where Preston Catholic College once existed, and I cannot help but smile at the memories of the special times we had. Bonds were formed that will never be broken, and fortunately we now have the maturity to realise that the most important things we need to learn and know cannot really be taught!

APPENDICES

PRESTON CATHOLIC COLLEGE HEADMASTERS

1865 - 1870 Fr. Wm. Cobb

1870 - 1878 Fr. Henry Martin

1878 - 1884 Fr. Charles de Lapasture

1884 - 1898 Fr. Francis Payne

1898 - 1899 Fr. Patrick Flynn

1899 - 1907 Fr. John Wright

1907 - 1907 Fr. Henry Meyer (two terms)

1907 - 1915 Fr. Joseph Welsby

1915 - 1918 Fr. James Bridge

1918 - 1922 Fr. Henry Irwin

1922 - 1940 Fr. Francis Grafton

1940 - 1947 Fr. Bernard Malone

1947 - 1956 Fr. John Duggan

1956 - 1961 Fr. Robert Carty

1961 - 1972 Fr Richard Wren

1972 - 1975 Fr. Peter Hackett

1975 - 1978 Fr. Richard Wren

NOTABLE ALUMNI

Leo Baxendale – Cartoonist best known as the creator of 'Bash Street Kids' and 'Minnie the Minx'.

Michael Carr – Liberal Democrat MP for Ribble Valley, 1991-92.

Joseph Delaney – Author of the 'Wardstone Chronicles'. Also known for his dark fantasy 'Spooks'.

Gregory Doran – Artistic director of the Royal Shakespeare Company. The Sunday Times called him 'One of the great Shakespearians of his generation.'

Patrick Kelly – Archbishop Emeritus of the Archdiocese of Liverpool.

Mark Lawrenson – Professional footballer for Preston North End, Brighton, Liverpool and the Republic of Ireland.

George Robinson – Former first-class cricketer who played for Oxford University in 1970 and 1971.

NOTABLE ACHIEVEMENTS COVERING THE LAST TEN YEARS OF THE COLLEGE, 1968-78

School Choir

The choir was very successful during the 1970's at the Pontrhydfendigaid Eidsteddfod in Wales, winning first prize on three separate occasions. Magazine records show that they were awarded the Catherine James and Davingon Hall trophies. The choir won many prizes at music festivals, including the Southport and Birkdale Ladies' Shield, and appeared on the television shows *Stars on Sunday* and *Granada Reports*. It also recorded the LP *The Choir of Preston Catholic College sings Advent and Christmas Music.*

The record of the choir at the Pontrhydfendigaid Eisteddfod in the 1970s (courtesy of Selwyn & Neli Jones, General Secretaries, Eisteddfodau Teulu James Pantyfedwen, Pontrhydfendigaid):

1970 - 4th
1972 - 1st
1973 - 1st
1974 - 2nd
1975 - 1st
1976 - 2nd
1978 - 3rd

Neli remembers the choir competing at the events in the 60's and 70's and said, 'There were many choirs competing at these competitions in those days, and your college did really well and were very popular competitors'.

Football

Between 1968 and 1978, the first team notched up 18 Preston and Lancashire Football Association cup final victories.

Cricket

Winners of the Houghton Shield and Preston Challenge Cup on 12 occasions between 1968 and 1978.

Chess

1978 – Winner, Preston under 13 knockout competition.
Also in that year, 2 x winners at the Fulwood Congress.

Drama

Winners of the Drama Club Trophy at Blackburn Festival, 1968.

Scouting

23 Queen's Scouts and 31 Duke of Edinburgh Gold Awards.

Badminton

1978 – Winners, Preston Senior Badminton Competition.